84   49.95
                    80E

D0849292

HANDBOOK OF
ACADEMIC ADVISING

HANDBOOK OF ACADEMIC ADVISING

Virginia N. Gordon

The Greenwood Educators' Reference Collection

GREENWOOD PRESS
Westport, Connecticut • London

Library of Congress Cataloging-in-Publication Data

Gordon, Virginia N.
    Handbook of academic advising / Virginia N. Gordon.
       p.   cm. — (The Greenwood educators' reference collection,
  ISSN 1056–2192)
    Includes bibliographical references and index.
    ISBN 0–313–28458–X (alk. paper)
    1. Personnel service in higher education—United States—
  Handbooks, manuals, etc. I. Title. II. Series.
  LB2343.G638   1992
  378.1′94—dc20   91–47558

British Library Cataloguing in Publication Data is available.

Library of Congress Catalog Card Number: 91–47558
ISBN: 0–313–28458–X
ISSN: 1056–2192

First published in 1992

Greenwood Press, 88 Post Road West, Westport, CT 06881
An imprint of Greenwood Publishing Group, Inc.

Printed in the United States of America

The paper used in this book complies with the
Permanent Paper Standard issued by the National
Information Standards Organization (Z39.48–1984).

10 9 8 7 6 5 4 3 2 1

This book is dedicated to my family, whose loyalty, patience, and love have inspired me more times than they know.

Contents

Illustrations

Preface

Academic advising is receiving renewed attention as an important function in higher education. Once the purview of faculty only, in recent years a new full-time professional has evolved out of the need for extended and more specialized services. While faculty members are projected to remain the dominant advising source, the new professional adviser serves as a stabilizing, enriching force in many delivery systems.

Students are becoming more aware of the need for advice in traveling through the maze of general and graduation requirements that exist on many campuses today. In some institutions, many academic programs are selective or oversubscribed, and students need expert advice as they engage in exploring alternatives. Academic advisers are increasingly viewed as resources for academic, career, and life planning. As students prepare for a changing world, their need for help in defining and working in that world places renewed responsibility on institutions to provide the best advising and counseling services possible. It is in this milieu that advising enters the twenty-first century.

This book is intended to assist practitioners in the intricacies of advising students. It outlines different organizational approaches for delivering advising, describes the basic tasks involved in the advising process, and summarizes advising approaches for the many special and diverse populations that advisers encounter.

Any faculty member, administrator, or student affairs or other professional working with college students will find practical strategies for engaging them in any campus setting. These approaches are based on a renewed appreciation and respect for students' uniqueness and special needs. The vast wellspring of literature applying to academic advising from many disciplines is the foundation supporting the information imparted in this book.

Chapter 1 traces the origins and growth of academic advising in America from the colonial colleges through the ensuing decades, reflecting the changes in higher education itself. The history of academic advising from its status as a faculty responsibility to the current trend toward professional advising is discussed. Definitions of academic advising are outlined, indicating that it is no longer just a "scheduling" function but one that incorporates a total student development approach. The diverse theoretical frameworks on which the advising process is now based are discussed in detail.

Chapter 2 discusses the many organizational and administrative approaches now used to deliver academic advising. "The building blocks of academic advising" form a model for examining the objectives or goals of an advising program, functions or tasks involved, the personnel who provide the services, the location and timing of advising services, and the various methods by which advising is delivered.

The heart of academic advising is the exchange between adviser and student, and this process is described in Chapter 3. A detailed profile of the various types of students who are the recipients of advising efforts is provided. The relationship between adviser and student is described, including both adviser and student roles and responsibilities. How to conduct an advising interview is described as a decision-making process, including a recognition of student problems. Advising skills, materials, and resources are discussed. Advising settings, including precollege contacts, orientation, advising courses, and group advising, are described in detail. This chapter provides practical approaches to the advising function.

Academic advising must incorporate a career perspective if it is to accommodate students' needs and expectations for help in making important academic, career, and life decisions. Chapter 4 discusses advisers' need to be informed about the changing workplace and the vocational relationships between majors and occupations. The important elements of career planning are detailed. These include self-assessment, the acquisition of occupational and educational knowledge, and the ability to make realistic and satisfying decisions. Advising undecided students and students who are in a transition from one major to another requires special advising skills and knowledge.

There are many special groups of students on today's campuses. Chapter 5 offers practical techniques for advising students who have unique needs. These special groups include adult students; student athletes; commuter students; disabled students, including those with learning disabilities; high-ability students, transfer students; and academically-at-risk students. This chapter describes the special academic, career, and personal needs that may surface in the advising exchange and offers suggestions for responding to them.

Advisers are finding themselves working with increasing numbers of culturally diverse students. Advising students from a culture different from one's own requires a sensitivity to these students' needs and perceptions of the college experience. The culturally diverse students discussed in Chapter 6 include African-American, Asian American, Hispanic, Native American, and international students. Advising implications are offered for each of these special groups.

The importance of a well-trained advising staff cannot be overemphasized. Chapter 7 discusses the issues involved in adviser training programs, including who needs them, who is responsible, and how often and where they should take place. Different types of training activities are described. The content for both preservice and in-service training is outlined. Training methods and materials are described in detail. Evaluation approaches are also included.

Chapter 8 discusses the need for evaluating advising programs as well as for the evaluation of individual advisers on a regular basis. Evaluation should be based on the behavioral objectives set forth for the total advising program. Formative and summative evaluation methods are described. Student, peer, and supervisory evaluations of individual advisers provide excellent feedback to advisers who wish to improve their advising knowledge and skills. Evaluation based on nationally set standards is detailed. Examples of evaluation instruments are provided.

The advent of the full-time professional adviser, while not new, has increased dramatically over the past decade. Chapter 9 explores advising as a professional career and the issues involved, such as setting standards, professional preparation, and title and salary issues. The diversity of backgrounds among professional advisers emphasizes the heterogeneity of the group which is discussed in terms of advantages and disadvantages to the profession. A current trend is for professional advisers to become increasingly specialized (e.g., honors advising, minority advising, athletic advising). As the number of professional advisers grows, there will be increased interest in examining the many issues involved in professional identity and recognition.

Chapter 10 attempts to forecast the growth, changes, and needs of advisers and students into the next century. Faculty advising will remain the major delivery system for advising, but increased needs for training will improve the quality and commitment for this function. Professional advisers will become increasingly specialized as the makeup of the student body will include more first-generation, minority, adult, and other students with special needs. Advising will incorporate a student development perspective as the rule rather than the exception. Advising as a function will increasingly be recognized as one of the most important services on the campus.

The author would like to acknowledge the contributions and support of colleagues and students who made this book possible. The intellectual stimulation of ideas from advisers and the real-life, daily concerns of students have served to encourage and support the need for a book that can convey the importance, the complexity, and the need to espouse academic advising as a critical force in the life of higher education and the students it serves.

HANDBOOK OF
ACADEMIC ADVISING

1

The History and Roots of Academic Advising

THE HISTORY OF ACADEMIC ADVISING

The history of higher education in the United States and academic advising are inextricably entwined. Some of the early colonial colleges were already established on the eve of the American Revolution. According to Rudolph (1962), a group of Cambridge- and Oxford-trained graduates created Harvard (with the passing of legislation by the Massachusetts General Court) to preserve one of the many traditions of the England they left behind. More important, they knew that education was the only way to establish "a learned clergy and a lettered people." These purposes also permeated the establishment of eight subsequent colonial colleges.

Early academic advising was performed by the president of the college and later by the faculty. Since many of the earliest American colleges were predominantly private and controlled by clergy, their mission was to save "students' souls" and guide their private lives. The president was accountable to the parents for the education of their children and was also the primary disciplinarian. Later this responsibility was delegated to a personnel administrator or dean who saw to the enrollment and teaching of students (Rudolph, 1962).

Aspects of advising can even be traced back to the concern for women students who sought admission in increasing numbers to men's institutions after the Civil War (Reed, 1944). The creation of Lady Principals, Lady Assistants, or Matrons could be considered the forerunners of advisers. By 1900 a new type of Lady Principal was called for since the variety of curricular offerings in the college catalogs (as well as inadequate housing facilities for women and the increased importance of social activities) created a need for a more broadly trained individual. The title of Dean of Women evolved out of these complex developments, and these deans were charged to handle disciplinary duties and extracurricular activities, as well as to resolve academic problems (Potter, 1927).

Faculty with a reputation for being empathic, caring advisers were excellent candidates for appointments as deans of men. President Charles W. Eliot of Harvard characterized these unofficial advisers who served students as "advising . . . rather than controlling." His description of Dean LeBaron Briggs is an example: "He possesses a high honesty, a readiness to give himself to others and a certain kindliness of character which made [students] at ease in his presence. . . . They were going to him for counsel for every kind of problem" (Brown, 1926, p. 11).

The first system of faculty advisers was initiated at Johns Hopkins in 1876, partially because of the increased growth of the student population. In 1899 the first "chief of faculty advisers" was appointed by the president. This appointment provided official recognition of the important institutional need for academic counseling and advising (Cowley, 1949). Freshman advisers were appointed at Harvard in 1888 because of the increased size and elective additions to the curriculum, which required closer attention to undergraduate guidance (Rudolph, 1962).

The rapid proliferation of institutions of higher learning in America is unique in the history of higher education (Mueller, 1961). The evolution of academic advising services reflects a variety of settings, including small liberal arts colleges, state universities, church-supported schools, municipal institutions, and technical and community colleges. The very nature of American democracy dictated that the concept of education extend far beyond old-world traditions to include students of all socio-economic and cultural backgrounds. This diversity carried over into institutional goals and objectives, curricula, organization, and means of financial support. This diversity also influenced the type of advising delivery systems that were created to meet the unique needs of each institution.

Academic advising also evolved out of the need for interpreting more complex and varied curricula. Curricula, according to Clark Kerr, are "a statement a college makes about what out of the totality of man's constantly growing knowledge and experience, is considered useful, appropriate, or relevant to the lives of educated men and women" (Rudolph, 1977, p. 24).

The evolution of the curricula in American colleges and universities can be traced from the highly structured offerings of the colonial colleges and the classical curriculum of early nineteenth century, to the comprehensive university exemplified by Cornell and the research university created at Johns Hopkins in the middle of that century. It continued to evolve with the experiments with interdisciplinary, competency-based curricula, and core courses initiated in the twentieth century. As the breadth and complexity of the curricula increased, the need for extended educational counseling became more critical. After World War I, counselors were trained to complement faculty advising. Feelings and attitudes of students were taken into account in addition to aptitudes for study (Rudolph, 1977).

MacLean (1949) bemoaned the fact that after World War II there was an "overwhelming embarrassment of curricular riches" that made it difficult for a student to choose courses. On the other hand advisers "were sure they should be able to find a course of study to fit the need and abilities of almost any individual student," even though "[the student] might not know what each course contains or who the teacher is." MacLean echoed William Rainey Harper's concern that specially trained professionals would be needed to help students through the maze of course selection based on the individual's unique intellectual, personal, and social makeup.

The forerunner of developmental advising may be traced to the thinking of Harper (1905), who delivered a lecture in 1899 at Brown University entitled "The Scientific Study of the Student." He discussed the many features he thought would characterize twentieth-century college education. One of these was individualism in education as opposed to collectivism. Individualism, as espoused by Harper, meant the introduction of an elective system of courses and the encouragement of the faculty to specialize in their respective departments. This doctrine of individualism altered the student's work load by the many courses from which to choose and the freedom to make that choice. Harper prophesized:

In order that the student may receive the assistance so essential to his highest success, another step in the onward evolution will take place. This step will be the *scientific study of the student himself.* . . . In the time that is coming provision must be made, either by the regular instructors or by those appointed especially for the purpose, to study in detail the man or woman to whom instruction is offered. (Cowley, 1949, p. 22)

The "general diagnosis" that Harper predicted would include five considerations in addition to physical health: (1) his character, (2) his intellectual capacity, (3) his "special intellectual characteristics," (4) his special capacities and tastes, and (5) "the social side of his nature." "This feature of twentieth-century education," he said, "will come to be regarded as of greatest importance, and fifty years hence will prevail as widely as it is now lacking" (Cowley, 1949).

In the 1960s Mueller (1961) contended that curricular offerings of the colleges were reflected in the problems brought to advising and counseling offices. She suggested that if students were involved in professional schools, they were likely to spend more of their leisure time in activities related to their curriculum. Students enrolled in a more general or liberal arts curriculum spent more time exploring their interests and aptitudes since their vocational goals were more uncertain. This observation is still true today, since the majority of students need vocational and placement counseling to prepare for the complicated job market they are about to enter.

The increasing heterogeneity of student populations across campuses over the years demanded the creation of many different and sometimes complex types of services. The relationship between teacher and students is no longer "close or frequent," according to Mueller. Most of the factors that made teaching informal and individualized no longer exist on many campuses today, especially large ones. Faculty members have become as heterogeneous as their students, and their motivations, goals, and abilities are just as diverse as those of their students. This situation has led to the need for many new services, such as testing and advising for orientation, a knowledge of the needs of special populations, and a knowledge of career options. The academic adviser today must be trained in a variety of knowledge and skill areas that were unnecessary when colleges, faculties, and students were more homogeneous. We are entering into the era of specialists in the advising field.

The decades of the 1960s and 1970s saw an increasing demand for academic advising on the part of students. Along with student services, it had not received high priority during the years when enrollments increased dramatically. Colleges and universities were continuing to expand with limited resources. The advent of the community college brought a recognition of the great diversity among the "new" students enrolling in college (Cross, 1974). The "new" students were characterized as first generation and from lower-income families. Many were poorly prepared academically. The returning older adult also had special needs and expected a quality education, including supportive services. Minorities, disabled, international, and other special populations also required special services. Academic advising became an important vehicle for individualizing academic adjustment and planning for these groups.

The issue focused upon in the 1980s was a decreasing pool of students and the need to retain the ones currently enrolled. Retention focused on a quality learning experience emphasizing outcomes that include student success and satisfaction. Once again, academic advising was considered a critical service in assisting students with educational planning that incorporated their personal goals and aspirations.

One of the most important aspects to be recognized in the field of advising in the 1970s and 1980s was "developmental advising." The theoretical frameworks set forth by William Perry, Arthur Chickering, Lawrence Kohlberg, Carol Gilligan, and others, as well as the vocational theories of Donald Super, John Holland, and David Tiedeman, were adapted to personalize advising in an approach that went far beyond the traditional advising agenda. Students were espoused as individuals with unique needs and concerns, and advising practices were broadened to include educational and vocational goal setting as well as the traditional scheduling of classes.

While faculty advising has remained the primary delivery system for advising, a dramatic increase in the number of full-time professional advisers has taken place. The "advising center" as a delivery system has become an accepted vehicle for emphasizing and concentrating advising services that have become fragmented or nonexistent on many campuses.

The future of advising can only be speculated, but it will continue to be an important part of college life into the next century. The trend toward more centralized services, more professional staffing, and more specialization will continue. The individualization of advising will be just as important in the twenty-first century since the number of minorities attending college will continue to grow and retention concerns will remain. In fact, advising, like many student services, will need to become more specialized to serve the continuing growth of special populations. Developmental advising will become the only acceptable approach, and eventually "developmental" will be dropped when the term "advising" and "developmental" become synonymous.

DEFINITIONS OF ACADEMIC ADVISING

The need to define advising did not seem necessary until a developmental perspective was espoused. Advising has always been a function in which faculty and students consulted about the students' selection of major and courses and proceeded through the scheduling process. In the early 1970s two classic articles defined advising in broader terms and thus reintroduced a concept of advising that had been a part of earlier faculty-student relationships. O'Banion (1972) outlined the skills, knowledge, and attitudes required for good academic advising and, in so doing, defined the functions in a much broader context. The five steps, which were in priority order, included (1) exploration of life goals, (2) exploration of vocational goals, (3) program or major choice, (4) course choice, and (5) scheduling courses. While the last three are typically within the purview of traditional advising, the first two added a new dimension to the advising process.

Crookston (1972) reflected the dissatisfaction of the students of the 1960s by describing a more personal view of advising. Prescriptive advisers were characterized as those who assumed authority and responsibility for students' progression through academic programs. They were interested only in students' academic problems. Developmental advisers, on the other hand, were interested in a holistic approach and shared responsibility for students' adjustment and progression through college in a number of academic, social, and vocational arenas. The adviser assumed a teaching role in the advising exchange and respected the uniqueness of each individual student.

The individualized approach to academic advising is, of course, not new. Many advisers through the years held great respect for students' unique characteristics and were sensitive to their concerns. As indicated earlier, small groups of students and faculty were interacting in the earliest colleges. Students' cognitive and affective concerns were assumed by faculty to be within their responsibilities as advisers. This emphasis was not placed on advising in more recent decades, when the adviser's major duty was to "keep records of students' progress toward their degree and make sure that students fulfilled both college and major requirements" (Walsh, 1979, p. 446).

Winston, Ender, and Miller (1982) provided a more refined definition of the developmental advising process by including the following characteristics:

• Developmental advising is a process, not a one-step, paper endorsing activity
• Developmental advising is concerned with human growth

- Developmental advising is goal related
- Developmental advising requires establishment of a caring human relationship
- Advisers serve as adult role models and mentors
- Developmental advising is the cornerstone of collaboration between academic and student affairs
- Developmental advising utilizes all campus and community resources (pp. 7–8)

They continue to give an operational definition of developmental advising: "Developmental advising both stimulates and supports students in their quest for an enriched quality of life; it is a systematic process based on a close student-adviser relationship intended to aid students in achieving educational and personal goals through the utilization of the full range of institutional and community resources" (p. 8).

Crockett (1979) describes academic advising as a multi-faceted activity. Academic advising should assist individual students to realize the maximum educational benefits to them. It accomplishes this goal by:

1. helping students to clarify their values, goals, and better understand themselves as persons;
2. helping students understand the nature and purpose of higher education;
3. providing accurate information about educational options, requirements, policies, and procedures;
4. helping students plan an educational program consistent with their interests and abilities;
5. assisting students in a continual monitoring and evaluation of their educational progress; and
6. integrating the many resources of the institution to meet the student's special educational needs and aspirations.

In brief, the academic adviser serves as a coordinator of the student's educational experience, according to Crockett.

Some of the benefits students derive from an effective advising program include

1. successful attainment of their educational and career objectives;
2. achievement of grade point averages (GPAs) consistent with their ability;
3. greater likelihood of completing a degree;
4. satisfaction with the process and development of a positive attitude toward the institution; and
5. development of a meaningful relationships with their adviser.

Grites (1979) defines advising as "assisting students to realize the maximum educational benefits available to them by helping them to better understand themselves and to learn to use the resources of an educational institution to meet their special educational needs and aspirations'' (p. 1). That this definition and the others indicated above needed to be stated reflects the condition of advising on many campuses during this period. While the mission statements in the catalogs of many institutions promise to provide an atmosphere of nurturing the whole student, few have systematically integrated academic and student services to accomplish this purpose. Advising is the one service that spans both areas and deals with students from the day they set foot on campus to the day they graduate.

While each institution must state advising objectives and policies that reflect its individual character, there are many common tenets and theoretical underpinnings upon which to base these goals. As Winston, Ender, and Miller (1982) indicate, ''The integration of personality and intellectual development [among students] is an essential and viable goal of higher education. . . . Such an integrated approach is not only possible, but its touchstone is the academic advising process'' (p. 4).

THEORETICAL UNDERPINNINGS

Academic advising draws from many theoretical frameworks and perspectives for its rationale and for the definitions of its functions and processes. The evolution of academic advising philosophies or objectives has been closely linked to the proliferation of many of the theoretical frameworks presented in the last 30 years. These include theories concerning student development, adult development, career development, decision-making theory, and learning theory. Harper's prophecy in his 1899 speech at Brown University of teachers and advisers ''getting to know students'' has gone far beyond what he envisioned. Theoretical frameworks provide an understanding of every facet of a student's growing, ever-changing life.

Many of the theories that relate to college students emerged in the late nineteenth century and continue to develop today. Moore (1990) traces the writings relating to student development back to Carl Jung, Sigmund Freud, and B. F. Skinner. Carl Rogers (1961) is noted as having great influence on student affairs professionals with his ''client-centered'' approach. Erik Erikson (1968) and Jean Piaget (1964) are also cited by Moore as having great influence on the way we perceive college students' personal and intellectual growth.

Other theorists who have written about college students are Roy Heath (1964), who observed different ways college males approached the decision-making process; Berton Clark and Martin Trow (1966), who studied student subcultures; and Douglas Heath (1968), who wrote about maturity and development.

Many theories can provide academic advisers with the knowledge that leads to a deeper understanding of the students with whom they are engaged. A brief overview of some of these theoretical frameworks are provided below with suggestions for applying some of their tenets to advising situations.

Student Development Theory

Many changes take place in the traditional-aged student during the college years. Advisers need to be aware of these differences in growth and development since insights about a particular student's concerns may be gleaned from this knowledge. Two developmental theories in particular have relevance for academic advisers. Chickering (1969) discusses the tasks that students must resolve during the college years, and Perry (1970) outlines the cognitive and moral development of students during this time.

Arthur Chickering. Chickering provides an outline of developmental tasks that students need to accomplish if they are to move smoothly into adulthood. These seven tasks or vectors have some elements in common. Each has content and directionality; each ascends into focus at certain times and needs to be resolved at those times. How students resolve each vector will affect how future vectors are accomplished. If a vector is not resolved adequately at the time it is in focus, it may cause problems later at a time of crisis. Even though a vector is resolved adequately, it may reappear later and need to be resolved at a different level.

Chickering identifies seven developmental tasks that college students need to resolve:

1. *Achieving Competence*. The areas in which college students need to achieve competence are intellectual, physical, social, and interpersonal. While many students enter college with some competencies in these areas, the college years are a time for refining and mastering them at a higher order. Intellectual competence is an essential task for college students, as the capacity for mature thought is at the heart of becoming a successful learner. Physical competence is refined while in college, and lifetime skills in recreational and leisure time pursuits are learned. Students consider social and interpersonal competencies as important in their adjustment and enjoyment of college life. Achieving competence means that students are comfortable and confident that they can meet any challenge that is placed before them.

2. *Managing Emotions*. Neville Sanford (1966) describes the typical freshman as authoritarian, rigid, submissive, and anti-intellectual. All of these are repressive forces, so that students' first task is to become aware of their feelings and learn to trust them more. Two major impulses need to be managed—aggression and sex. Maturity implies that legitimate ways to express anger and hate have been found. Sexual impulses are more insistent than before. Issues of interpersonal relationships, value, and identity are raised, and students feel pressured to find answers.

3. *Becoming Autonomous*. During the first weeks of college students are hesitant to try new activities or approaches, but they soon change. Although they become more independent, they are shaky at first. For the first time there are no restraints or outside pressures. Once they are on their own, they may flounder. Eventually recognition and acceptance of interdependency bring autonomy. Once interdependence is recognized and accepted, the boundaries of personal choice become clearer and the ranges within which one can give and receive become more settled.

4. *Establishing Identity*. The establishment of identity will depend on the resolution of previous vectors. In addition to the inner changes, college students also need to clarify perceptions of physical needs, personal appearance, and appropriate roles and behavior. Once a sense of identity is achieved, the other major vectors may be dealt with. Identity is the hinge upon which future development depends.

5. *Freeing Interpersonal Relationships*. Once identity is achieved, relationships become less anxious, less defensive, more friendly, spontaneous, and respectful. Students are more willing to trust and are more independent. Students can now develop the capacity for mature intimacy.

6. *Clarifying Purposes*. Interests tend to stabilize at this point, and vocational alternatives are explored. A general orientation is achieved first, and then more specific career decisions are made. Students formulate plans and integrate vocational and life-style considerations into their future goals.

7. *Developing Integrity*. Students need to clarify a personally valid set of beliefs that have some internal consistency. This clarification happens in three stages: humanizing values, personalizing values, and developing congruence between beliefs and behavior. Students examine the values they grew up with and either retain or reject them. They are then able to act out their very own beliefs in an active way.

More recently Chickering (Thomas & Chickering, 1984) has suggested some revisions to his earlier work. He acknowledges that if writing *Education and Identity* today, he would place more emphasis on intellectual and interpersonal competence. Cultural changes make managing emotions more complex since the range of alternative behaviors has become more evident and acceptable. He would relabel the autonomy vector as interdependence, emphasizing the capstone of the task.

Clarifying purpose would still reflect the integration of work, leisure, and life-style orientation but would recognize its difficulty in an era of economic constraints. The last vector, integrity, would be expanded to include the work of Kohlberg and Perry. Gilligan's work concerning women would also be recognized.

Chickering emphasizes the need to acknowledge the diversity of today's college population. He suggests that orientation and advising are critical, as retention studies have shown, and that more emphasis and resources need to be placed in these areas.

Advisers are often caught up in helping students resolve problems dealing with the developmental tasks that Chickering has outlined. For example, a student who is homesick may be dealing with issues of autonomy. A student who cannot choose a major may not have established an identity. Understanding the normal tasks that students need to accomplish may offer insights into an advising approach or indicate a referral source. Listening to the meaning of words beneath a presented problem may lead to a discovery of a developmental concern that can be resolved once adviser and student acknowledge it.

William Perry. Perry's (1970) theory of cognitive and moral development can also provide insights into students' intellectual growth and behavior. Perry developed a scheme to describe the development of the thinking and reasoning processes that take place naturally as students mature and grow intellectually. Each phase of this development may be likened to a set of filters through which students see the world around them. Perry's stages or positions are cognitive structures that operate like a lens. First students perceive, then organize and evaluate what is perceived. These perceptions shape the way they learn.

Dualistic students see the world around them in polar terms. All questions have either a right or wrong answer, and they are looking for simplistic ones. They know hard work and obedience pay off. They are externally controlled. They see advisers as authorities having the "right" answers.

As students develop, they become capable of more complex reasoning and are dissatisfied with simplistic answers. They are moving into a "multiplistic" view of the world. They begin to see and understand cause and effect relationships. Diversity becomes legitimate because they realize that no one has all the answers. However, they still depend on others to make decisions for them. Some freshmen and sophomores view their experiences through this multiplistic lens.

The next stage Perry identifies is termed "relativism." Students can now begin to synthesize diverse and complex elements of reasoning. They are able to view uncertainty as legitimate. They now understand that they are responsible for making their own decisions. Many juniors and seniors are "relativistic" thinkers.

In the most advanced stage, according to Perry, individuals make a commitment to a personal identity and its content and style. They develop a sense of being "in" one's self, along with an awareness that growth is always transpiring and that change is inevitable and healthy. Students make a commitment to a defined career area and are able to develop a life-style that is uniquely theirs. Many students continue in this state of development after college.

Perry theorizes that growth occurs in surges, with pauses between that allow for reflection on the growth that has just occurred. During these pauses some students feel the need to detach themselves for awhile, while others even retreat to the comfort of their past ways of thinking. All students have the freedom to choose what kind of persons they will become, but the forces of growth, according to Perry, will not be denied.

When advisers recognize these stages of development in individual students, certain responses may challenge students to move forward. For example, dualistic students need to be encouraged to become more independent. They need to increase their personal insights and become more aware of self. Structured, experiential activities can be developed to challenge them to think in more multiplistic terms.

Multiplistic students may be challenged by an adviser who can provide supporting evidence for a change of view. Advisers need to use concrete examples to teach new ideas. Introspection should be encouraged. Late multiplistic students may be helped to discriminate between competing choices, and advisers can provide loose structure to help accomplish this discrimination. Advisers should encourage students to analyze and evaluate problems or issues from the students' own perspective and experiences.

Relativistic students can focus or narrow down a variety of alternatives when making a decision. They have an internal locus of control and are capable of analytical reasoning. Advisers can often act as sounding boards for their ideas. Advisers can be used as resource persons and can encourage students to orient themselves in a relativistic world through some form of personal commitment. Some students reach commitment only in the years after graduation.

Adult Development Theory

While some of the tenets of student development theory may apply to non-traditional students, there is a large body of theory to explain many adult students' motivations, aspirations, and behaviors. Older adults returning to college comprise a large portion of today's student population, and their special needs must be recognized. Programs and services designed to incorporate the adult student's unique concerns have increased significantly over the past two decades. Adult development theory provides many insights into the older student's perspectives and concerns. Advisers who are familiar with adult development concepts understand how adults adjust to the college environment and why some succeed and some do not.

Three theoretical areas paint a broad picture of adult development: psychosocial, cognitive, and physical development. Psychosocial theorists focus on individuals' interaction with their social environment. Cognitive theorists look at how people make meaning of their experiences as well as changes in intelligence, memory, and approaches to learning. Physical changes also have an impact on adults' development and influence psychosocial and cognitive development.

Schlossberg (1984) provides four perspectives on adulthood: cultural, developmental, transitional, and life span. Some adults, for example, may return to school because of a midlife crisis brought about by a change in the organizational structure in which they are working rather than because of the aging process. Levinson et al. (1978) provide an example of the developmental perspective and postulate sequences of development based on age-related stages. Neugarten (1971) exemplifies the transitional approach to development. Many adults return to school because events in their lives trigger a transition that must be dealt with. Divorce, death, or other major life crises may pressure an individual to make a decision about a change whether they want to or not. Schlossberg (1984) also presents a transition model that includes how transitions affect people's lives and how they cope with them. Eventually an individual becomes integrated into a new environment, and the assimilation process replaces the earlier uncertainty characterized by most transitions.

Life-span theorists emphasize continuity and change. Vaillant's study (1977) confirms the individuality and variability in the adult experience. Today's changing life patterns emphasize the need for fluidity and flexibility as life roles change. Transitions are not seen as happening in age-related sequences.

Since academic advisers often see adults in a transition phase (i.e., entering college for the first time or reentering with different motives and objectives), it is critical to understand the reason for the transition, the coping strength of the individual, and the student's support systems (Schlossberg, 1984). An accepting, supportive adviser can often make the difference between a successful student and one who becomes discouraged and leaves.

Career Development Theory

There are many views about how individuals choose careers and how a career develops over a lifetime. Career development theorists provide insights into this process through a number of approaches. A description of some of the theories follows.

Trait-Factor Approach. Trait-factor theory matches an individual's interests and aptitudes with occupational traits. It assumes that these personal traits can be measured accurately and reliably. In turn each occupation has a set of measurable trait requirements that are necessary to perform the job. This approach assumes that a close match between personal and job traits will produce a productive and satisfied worker. Holland's model exemplifies this approach.

Holland (1985) assumes that in our culture, individuals can be categorized by six personality types. Holland also categorizes work environments by the same six types. The descriptions of the environments and the types of people working in those environments are similar. The following summarizes each of the six personality types and identifies some work environments for each type.

1. *Realistic.* These individuals prefer to work with things rather than ideas or people; have structured patterns of thought; often have mechanical and athletic ability; value concrete things, like money, power, and status. They tend to be more conventional in their attitudes and values and are persistent and mature. "Realistic" people prefer to work in areas like agriculture, engineering, natural resources, and technical fields.

2. *Investigative.* These individuals are analytical and need to be challenged intellectually. They are scholarly, often having mathematical and scientific ability. They tend to avoid interpersonal relationships with groups or new individuals. They are original and independent. They prefer to work in occupations related to math, science, and technical areas.

3. *Artistic.* Artistic types are sensitive, nonconforming, original, intuitive, and independent and often have artistic or musical ability. They tend to value esthetics and place less importance on material things. They avoid direct relationships and often relate through artistic media. They prefer to work in occupations related to music, literature, theater, and other creative fields.

4. *Social.* Social personalities have a high interest in people and are sensitive to the needs of others. They have teaching abilities and value social activities, social problems, and interpersonal relations. They have good verbal and social skills. They are scholarly

and verbally oriented. They prefer occupations related to teaching, social welfare, and those involving a helping relationship.

5. *Enterprising*. These people are adventurous, dominant, and persuasive. They place high value on political and economic matters and are drawn to power and leadership roles. They are aggressive, popular, self-confident, and social and have good leadership and speaking abilities. They prefer occupations related to sales, supervision of others, and leadership roles.

6. *Conventional*. These types tend to be practical, neat, and organized and prefer to work in a structured situation. They are conforming and orderly and have clerical and numerical abilities. They value business and economic achievement, material possessions, and status. They prefer accounting, business, computational, secretarial, and clerical vocations.

An important element of Holland's theory is the concept of "congruence," which means that different types flourish in work environments that provide the opportunities and rewards that meet particular individual needs. Vocational satisfaction, stability, and achievement depend on the congruence between one's personality and the environment in which one works.

Advisers using the trait-factor approach could help students identify their personal strengths and limitations through careful assessment of their interests and abilities. This will often mean referring students to the career counseling and planning resources on campus. Advisers may also provide information about occupations related to various majors. They can help students gather, understand, and apply information so that new fields can be generated or alternatives can be substituted for earlier unrealistic or unattainable ones.

Developmental Theory. Developmentalists view a career as happening over the entire life span. Throughout each life stage individuals are seen as attempting to implement their self-concept through work. Super and Nevill (1984) describe career maturity as a readiness to engage in developmental tasks appropriate to the age and level in which one finds oneself. Career development is not static but continues over the life span. Persons at different stages of development need to be counseled in different ways. Super views college students as being in the "exploration" stage, where self-examination, role tryout, and occupational exploration take place. In this stage tentative choices are made and tried out. Reality factors are taken into account as the student enters the work force.

Advisers using a developmental perspective will understand the particular stages, tasks, and roles in which college students are involved in developing their careers. They view college students in many roles and understand that many aspects of students' lives come into play in the advising exchange. Advisers also understand that changing occupations during one's lifetime is a natural phenomenon and that students need to learn how to manage a lifetime of career adjustment and change.

Decision-Making Theory. While career development is a continuous process, there are critical decision points along the way; many of these occur during the college years. Tiedeman and O'Hara (1963) provide a model that takes into account all the factors inherent in making decisions. When individuals are fully aware of these factors, they will be able to base choices on full knowledge of themselves and appropriate external information as well. Their model divides decision making into two aspects: anticipation and accommodation. In anticipation the individual becomes aware of the problem, identifies alternatives, moves toward a choice, and implements a decision. The accommodation phase incorporates contact with a real work environment and the adjustment and integration into that environment.

Harren (1979) identifies some of the factors that influence the effectiveness of an individual's decision making. He outlines three decision-making styles that students may use in the decision-making process: rational, intuitive, and dependent. Rational decision makers use systematic and logical strategies while intuitive decision makers rely on how a decision "feels" and are often impulsive. The dependent style denies responsibility for choices and complies with the authority of others. Harren believes that the rational style is most effective since the strategies used are more thoughtful and logical. Phillips, Pazienza, and Ferrin (1984) found that while rational decisional strategies generate problem-solving confidence, the intuitive style was associated with both the rational style and a confident approach to problem solving. They suggest that perhaps the intuitive strategy might offer an emotionally satisfying alternative.

Using decision-making theory, advisers can provide experiences through which students could contribute to their emotional maturity, self-concept, and values orientation. Advisers can help students identify resources and teach them how to use them. They can help students analyze their own strategies for making decisions and help them improve these strategies. They can teach decision-making skills. They can also help students take responsibilities for the decisions they have made.

Crites (1981) suggests at least three outcomes of career counseling: making a choice, acquiring decision-making skills, and enhancing general adjustment. These are outcomes for academic advising as well. The knowledge advisers can gain from career and decision-making theorists is useful in accomplishing these outcomes.

Moral Development Theory

Kohlberg (1981) indicates in discussing moral development that individuals progress from a reliance on outside authority and others' judgments to a higher state of taking responsibility for their own actions. Kohlberg outlines four stages in moral development. An individual in the premoral stage neither understands rules nor judges good or bad in terms of rules and authority. At the preconventional level, an individual has either a punishment and obedience orientation or an instrumental relativist orientation. In the first, the physical consequences of action determine its goodness or badness regardless of human values or meaning. In the second, there is an awareness of the elements of fairness, reciprocity, and equal sharing, but they are interpreted in a physical or pragmatic way.

The third level, according to Kohlberg, is the conventional level, where the expectations of the individual's family, group, or nation are perceived as valuable in their own right, regardless of immediate and obvious consequences. The two stages at this level use conformity to stereotypical images of what is "natural" behavior, with the second stage oriented toward law and order. The existence of authority, fixed rules, and the maintenance of the social order is important. The last stage is called postconventional where there is a clear effort to define moral values and principles that have validity and application apart from the authority of groups or persons holding these principles and apart from the individual's own identification with these groups.

Kohlberg espouses moral education and indicates there are ways to develop sound value systems by being a good example; assisting young people to assess conflict situations and to gain insights into the development of constructive values and beliefs; helping students acquire an understanding of the importance of values that society considers worthwhile; and aiding students to uphold and use positive values when confronted by adverse pressures from peers.

Educational and real life experiences can stimulate moral development. The focus is on moral reasoning and conflict of issues involved in a given situation. Cognitive development is a necessary but insufficient condition for moral development. The extent of social participation has been positively related to moral development (Kohlberg, 1981).

Gilligan (1982) indicates that women's moral development begins with a concern for survival where there is a concern for not hurting others and for taking care of oneself. Individuals are constantly renegotiating interdependence and caring within widening circles of attachment.

While advisers sometimes hear students describe moral dilemmas in which they are involved, some advisers are often unsure of their role or authority in their responses. While some advisers are very careful not to offer their own moral "truths," personal opinions, when labeled as such, might help young college students to gather insights into a particularly troublesome situation (e.g., roommate problems, critical relationships, academic misconduct).

Learning Theory

Understanding learning behavior is critical in understanding the academic development of many students. Jean Piaget (1968) identifies two dimensions representing the major directions of cognitive development. The course of individual development from birth to adolescence moves from a concrete view of the world to an abstract perspective. It also moves from an egocentric (active) view to a reflective mode. Other theorists have identified a concrete-abstract dimension in cognitive growth and learning (Brunner, 1966; Harvey, Hunt, & Schroeder, 1961).

A practical application of these principles is embodied in the variety of learning style theories presented. The Dunns' model (1978) concentrates on learning conditions that encompass environmental, emotional, sociological, physical, and psychological factors. For example, some students indicate they cannot study without a radio playing, while others need absolute silence. Some students learn better in groups while others prefer to learn alone. The Dunns believe that students should be taught according to how they learn most effectively.

Gregorc's (1979) learning style model reflects how students relate to the world. He discusses four learning styles, which are combinations of two dualities, one relating to perception (concrete versus abstract) and the other relating to ordering abilities (sequential versus random). Although Gregorc believes there are no pure types, his four learning styles can provide insights into how students learn best. Matching teaching and learning styles can be boring if they are too much alike, while a continuous mismatch can often cause discomfort and stress for the learner (and the teacher). He believes students should be aware of their own learning styles since they may be encouraged to take responsibility for their own learning if this process were known.

A well-known learning style model is that of Kolb (1981), who has drawn upon Jungian psychology and the tenets of Piaget for his work. Kolb focuses on the process of learning. He identifies four types of learners: convergers, divergers, assimilators, and accommodators. These styles result from choices made between processing abstract or concrete content through active and reflective behavior. Convergers, for example, prefer abstract concepts through experimentation, while divergers prefer concrete experiences through observation. Assimilators, on the other hand, prefer abstract concepts through observation, while accommodators process concrete experience through experimentation.

Advisers can sometimes point out to students, for example, that learning style preferences might account for why they do well in the laboratory part of a chemistry course while having more difficulty understanding the concepts in a chemistry lecture. Discussing the physical aspects of studying might be useful for other students whose optimal conditions might include quiet (as opposed to noise) or eating to release nervous tension. Strongly emphasizing one style of learning might mean another dimension of learning needs to be developed. Advisers can sometimes recognize a student who is totally unaware of how he approaches the learning process. Discussing the various possibilities might provide the insights a student needs to seek further help.

SUMMARY

Academic advising has its roots in the early colonial colleges where faculty were closely tied to students both personally and academically. The evolution of academic advising services reflects a variety of settings and changing institutional goals and objectives. The emphasis or deemphasis advising received over the years reflects the trends toward and away from student centeredness. Advising was reaffirmed as an important function during the 1970s when students demanded more personalized attention to their academic, career, and personal needs. Today a more developmental perspective is used to assist students in decisions relating to academic and life goals and as a critical function in the retention of students.

There are many definitions of advising, but most stress the importance of understanding individual students and their unique needs. Academic advising is often referred to as a process that involves a close student-adviser relationship. Advising is seen as an important vehicle for helping students achieve educational and personal goals through the use of campus and community resources.

While academic advising incorporates many theoretical perspectives, many advisers are generally not experts in these broad-ranging frameworks. Becoming familiar with them can enhance advising techniques and skills by applying ideas derived from this knowledge.

Advising has generated some approaches (e.g., O'Banion and Crookston), but conceptualizations of relationships between events that lead to causes and effects have not been devised. Theories can serve as starting points from which new ideas and practices can be generated and validated. Perhaps in the future, advising theory will help to identify new relationships within advising processes and new practices can be founded on valid research of these theories.

REFERENCES

Brown, R. W. (1926). *Dean Briggs*. New York: Harper & Bros.

Brunner, J. (1966). *The process of education*. New York: Atheneum.

Chickering, A. W. (1969). *Education and identity*. San Francisco: Jossey-Bass.

Clark, B. R., & Trow, M. (1966). The organizational context. In T. M. Newcomb & E. K. Wilson (Eds.), *College peer groups: Problems and prospects for research* (pp. 17–70). Chicago: Aldine.

Cowley, W. H. (1949). Some history and a venture in prophecy. In E. G. Williamson (Ed.), *Trends in student personnel work* (pp. 12–27). Minneapolis: University of Minnesota Press.

Crites, J. O. (1981). *Career counseling: Models, methods and materials*. New York: McGraw-Hill.

Crockett, D. (Ed.) (1979). *Academic advising: A resource document*. Iowa City, IA: American College Testing Program.

Crookston, B. B. (1972). A developmental view of academic advising as teaching. *Journal of College Student Personnel. 13*. 12–17.

Cross, K. P. (1974). *Beyond the open door: New students to higher education*. San Francisco: Jossey-Bass.

Dunn, R., & Dunn, K. (1978). *Teaching students through their individual learning styles: A practical approach*. Reston, VA: Reston.

Erikson, E. H. (1968). *Identity: Youth and crisis*. New York: Norton.

Gilligan, C. (1982). *In a different voice*. Cambridge: Harvard University Press.

Gregorc, A. F. (1979). *Learning/teaching styles: Diagnosing and prescribing programs*. Reston, VA: National Association of Secondary School Principals.

Grites, T. J. (1979). *Academic advising: Getting us through the eighties.* Washington, D.C.: AAHE-ERIC Higher Education Research Report, no. 7.

Harper, W. R. (1905). *Trends in higher education.* Chicago: University of Chicago Press.

Harren, V. A. (1979). A model of career decision making for college students. *Journal of Vocational Behavior. 14.* 119–133.

Harvey, O. J., Hunt, D. E., & Schroeder, H. M. (1961). *Conceptual systems and personality organization.* New York: Wiley.

Heath, D. (1968). *Growing up in college.* San Francisco: Jossey-Bass.

Heath, R. (1964). *The reasonable adventurer.* Pittsburgh: University of Pittsburgh Press.

Holland, J. L. (1985). *Making vocational choices.* Englewood Cliffs, NJ: Prentice-Hall.

Kohlberg, L. (1981). *The philosophy of moral development.* San Francisco: Harper & Row.

Kolb, D. A. (1981). Learning styles and disciplinary differences. In A. W. Chickering, *The modern American college* (pp. 232–255). San Francisco: Jossey-Bass.

Levinson, D. J., Darrow, C. M., Klein, E. B., Levinson, M. A., & McKee, B. (1978). *The seasons of a man's life.* New York: Knopf.

MacLean, M. S. (1949). Adolescent needs and building the curriculum. In E. G. Williamson (Ed.), *Trends in student personnel work* (pp. 27–39). Minneapolis: University of Minnesota Press.

Moore, L. V. (Ed.). (1990). *Evolving theoretical perspectives on college students.* New Directions for Student Services, no. 51. San Francisco: Jossey-Bass.

Mueller, K. H. (1961). *Student personnel work in higher education.* Boston: Houghton Mifflin.

Neugarten, B. L. (1971). Adaptation and the life cycle. *Journal of Geriatric Psychiatry, 4,* 71–87.

O'Banion, T. (1972). An academic advising model. *Junior College Journal, 44,* 62–69.

Perry, W. G. (1970). *Intellectual and ethical development in the college years.* New York: Holt, Rinehart, & Winston.

Phillips, S. D., Pazienza, N. J., & Ferrin, H. H. (1984). Decision-making styles and problem-solving appraisal. *Journal of Counseling Psychology, 4,* 497–502.

Piaget, J. (1964). *Judgment and reasoning in the child.* Patterson, NJ: Littlefield Adams.

Piaget, J. (1968). *Structuralism.* New York: Harper & Row.

Potter, M. R. (1927). History of conferences of Deans of Women to the organization of the National Association in 1917. *Fourteenth Yearbook of the National Association of Deans of Women,* pp. 212–227.

Reed, A. Y. (1944). *Guidance and personnel services in education.* Ithaca, NY: Cornell University Press.

Rogers, C. (1961). *On becoming a person.* Boston: Houghton Mifflin.

Rudolph, F. (1962). *The American college and university.* New York: Vintage Books.

Rudolph, F. (1977). *Curriculum.* San Francisco: Jossey-Bass.

Sanford, N. (1966). *Self and society: Social change and individual development.* New York: Atherton.

Schlossberg, N. K. (1984). *Counseling adults in transition.* New York: Springer.

Super, D. E., & Nevill, D. D. (1984). Work role salience as a determinant of career maturity in high school students. *Journal of Vocational Behavior, 25,* 255–270.

Thomas, R. & Chickering, A. W. (1984). Education and identity revisited. *Journal of College Student Personnel, 25,* 392–399.

Tiedeman, D. V., & O'Hara, R. P. (1963). *Career development: Choice and adjustment.* New York: College Entrance Examination Board.

Vaillant, G. E. (1977). *Adaptation to life.* Boston: Little, Brown.

Walsh, E. M. (1979). Revitalizing academic advisement. *Personnel and Guidance Journal, 57,* 446–449.

Winston, R., Ender, S., & Miller, T. (1982). *Developmental approaches to academic advising.* New Directions for Student Services, no. 17. San Francisco: Jossey-Bass.

2

Delivering Academic Advising Services

A discussion of advising delivery systems encompasses many complex organizational characteristics and a variety of personnel who perform advising tasks. It must also take into account the traditions and organizational structure of each campus that make it unique. Advising, once viewed as a simple exchange of curricular information between a faculty member and a student, is now defined in a broader context that includes, in addition to the scheduling function, the tasks of interpreting institutional procedures, providing career information, counseling students about adjustment concerns, and helping them make many kinds of academic decisions.

There are as many types and structures of delivery systems for advising as there are campuses that provide them. Although faculty advising systems have been the traditional means of delivery for most institutions, there is now a proliferation of other models, such as advising centers, systems using professional advisers, combinations of faculty and full-time professional staff, and peer or paraprofessional advisers. Habley (1983) contends that a distinction should be made between the structure within which advising takes place and the identification of the people who actually deliver the services. The overall make-up of an institution (size, type, location, mission) will influence the type of delivery system that is used. The uniqueness of each campus, including the emphasis placed on advising, will be reflected in the method by which advising is delivered (or not delivered) (Wilder, 1981).

Frank (1988) has outlined a theoretical model for advising program development. The Four-Stage Model includes the direction, nature, and scope of changes that have an impact on the effectiveness of an established organizational system. The four stages include (1) increasing access, (2) upgrading services, (3) coordinating programs, and (4) enabling advisers.

Frank tested the model by surveying a cross-section of institutions and found that while the essence of the theoretical model was validated, there was disagreement about the exact parameters of the four stages and where they overlapped. A revised model was developed as a result of this input. The revised model emphasizes the interconnection of stages and adds a time dimension to the process.

The Council for the Advancement of Standards for Student Services/Development Programs (1990) has set standards and guidelines for institutional academic advising programs. Included are guidelines for mission statements, program, leadership and management, organization and administration, human resources, equal opportunity, access and affirmative action, campus and community relations, multicultural programs and services, ethics, and evaluation. The standards were designed to improve the quality of advising and other services and the training of professionals involved in advising. An institution can examine its advising program by these standards and can adapt various aspects of its delivery system to them.

There are many factors to consider when describing advising systems. These include stated objectives or goals, the tasks or functions involved in the advising process, the personnel who perform these tasks, and the timing, location, and method for delivering systems. Figure 2.1 outlines these building blocks of advising delivery systems. Each block is a critical part of the whole, and when all aspects are coordinated and work in harmony, an effective service is usually in place. The student is always the focal point for these efforts and whether the developmental needs of freshmen or services for a group of students with special needs are included, students' reactions and satisfaction with advising services are the real test of a program's value, vitality, and effectiveness.

This chapter discusses the various aspects of delivering advising services and the critical components making up an overall program. As shown in Figure 2.1, these advising blocks not only build upon each other but interact at many points.

WHY ADVISING?

What is the purpose of advising? What are desirable outcomes of effective advising? These questions must be approached from three perspectives: the student's, the adviser's, and the institution's. The needs of all three must be reflected in the goals stated for an advising program.

Student Needs

Students' expectations of advising have been discussed by numerous authors (Hornbuckle, Mahoney, & Borgard, 1979; Kramer & Washburn, 1983; Stickle, 1982; Teague, 1977; Trombley, 1984; Walsh, 1979; Witters & Miller, 1971). Abel (1980) developed a model for delivering academic advising based on students' needs and progress toward selected academic goals. The goals in her

Figure 2.1
The Building Blocks of Academic Advising

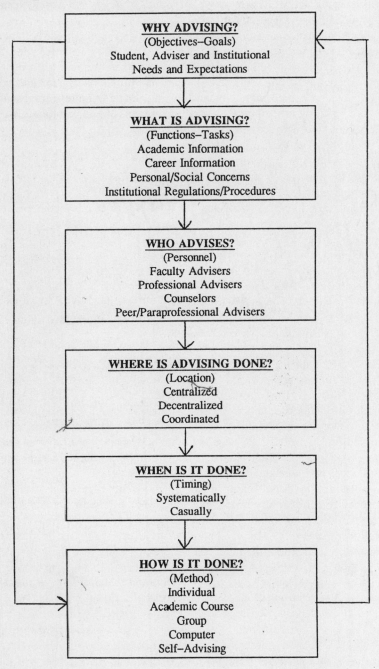

model are developmental in nature: providing opportunities for students to select and plan their academic programs, to evaluate their progress, and to identify special learning needs. The model incorporates a variety of support systems to which students may be referred.

Students' needs for advising change as they progress through the college years. Freshmen frequently need assistance during their initial encounter with the college environment. Problems of adjustment may often be identified by a competent, caring adviser (Iaccino, 1987). Students' problems sometimes surface in an advising conference that is ostensibly intended for more practical matters such as scheduling or dropping a course. Freshmen often need to talk with, ask questions of, and try ideas out on someone with whom they feel comfortable and whom they can trust.

Freshmen need help in formulating educational and career goals since they often lack the knowledge and skills to do this. Academic advisers must recognize the inherent need for accomplishing this important life task and be prepared to help freshmen assume responsibility for this critical process. Sophomores, on the other hand, may begin to question their initial choice and may need help in confirming earlier decisions. Sophomores have more real academic experiences upon which to base the appropriateness of a choice. Students at this level often need assistance in gathering information in more depth and help in evaluating each possible option in terms of this new information. Sometimes changes are apparent to students, and they will seek help. Others need to be confronted with the need to seek alternatives. Advisers must be sensitive to some students' lack of ability to assess their own needs realistically.

A few juniors may also need alternative academic counseling since they may be dissatisfied with their choice or are not performing well academically. The majority of juniors and seniors, however, are looking ahead to graduation and need help in establishing more specific occupational goals and in preparing for eventual entry into the work force. Upperclass students feel more settled into the routine of the academic environment, and their advising needs are less concerned with schedule planning and other structured advising tasks than with learning ways to strengthen their academic programs, improve their academic performance, and enhance their marketability after graduation.

Advisers who work with both freshmen and seniors are quite aware of their differences. Freshmen are more dependent and more distracted and need more structure in academic planning. Their need for regular advising contact and support is greater than that of upperclass students, who have learned how to negotiate the academic milieu and can take responsibility for their own decision making and goal setting. Advisers who have conveyed the importance of independence and academic integrity to their advisees will see this come to fruition in their seniors.

Adviser Needs

Adviser needs must be acknowledged in setting goals and objectives for an advising program. Adviser needs may be addressed with clear and comprehensive policies, adequate resources, and a reward system appropriate to the setting. While a great deal of information has been gathered about student needs in the advising setting, adviser needs have been studied infrequently. Kramer and Gardner (1983, p. 18) discuss the various roles imposed on a faculty adviser from both within and without the institution. These include the following:

1. *Adult*—one who combines age and experience to cope successfully with life; grown; mature.

2. *Expert*—one whose training, achievement, and position signify master of a subject matter; specialist.

3. *Teacher*—one who is charged by an institution with transmission of skills, knowledge, or information to others; educator, instructor; tutor.

4. *Researcher*—one who has past or present involvement with functions and activities that may be so labeled; investigator; explorer.

5. *Friend*—one with whom one has an emotional and personal attachment (affection); companion; confidant; comrade; associate.

6. *Judge*—one who by virtue of special skills, training, or position is afforded the activity of evaluating or assessing; arbiter; judicator; critic.

7. *Authority*—one who has prestige and/or power and/or is accorded sanction by an institution to give directions and have them carried out; official.

8. *Rubber Stamp*—one who confirms, agrees, or affirms the position of another.

9. *Lecturer*—one who is charged with the responsibility of providing systematic instruction in a body of knowledge using a formal verbal presentation.

10. *Citizen, parent*—one whose residence is a country or acquisition of position of parenthood.

Faculty advisers, according to Kramer and Gardner, respond to students differently depending on the situation or setting. Adviser needs in each of these roles are also different. Some roles are more comfortable and easier to accept than others. Often a conflict in roles is felt by advisers (e.g., being an authority when wanting to be a friend). If advisers are the sanctioned representatives of the institution in procedural matters, knowing the regulations and support systems for carrying them out is critical. The roles of teacher and researcher require the time to perform the duties implicit in these roles. In some instances, advisers assume the role of arbitrator or advocate on the student's behalf. This implies a need for authority and the ability and freedom to fulfill that role.

Hardee (1970) also discusses faculty in terms of advising roles. These roles will be influenced by objective interests of the faculty, which in turn are influenced by the role of the college and by the structure of the reward system. The expectations of faculty advisers will also be influenced by the scale and autonomy of the institution (Lunsford, 1963).

Full-time professional advisers also assume certain roles, and their needs, like those of faculty, must be acknowledged through administrative support. The need for professional development must be recognized and provisions made to provide the opportunity and time for this professional growth.

Dressel (1980) claims advising is often not recognized as a critical task requiring both commitment and skill. Rewards of any type are generally not provided. According to Dressel, advising deserves recognition and should be rewarded as a "quasi-administrative function." Advising should be viewed as an important assignment, and advisers should be granted the time, autonomy, and recognition that this task requires.

Institutional Needs

An institution's perspective on advising may be offered in a philosophical statement in the catalog or bulletin or in an advising manual. This philosophy will have great bearing on the functional model that is selected (Crockett, 1982). The objectives or desired outcomes of an advising program must be clearly stated before an optimal delivery system may be identified. A statement of objectives reviewed periodically may also be used to evaluate an existing program as well as updating, expanding, or improving one.

Retention studies frequently discuss academic advising as an important ingredient in successfully retaining students (Beal & Noel, 1980; Habley, 1981; Kapraun & Coldren, 1982; Noel, Levitz, & Saluri, 1985; Tinto, 1982). An institution's concern for the retention and well-being of its students is often implicit in the philosophy or set of objectives it sets forth. Advising can be a powerful force in personalizing the institution's purposes and in disseminating important procedural and resource information. Advisers act as interpreters of the institution's climate and culture as well as its curriculum and regulations (Hardee, 1970).

Glennen et al. (1989) examined the need to expand the advising team to include presidential support, enrollment management, centralized advising, and faculty involvement. They conclude that central administration's commitment to advising is critical to an effective program. A centralized, intrusive advising center can be the catalyst for including the many levels of institutional involvement necessary to the advising function.

WHAT IS ADVISING?

There are many functions associated with academic advising. Providing academic information is often perceived as the primary task in an advising exchange, but this information must also be interpreted within the students' personal context. The need to integrate academic and occupational information is implicit in many students' questions as well. The adviser is often the monitor of institutional procedures and regulations as they affect a student's curricular or personal needs. Beyond informational needs, students may have personal or social concerns that must be acknowledged since they often distract or impede academic progress.

In a national survey of two-year colleges (O'Banion, Fordyce, & Goodwin, 1972), advisers were asked to name the advising function. The majority used the terms academic advising, counseling, faculty advising, or academic counseling. Other terms used were educational planning and career planning. The varied terms offered by these respondents demonstrate the diversity with which advising functions are perceived.

There are also differences between the advising and counseling functions. Advising is often conceived as simple information giving while counseling is an integration of this information into an individual's personal frame of reference (e.g., taking into account personal characteristics and values). The following describes the functions often associated with advising:

Providing Academic Information. Perhaps the most apparent reason for advising is to provide students with relevant and current information about curriculum, courses, academic majors, and degree requirements. Providing a rationale for these curricular requirements from an institutional perspective is also important. Academic advisers are probably best equipped to perform this function.

Academic Counseling. When information needs to be interpreted in personally relevant terms, academic counseling begins. Academic counseling helps the student use the information in a personal context. For example, a discussion of the math requirement in engineering may evoke in certain students doubts about their capabilities to achieve in this subject. The ensuing discussion may center on students' feeling of inadequacy in this area and the implications it might have on future course selection and scheduling and even major choice. Academic counseling may be performed at many levels, and when the content becomes too personal, proper referrals may need to be made. Most experienced advisers use advising techniques that border on counseling, even though they may not consider themselves trained experts in this area. There is often no way to separate academic information dissemination and academic counseling when working with a particular student's problem.

Providing Career Information. It is often difficult to separate academic and career information since students frequently perceive them as the same. Information about specific occupations is critical in making career decisions. This information may include the characteristics of successful workers, educational prerequisites, descriptions of work environments, the tasks involved, salaries, and job outlook. Some advisers have access to this information, particularly in their own disciplines, while others must refer students to other campus agencies such as career libraries or computerized career information systems for this information. Students consider career information to be a vital part of academic advising.

Career Counseling. Like academic counseling, career counseling provides the interpretation of information about work and career opportunities within a personal framework. Specific knowledge and skills are needed for career counseling;

therefore many academic advisers will refer students to other campus resources when the need arises. Many skills needed in academic counseling are also used in career counseling, such as communication techniques and knowledge of information resources. An assessment of personal strengths and limitations is usually performed in a more organized and thorough fashion in career counseling, which often includes testing. Crites (1981) discusses career counseling as both comprehensive and complex. In an advising context, career counseling is helping students explore and define their roles in one of the most important areas of their lives—the work world.

Personal and Social Concerns. While many academic advisers do not have the background or training to counsel students with personal problems, these concerns may surface during an advising session. Student problems may vary from lack of study skills or roommate conflicts to thoughts of suicide. Two advising skills are used: communication and referral. No student problem should be taken lightly. An adviser is in a position to help a student secure immediately the type of help that the problem warrants.

Institutional Regulations and Procedures. While many advisers prefer not to handle institutional paperwork, it remains a function of advising in many cases. Advisers may feel on occasion that they are in an ambiguous role, as a student advocate on one hand and as a representative of the institution on the other. Advisers often need to interpret faculty rules to students so that they may learn to negotiate successfully the policies set forth by the institution. Knowledge of institutional procedures is an important tool since it can often be used to help a student resolve a particular problem.

WHO ADVISES?

Although the traditional faculty advising system still predominates (Habley & Crockett, 1988), other personnel have increasingly been given responsibility for advising tasks. Institutions may use counselors, academicians, student personnel professionals, student advisers, or paraprofessionals to perform advising services. Some use a combination of these personnel. O'Banion (1972) questioned the appropriateness of faculty advising for community colleges and developed a team model. O'Banion suggested that who performs advising is not as important as the philosophy and commitment of an institution to advising services. Teague (1977) agrees that the type of personnel who advise is not as important as having a specific person responsible for the advising of a specific student.

Crockett (1982) presents a model delivery system that includes the services of many types of advisers within a centralized advising center. While an institution's selection of a delivery mode for advising is important, Crockett views institutional commitment and the personalization of advising as more important to achieving an effective program.

The following sections discuss various types of advising personnel and their contributions to the advising process.

Faculty Advisers

As outlined in Chapter 1, the first faculty advising system was developed at Johns Hopkins University in 1877; Harvard appointed freshman advisers in 1899 (Rudolph, 1962). This was the first acknowledgment that students—freshmen in particular—needed guidance in the selection of courses for increasingly complex academic programs.

Although a great deal of research is available concerning faculty advising, much of it has been confusing because of the variety of definitions and descriptions of functions assigned to it (Biggs, Brodie, & Barnhart, 1975; Borland, 1973; Dehn, 1987; Lumpkins & Hall, 1987). Hardee (1970) describes faculty advising as an activity with many dimensions and views the faculty as the coordinator of the student's learning experiences. As coordinators, faculty can assist students in implementing their choice of program and can help them set long-range occupational and professional goals. The advantages of a faculty advising system, according to Hardee, are that (1) students will know at least one faculty member in an out-of-class setting, (2) students may receive help with occupational plans, (3) faculty can provide input into administrative processes by reflecting student needs, and (4) students will have access to a role model who can be a stabilizing influence.

Other proponents of faculty advising systems point out the similarity of the teaching and advising functions, the frequency of contact between faculty and student via the classroom, the knowledge of academic programs that faculty possess, and the positive effect that faculty have on the intellectual growth of students (Evans & Neagley, 1973; Gallagher & Demos, 1970; Hallberg, 1964; Pascarella et al., 1983; Vowell & Karst, 1989). Beasley-Fielstein (1986) indicates the quality of student-faculty interaction is a major contributing variable in institutional holding power. Endo and Harpel (1982) found that informal contact with faculty had more effect on personal/social and satisfaction outcomes than on intellectual or achievement outcomes.

Many studies deal with perceptions of advising by both faculty and students (Donk & Oetting, 1968; Mahoney, Borgard, & Hornbuckle, 1978; Rossman, 1968; Sanborn & Taylor, 1975; Stickle, 1982; Teague, 1977). Students report satisfaction with faculty advising when more time is spent with them personally (Rossman, 1968). Faculty are seen as important by students in helping them further their intellectual development and in helping them with career decisions (Astin, 1977; Feldman & Newcomb, 1969; Morstain, 1977). Hornbuckle, Mahoney, & Borgard (1979) found that students had difficulty in evaluating faculty advisers on the basis of technical competence such as planning course schedules and interpreting regulations but could evaluate their advisers on the basis of personal likes or dislikes. Stickle (1982) found that students and faculty perceptions of the effectiveness of advising were very different, with faculty rating their own effectiveness much higher than did their advisees. Kramer, Arrington, & Chynoweth (1985) studied the perceptions of students, faculty, and administrators of the role and success of academic advising centers and faculty advisers. Results indicated significant differences in perceptions across groups.

Borgard, Hornbuckle, and Mahoney (1977) studied faculty's perceptions of advising and found that faculty had mixed feelings about their advising role and that many even questioned the philosophical issue of the necessity for faculty advising. Institutions need to address the issue of faculty satisfaction and fulfillment with advising if this, indeed, is an important role for them to play (Larsen, 1983). Kramer, Arrington, & Chynoweth (1985) found that faculty advisers in their study tended to accept credit for positive outcomes and deny responsibility for poor advising sessions.

Teague and Grites (1980) found that half the faculty contracts they examined contained no mention of advising as a responsibility. They concluded that faculty advising is not considered a responsibility by many institutions in contracts, collective bargaining agreements, or faculty handbooks.

Regardless of what students regard as the advantage or disadvantage of faculty as advisers or how the faculty themselves perceive their role in the process, faculty are still the most frequently used advising personnel on campuses today. Continued research will help to clarify the role of faculty advisers and help to determine the type of extended responsibilities called for by those who espouse developmental approaches. The type of training and in-service programs that can improve and refine faculty expertise and satisfaction in performing advising tasks also needs careful study.

Professional Advisers

Nonfaculty advisers come from a wide variety of academic backgrounds. Some have degrees in disciplines such as history or science, while others have backgrounds related to student personnel and counseling. Many times the use of nonfaculty advisers is the result of large enrollments or the lack of interest and availability of faculty. More recently professional advisers are viewed as better qualified to provide the broader range of advising services that a more heterogeneous population of students needs, such as developmental skills or career advising (Meskill & Sheffield, 1970; Sheffield & Meskill, 1972).

Moore (1976) discusses the importance of using student personnel–trained professionals in advising. She found that faculty advisers tend to define their responsibilities within a narrow range of academic topics and concerns. The extent of their knowledge and their ability to refer depended on the length of time they had been on campus. Although the need for concentrated vocational or developmental counseling is vital to many students, faculty do not traditionally fulfill these needs.

Olson (1981) describes a model that integrates advising, curricular planning, and career guidance. She argues that professional academic counselors can most effectively facilitate communication, coordinate the student's learning experiences, and act as referral agents. Though the professional advisers in this departmental model had master's degrees in the academic discipline, they also demonstrated competence in independent, cognitive, and innovative thinking. Curriculum development that reflected student needs and interests was an important part of the adviser's responsibility. This led to more diverse degree options within the department. This successful program helped achieve the developmental integration of students' academic, career, and life goals through a centralized service.

Walsh (1979) proposes that advisers must expand and broaden the type of functions they provide. To do this, advisers need to be trained in counseling techniques and approaches. An important part of advising must be to teach students the process of goal identification and implementation. One of the strengths of professional advisers is that they are often trained in these areas and have the time to help students develop these life skills. According to Walsh, instructors may teach content, but advisers need to teach a process.

King (1988) provides an excellent summary of the strengths and weaknesses of a system using professional advisers. On the positive side they are more accessible to students than other types of advisers and have more opportunity to be proactive with their advisees. Adviser loads can, however, become a negative factor since the use of full-time professional staff trends to create overloads.

Counselors

While college counselors are typically engaged in helping students with their personal and social concerns (Carney & Barak, 1976; Dameron & Wolf, 1974), some institutions use counselors as academic advisers. Two-year colleges in particular use professional counselors in this role (Carstensen & Silberhorn, 1979). Advising services may be housed in student counseling centers or similar offices. Professionals involved in these systems usually have backgrounds in counseling psychology, guidance and counseling, or related fields. While these advisers are primarily trained for psychological or therapeutic counseling, they may learn the academic information necessary for advising.

Dameron and Wolf (1974) point out the advantages of this type of adviser. Their training, experience, and understanding of student development are important credentials for advising. A more comprehensive knowledge of career development and counseling and an understanding of employment trends are other advantages. Professional counselors' knowledge of student development can be particularly useful when working with students who are making educational, occupational, and life-style choices. If personal adjustment counseling is required, this may be integrated into the advising approach as well.

Some disadvantages of using counselors as advisers are cited by Crockett (1982) and Grites (1979). Some counselors are more interested in pursuing psychological concerns than academic concerns of students. Knowledge of specific curricula, course and graduation requirements, choice and use of electives and an understanding of the rationale for certain requirements may not be as extensive as with faculty advisers who are experts in their disciplines.

Kapraun and Stephenson (1983) describe a plan to integrate counseling into instructional units. The counselor is viewed as a generalist-specialist adviser. A rotation plan was initiated so that certain counselors spent each semester in a different instructional unit to increase their knowledge of academic programs. In this way they were generalists in their ability to counsel any student about all programs. They were also specialists in a functional area of the counseling division.

Integration of academic information with students' learning experiences is called for by Walsh (1979), who maintains that advisers must become counselors, advocates, and guardians in their helping role. A new repertoire of adviser behavior and skills is essential if advising is to become an important force in the lives of students. These extended responsibilities are often difficult for faculty to assume because of other pressures put upon them to teach, research, and perform public service. These duties often take precedence over advising. The professional counselor's expertise and training must be taken into consideration if developmental advising is considered important to the growth and success of students.

Peer Advisers

The value of peer advising by undergraduates has been clearly established (Conroy, 1978; Davis & Ballard, 1985; Delworth, Sherwood, & Casaburri, 1974; Ender, McCaffrey, & Miller, 1979; Frisz & Lane, 1987; Gnepp, Keating & Masters, 1980; Habley, 1979; Presser, Miller, & Rapin, 1984; Stein & Spille, 1974; Upcraft, 1971; Zunker, 1975; Zwibelman, 1977). Peer advisers can be trained to provide basic academic information and referrals. They can also offer help from a student's perspective and facilitate students' orientation to college life. Some research has shown that students consider peer advisers more acceptable and effective than faculty (Brown & Myers, 1975; Murry, 1972). Seventeen percent of the institutions in the American College Testing (ACT) program's last national survey (Habley & Crockett, 1988) reported they used peer advisers as part of their advising system. This figure is down from 27 percent on the previous survey (Crockett & Levitz, 1983).

Habley (1979) discusses the advantages and disadvantages of using students as academic advisers. Students report great acceptance of the way peer advisers relate interpersonally and provide academic information. Peer advisers are more economical than faculty, although Habley cautions this factor should not be the primary reason for initiating a peer advising program. Student advisers are more readily accessible than faculty advisers. Peer advisers may be placed in residence halls and other convenient campus locations on a regular basis. They also provide the flexibility needed for particularly busy periods such as registration. The released time provided by peer advising offers faculty and other advisers the time for more in-depth contacts that some students require. A major disadvantage of peer advising is the lack of continuity since new students must be selected and trained on a continual basis. This process requires a great deal of staff time in training and supervision (Ender & McFadden, 1980; Kelly & Nolan, 1980; Levinson, 1976; Meadows & Higgins, 1976). Student adviser training programs need strong components in time management and referral skills so that the student's own status is not affected adversely by the time and commitment needed to perform advising tasks. They also need to be sensitive to the objectivity with which they provide information about teachers and courses. Students may provide advisees with more subjective, experiential advice than objective advice (Upcraft, 1971; Zultowski & Catron, 1986).

Frisz (1984) found that peer advisers who had graduated indicated their past experiences had provided them with important skills that carried over into their professional lives. The peer adviser training and experience had helped to reinforce a previously determined career choice for some and helped others acquire interpersonal and communication skills that were useful in their careers.

Habley (1979) summarizes the contributions that peer advising can offer an advising program. In addition to effectiveness, economy, availability, and flexibility, peers can provide important input into the organization and effectiveness of an advising program. The importance of selection, training, and supervision, however, must be emphasized since the lack of continuity, accountability, and objectivity can have negative effects if not acknowledged and properly dealt with.

Paraprofessional Advisers

Another type of adviser needs to be acknowledged. Some institutions employ professionals to be advisers on a part-time basis (Burns & Kishler, 1972; Kerr, 1983). These are often persons with baccalaureate or master's degrees who generally work 20 to 30 hours a week. They are sometimes retired faculty who are used on an "as needed" basis. The reasons for using part-time advisers are often economical but may reflect the desire of certain qualified individuals who prefer part-time employment. The advantage of part-time professionals is the freshness and commitment they often bring to students and the continuity and maturity they offer when compared with student advisers.

Another type of adviser is the graduate student who works part-time while fulfilling the requirements for a master's or doctoral program. Both these types of paraprofessionals can become capable advisers with the expertise and commitment vital to an effective advising program.

King (1988) has summarized the strengths and weaknesses of each type of advising personnel. Seven criteria were used: accessibility, priority placed on advising, knowledge of discipline, knowledge of student development, need for required training, cost to institution, and credibility with faculty. While professional advisers rated highly on many dimensions, other types had strengths in different categories.

WHERE IS ADVISING DONE?

The physical location and organizational configuration of advising services will depend on the type and size of the institution as well as the objectives set forth for the advising program. Organizational patterns can range from highly centralized systems to very autonomous, decentralized ones. Large universities often use a decentralized arrangement, with colleges or schools providing a college office location along with coordinated departmental advising. Smaller campuses using faculty advisers often employ a departmental arrangement.

Hines (1984) suggests five factors to consider when choosing a delivery system: (1) characteristics of the students, (2) the advisers who are available to provide services, (3) the organizational structure of academic advising, (4) the budget, and (5) the facilities.

Centralized Advising

A centralized advising service is physically and administratively organized to serve all students at one location on campus. Centralized advising, such as an advisement center, can provide a wide range of services that may be coordinated and integrated. All students are served in a consistent manner, and duplication of services is eliminated. While many advising centers are staffed by full-time professionals, faculty may be assigned on a part-time, rotating basis.

Crockett (1982) lists some advantages of an advising center as easy accessibility, continuity of contact, accuracy of information, and focus on student rather than department. Another advantage of centralized advising is that students with special needs, such as undecided students, returning adults, or freshmen, may be served more effectively. Advisement centers often perform other services relating to advising such as orientation or adviser training.

A two-year model for community colleges (King et al., 1987) recommends a centralized advising center or office, which could reside in a counseling center, an admissions office, or an academic area. The center would advise new students until they are ready to be advised by faculty or a department. A director of advising would oversee training and evaluation and integrate related services such as career planning and academic support.

Some institutions use a residence hall approach as a way to deliver advising, where the students are most likely to find the services convenient. Gershman, Anchors, and Robbins (1988) describe a comprehensive advising program that is residentially based. The program for freshmen was developed in response to concern for retention of students as well as enhancing faculty-student relationships.

Abel (1980) describes a developmental advising program that is coordinated by a centralized advising staff. Residence hall coordinators serve as general advising staff and help students with personal and educational concerns. Peer advisers, working within the advising center, provide additional service. A centralized professional staff can coordinate its services with admissions, counseling, departmental advising, and student services (Burns & Kishler, 1972).

Decentralized Advising

A decentralized advising service is often maintained by a college, school, or department in a larger institutional setting. Decentralization is usually the result of tradition rather than being intentionally designed. Decentralized advising often provides close contact with faculty in a particular college or department. Its autonomous nature provides close control by the agency supporting it. It is often conveniently located in the student's educational area (Johnson & Sprandel, 1975). Each decentralized unit in large universities is often staffed by full-time professionals while smaller campuses may use departmental chairpersons or assign individual faculty to coordinate advising services.

Decentralization may cause expensive duplication of services, and the quality of services to students between difference academic units may be inconsistent. Decentralized advising often does not provide the special services needed by certain groups of students, such as those who are undecided or those needing learning skills. Special services may also be decentralized and often confuse students who must be referred to many physical locations.

An example of a departmental advising center is provided by Polson and Jurich (1979). The advising center is a clearinghouse for academic information and a centralized referral source for other campus resources. The center is also the depository for student records, helps students define career goals, acts as a liaison between students and faculty, coordinates field placement, and provides information about the job market.

A disadvantage of decentralized advising is that it may foster many independent advising offices with little contact with each other. Unless a concerted effort is made, little sharing of problems, ideas, methods, or resources will take place. A well-developed referral system needs to be established so that students may receive information and help in other areas when needed.

Coordinated Advising Services

Some large institutions have found a coordinated service more effective than a decentralized one. This structure maintains the autonomy of individual academic units but helps ensure the overall consistency and purpose of advising services.

A central coordinating office may serve as the conduit for important information common to all units such as institutional policies or student record information. The central authority for such an organizational structure can rest with an academic vice-president or dean or within a student affairs office.

The three organizational structures outlined above are oversimplified compared to the possible combinations that some campuses have established. At Brigham Young University, for example, advising centers are established in each of the academic colleges (Spencer, Peterson, & Kramer, 1982). A coordinator for advising helped to develop the centers and maintains a standard campuswide program, including responsibilities for training, policy information flow, orientation, curricular changes, and research and evaluation. The centers are placed organizationally under admissions and records. This organizational structure is an example of a coordinated system with the benefit of a strong central coordinating unit so that consistency and high levels of communication are present. This "hub-spoke" model has been used successfully at other universities for delivering student services in academic units as well (Appleton, Moore, & Vinton, 1978).

In a discussion of advising structures, it is important to note the advent of the full-time advising coordinator's position (Kramer, 1981). As the importance and complexity of advising services have become increasingly apparent, the need for responsibility, coordination, and accountability has been recognized. Twenty-one percent of the institutions in the ACT survey had designated an individual as director or coordinator of advising on their campuses. Four-year institutions reported this title more frequently than two-year colleges. These individuals typically held graduate degrees and worked on a 12-month basis. A more complex arrangement has been offered by Habley (1983, 1988), who suggests seven organizational structures for advising. Each model is based on the persons with whom students interact during the advising process, whether faculty, someone in an advising office, or both. There are many variables to consider before an effective organizational structure can be determined. These include student needs, staffing, adviser selection and training, accountability, coordination, evaluation, and economy.

Thirty-three percent of the respondents to the ACT National Advising Survey (Habley & Crockett, 1988) reported they used a faculty-only model. Twenty percent used an advising office in addition to faculty, and 22 percent used a "split" model where an advising office is responsible for a specific group of students such as undecided, underprepared, or nontraditional. The self-contained model in which all students are advised from entry to graduation within the same centralized unit was used by 11 percent. Four percent of the institutions surveyed indicated they used one of Habley's other three models: the dual, total intake, or satellite models.

The institutional environment consisting of the mission, norms, and scope of program offerings influences the type of organizational structure that evolves. Habley suggests that further research may identify the most effective organizational structure for institutions with certain characteristics in common. This could lead to the design of an optimal structure for a particular campus.

WHEN IS ADVISING DONE?

The time when advising takes place will depend on the tasks that need to be accomplished and the policies of the institution concerning important contact points. Many of these contact points will be dictated by institutional procedures such as withdrawal or declaration of major deadlines. Preregistration, for example, is probably the one advising contact that is made on a regular basis on many campuses. Some students make frequent adviser contacts; others may not require help except on rare occasions. The institution's policies concerning adviser signatures on certain forms will also influence the number of contacts. In some cases this enforced contact could be superficial; in others it may provide an opportunity for quality student-adviser interaction.

Some contact times may be initiated by the student as the need arises. These may be caused by personal needs as well as academic ones. Many institutions have published deadlines and required advising contact points. Other campuses have no established contact times. The relationship that has been established between adviser and student will often affect the timing and number of contacts that are actually made.

HOW IS ADVISING DONE?

The traditional method for advising has been the student and adviser on a one-to-one basis. Other methods used more recently have been group advising, computerized advising, self-advising, and even advising courses for credit. A combination of these methods is often used. The type and size of the institution, the numbers and types of students served, and the resources available often affect the primary and secondary approaches used.

While most advising contacts are individual in nature, group advising is recognized as an economical, effective method for providing academic information, career information, and other pertinent content. Computers are increasingly involved in advising, for record keeping and as an interactive tool. Self-advisement is another method used by some institutions and is recognized as a way to help students take responsibility for their own decisions, especially when printed materials are accessible and routinely updated.

Individual Advising

Academic advising is usually thought of as an exchange between an institutional representative (for example, faculty, counselors) and a student in which academic and related issues are discussed in regard to the student's needs and aspirations. The advantages of individual advising are many, but the personalization of academic and other information is considered a critical advising function. This is especially true if the adviser and student work together in an ongoing basis and a positive relationship has been established. Ender, Winston, and Miller

(1982) discuss advising as a developmental, student-centered process. This implies the presence of a concerned adviser who has an understanding of how students develop and has the time to devote to an individual student's needs.

When student-adviser ratios are extremely high, individual contacts may be limited in time but may still reflect a quality experience. Adviser training is important in this regard since a competent, well-trained adviser can bring a breadth and depth of knowledge and understanding to this relationship.

Group Advising

Although the individual approach is often perceived as the optimal method for advising, group advising has proved to be an effective method for certain tasks. Hutchins and Miller (1979) describe a group advising program in which faculty and upperclass students are trained in group techniques. An advantage of this group approach is that it provides a basic reference group in which students are able to share ideas, feelings, and concerns. The range of topics that are dealt with in a group setting can be expanded. Group support and the provision of a model of effective problem-solving behavior are also supplied by group interaction.

Group advising can provide basic information relating to students' academic areas (Bonar & Mahler, 1976; Katz, 1973). The group method can take the form of initial or orientation group advising, regularly scheduled advising groups with faculty advisers or professional staff, or groups formed for specific advising tasks such as preregistration.

Grahn, Kahn, and Kroll (1983) used a faculty team approach to group advising. When compared with traditional faculty advising, the group approach significantly reduced the amount of time needed to provide academic information with no loss of student satisfaction. An observed benefit was the camaraderie that developed among the students in the small group.

A study designed to compare small group and computer approaches (Glaize & Myrick, 1984) disclosed no differences in the effectiveness of these two methods on the maturity and career decision making of students. Combining the two approaches did not provide noticeable effects. The authors conclude that the approach used will depend on the availability of staff time, equipment, and materials. How these approaches are integrated into an overall program is an important consideration as well.

Academic Advising Courses

Another group approach is the advising course for credit. These courses may take many forms (Gordon & Grites, 1984), but they are often used to orient new students over an extended period of time. Some advantages of an advising course are as follows:

1. Academic information may be provided in depth. It would take a far greater amount of time to provide the same amount of information to students individually.

2. Students with adjustment concerns (such as study habits, homesickness) may not only receive assistance but receive support during a sometimes difficult period.

3. The course instructor may be the student's adviser, and an advising relationship may be developed very quickly over a concentrated period of time.

4. Receiving academic credit for the course often gives advising tasks credibility, and students are more apt to take the content seriously.

Computer-Assisted Advising

There are many uses of computers in academic advising, including record keeping (Aitken & Conrad, 1977; Guinn, 1983; Spencer, Peterson, and Kramer, 1983; Vitulli & Singleton, 1972), identifying students with special needs (Juola, Winburne, & Whitmore, 1968), and interactive academic programs (Fernandez, Brechtel, & Mercer, 1986; McCutchen, 1983; Rees & Fischer, 1983; Thompson, 1980).

Computer programs that provide a student database are used to match student records with degree requirements. This information includes an up-to-date record of students' course work and grades, credits for advanced placement, transfer information, current registration information, and the courses remaining to fulfill graduation requirements. Spencer, Peterson, and Kramer (1982) conclude that a computer-based system can improve the accuracy of advising information, increase the frequency of information provided, simplify access of information, and reduce personnel costs. It can free advisers from the monotonous, time-consuming clerical tasks that are necessary to advising. Ehl (1978) describes a process for implementing a computer-based program in which faculty advisers were involved in the planning process. The computer program had considerable impact on faculty, and they rated this tool more important than other program components such as workshops, handbooks, and faculty orientation.

Interactive programs directed toward special populations are a more recent development. These approaches provide students with academic and career information that can be integrated in a very personal way. Shell, Horn, and Severs (1988) describe a computer-based educational center that led to improved academic performance of disabled students. Milheim, Bredemeier, and Clemente (1989) describe a program that provides descriptions of different educational programs, deadlines, and application and other information. The system is easy to use and answers questions often asked by undergraduate students.

Interactive career guidance systems have been available for some years. DIS-COVER and SIGI-PLUS, for example, are career information systems in which students can assess their personal characteristics and search for occupational information from a vast database (Bowlsby & Rayman, 1980; Miller & Springer, 1986; Roselle & Hummel, 1988). Systems providing academic information can offer students the opportunity to gather information about major requirements, special programs such as honors opportunities, and how completed course work compares to graduation requirements in many majors. These and many other computer-assisted advising approaches have unlimited potential for the future.

Self-Advising

Some campuses provide self-help materials to students with the assumption that accurate printed materials such as bulletins, handbooks, and pamphlets will supply the information needed to perform certain advising functions. McCoy (1972) describes a scheduling kit, for example, that was mailed to new students. The kit contained information in a programmed format so that students could build a schedule with no assistance. It was found that the number of errors students made in scheduling with this well-designed material was minimal. McFarland and Daniels (1977) describe a personal plan and record book that was created so that self-advising strategies could be implemented during new student orientation. Over half the students reported using the book after the orientation program and indicate it was a helpful tool.

Self-advisement may be encouraged when students' responsibility for their own academic planning is considered important. Grites (1979) points out that self-advising is not intended to weaken the advisers' role but to strengthen it since students come to the advising session better prepared and ready to receive help.

SUMMARY

The components of an effective advising system are many and complex. An important initial step is to establish objectives and goals for the program. These must incorporate the needs of students, advisers, and institutions. Many organizational models are available for delivering effective advising services. The organization of advising on a given campus will depend on the tradition and emphasis placed on advising in that institution. As Habley and McCauley (1987) point out, how advising services are organized depends on many institutional characteristics.

The type of personnel performing advising services will also depend on the size and type of institution and the traditional way of providing advising services. Many different types of personnel currently deliver advising services. While faculty advisers are most commonly used, full-time professional advisers, students, and other paraprofessionals and counselors are often involved either independently or in combination. Advising may be provided through individual contacts, group advising, computerized advising, self-advising, and an academic course approach.

The tasks involved in advising include not only academic information giving but career and adjustment counseling as well. Enforcing institutional regulations and procedures must also be considered an advising function. The timing or established contact points for advising will depend on student needs and institutional deadlines. Casual advising contacts initiated by students will depend on their perception of the helpfulness and availability of services.

Advising services can be centrally located and administered, decentralized, or coordinated. Some institutions use a combination of approaches where coordination is under a single person or office. Each system is individualized to each campus's traditions and needs.

To create and sustain an effective advising program, all the elements described in this chapter must be carefully defined and coordinated. Many campuses have come to the realization that effective advising not only has great influence on students but has an impact on the institution's overall well-being as well.

REFERENCES

Abel, J. (1980). Academic advising: Goals and delivery system. *Journal of College Student Personnel*, *21*, 151–154.

Aitken, C. E., & Conrad, C. F. (1977). Improving academic advising through computerization. *College and University*, *53*, 115–123.

Appleton, J. R., Moore, P., & Vinton, J. (1978). A model for effective delivery of student services in academic schools and departments. *Journal of Higher Education*, *49*, 372–381.

Astin, A. W. (1977). *Four critical years*. San Francisco: Jossey-Bass.

Beal, P. E., & Noel, L. (1980). *What works in student retention*. Iowa City, IA: American College Testing Program and National Center for Higher Education Management Systems. (ERIC Document Reproduction Service No. ED. 197 635).

Beasley-Fielstein, L. (1986). Student perceptions of the developmental adviser-advisee relationship. *NACADA Journal*, *6*, 107–117.

Biggs, D. A., Brodie, J. S., & Barnhart, W. J. (1975). The dynamics of undergraduate academic advising. *Research in Higher Education*, *3*, 345–357.

Bonar, J., & Mahler, L. R. (1976). A center for undecided college students. *Personnel and Guidance Journal*, *54*, 481–484.

Borgard, J. H., Hornbuckle, P. A., & Mahoney, J. (1977). Faculty perceptions of academic advising. *NASPA Journal*, *14*, 4–10.

Borland, D. T. (1973). Curricular planning through creative faculty advising. *NASPA Journal*, *10*, 211–217.

Bowlsby, J. H., & Rayman, J. R. (1980). *DISCOVER: A computer-based career guidance and counselor support system. Professional Manual*. Washington, DC: Discover Foundation.

Brown, C. R., & Myers, R. (1975). Student vs. faculty curricular advising. *Journal of College Student Personnel*, *16*, 226–231.

Burns, K. N., & Kishler, T. C. (1972). *Centralized academic advising at Michigan State University*. East Lansing, MI: University College Student Affairs Office.

Carney, C., & Barak, A. (1976). A survey of student needs and student personnel services. *Journal of College Student Personnel*, *17*, 280–284.

Carstensen, D. J., & Silberhorn, C. (1979). *A national survey of academic advising*. Iowa City, IA: American College Testing Program.

Conroy, J. K. (1978). Paid student paraprofessionals. *NASPA Journal*, *15*, 18–24.

Council for the Advancement of Standards for Student Services/Development Programs (1990). *NACADA Journal*, *10*, 52–60.

Crites, J. O. (1981). *Career counseling: Models, methods and materials*. New York: McGraw-Hill.

Crockett, D. S. (1982). Academic advisement delivery systems. In R. B. Winston, S. C. Enders, & T. K. Miller (Eds.), *Developmental approaches to academic advising* (pp. 39–53). New Directions for Student Services, no. 17. San Francisco: Jossey-Bass.

Crockett, D. S., & Levitz, R. (1983). *A national survey of academic advising*. Iowa City, IA: American College Testing Program.

Dameron, J. D., & Wolf, J. C. (1974). Academic advisement in higher education: A new model. *Journal of College Student Personnel*, *15*, 470–473.

Davis, B., & Ballard, M. R. (1985). Peer advisers: Agents of change for high-risk students. *NACADA Journal*, *5*, 9–15.

Dehn, S. (1987). Using faculty to advise new students. *NACADA Journal*, *7*, 62–66.

Delworth, U., Sherwood, G., & Casaburri, N. (1974). *Student paraprofessionals: A working model for higher education*. Student Personnel Series, no. 17. Washington, DC: American Personnel and Guidance Association.

Donk, L. J., & Oetting, E. R. (1968). Student-faculty relations and the faculty advising system. *Journal of College Student Personnel*, *9*, 400–402.

Dressel, P. L. (1980). *Improving degree programs*. San Francisco: Jossey-Bass.

Ehl, C. C. (1978). *Academic advising and counseling: A computer assisted enhancement*. Paper presented at the annual meeting of the Association for Institutional Research Forum, Houston, TX. (ERIC Document Reproduction Service No. ED 161 332)

Ender, S. C., McCaffrey, S. S., & Miller, T. K. (1979). *Students helping students: A training manual for peer helpers on the college campus*. Athens, GA: Student Development Associates.

Ender, S. C., & McFadden, R. B. (1980). Training the student paraprofessional helper. In F. B. Newton and K. L. Ender (Eds.), *Student development practices: Strategies for making a difference* (pp. 127–142). Springfield, IL: Charles C. Thomas.

Ender, S. C., Winston, R. B., & Miller, T. K. (1982). Academic advising as student development. In R. B. Winston, S. C. Ender & T. K. Miller (Eds.), *Developmental approaches to academic advising* (pp. 3–18). San Francisco: Jossey-Bass.

Endo, J., & Harpel, R. (1982). The effect of student-faculty interaction on students' educational outcomes. *Research in Higher Education*, *16*, 115–138.

Evans, N. D., & Neagley, R. L. (1973). *Planning and developing innovative community colleges*. Englewood Cliffs, NJ: Prentice-Hall.

Feldman, K. A., & Newcomb, T. M. (1969). *The impact of college on students*. San Francisco: Jossey-Bass.

Fernandez, E., Brechtel, M., & Mercer, A. (1986). Personal and simulated computer-aided counseling: Perceived versus measured counseling outcomes for college students. *Journal of College Student Personnel*, *27*, 224–228.

Frank, C. P. (1988). The development of academic advising programs. *NACADA Journal*, *8*, 11–28.

Frisz, R. H. (1984). The perceived influence of a peer advisement program on a group of its former peer advisers. *Personnel and Guidance Journal*, *62*, 616–618.

Frisz, R. H., & Lane, J. (1987). Student user evaluation of peer advising services. *Journal of College Student Personnel, 28,* 241–245.

Gallagher, P. J., & Demos, G. A. (1970). *The counseling center in higher education.* Springfield, IL: Charles C. Thomas.

Gershman, E., Anchors, S., & Robbins, M. (1988). A multidisciplinary faculty and peer advising program for residentially based freshmen. *Journal of College Student Development, 29,* 167–168.

Glaize, D. L., & Myrick, R. D. (1984). Interpersonal groups or computers? A study of career maturity and career decidedness. *Vocational Guidance Quarterly, 32,* 168–176.

Glennen, R. E., Farren, P. J., Vowell, F., & Black, L. (1989). Expanding the advising team. *NACADA Journal, 9,* 25–30.

Gnepp, J., Keating, D. P., & Masters, J. C. (1980). A peer system for advising. *Journal of College Student Personnel, 21,* 370–371.

Gordon, V. N., & Grites, T. J. (1984). The freshman seminar course: Helping students succeed. *Journal of College Student Personnel, 25,* 315–320.

Grahn, J., Kahn, P., & Kroll, P. (1983). Faculty team approach to group advising. *Journal of College Student Personnel, 24,* 214–218.

Grites, T. J. (1977). Student development through academic advising: A 4X4 model. *NASPA Journal, 14,* 33–37.

Grites, T. J. (1979). *Academic advising: Getting us through the eighties.* Washington, DC: American Association of Higher Education. (AAHE-ERIC Higher Education Research Report, No. 7)

Guinn, D. (1983). *The adviser's use of the computer as a student information resource.* Paper presented at the NACADA National Conference, St. Louis, MO.

Habley, W. R. (1979). The advantages and disadvantages of using students as academic advisers. *NASPA Journal, 17,* 46–51.

Habley, W. P. (1981). Academic advising: The critical link in student retention. *NASPA Journal, 18,* 45–50.

Habley, W. R. (1983). Organizational structures for academic advising: Models and implications. *Journal of College Student Personnel, 24,* 535–540.

Habley, W. R. (1988). *The status and future of academic advising.* Iowa City, IA: American College Testing Program.

Habley, W. R., & Crockett, D. S. (1988). The third ACT national survey of academic advising. In W. R. Habley (Ed.), *Status and future of academic advising* (pp. 11–76). Iowa City, IA: American College Testing Program.

Habley, W. R., & McCauley, M. E. (1987). The relationship between institutional characteristics and the organization of advising services. *NACADA Journal, 7,* 27–39.

Hallberg, E. C. (1964). Realism in academic advising. *Journal of College Student Personnel, 6,* 114–117.

Hardee, M. D. (1970). *Faculty advising in colleges and universities.* Washington, DC: American Personnel and Guidance Association.

Hines, E. R. (1984). Delivery systems and the institutional context. In R. B. Winston, S. C. Ender, T. K. Miller, T. J. Grites and Associates, *Developmental academic advising* (pp. 317–346). San Francisco: Jossey-Bass.

Hornbuckle, P., Mahoney, J., & Borgard, J. (1979). A structured analysis of student perceptions of faculty advising. *Journal of College Student Personnel, 20,* 296–300.

Hutchins, D. E., & Miller, W. B. (1979). Group interaction as a vehicle to facilitate faculty-student advisement. *Journal of College Student Personnel, 20,* 253–257.

Iaccino, J. (1987). Developing an effective delivery system—The freshman advising program. *NACADA Journal, 7,* 41–42.

Johnson, J., & Sprandel, K. (1975). Centralized academic advising at the department level. *University College Quarterly, 21,* 17–19.

Juola, A. E., Winburne, J. W., & Whitmore, A. (1968). Computer-assisted academic advising. *Personnel and Guidance Journal, 46,* 146–150.

Kapraun, E. D., & Coldren, D. W. (1982). Academic advising to facilitate student retention. *NACADA Journal, 2,* 59–60.

Kapraun, E. D., & Stephenson, C. W. (1983). *Organizational plan and procedures for integration of centralized counseling with instructional divisions.* Paper presented at the NACADA National Conference, St. Louis, MO.

Katz, J. (1973). *Services for students.* San Francisco: Jossey-Bass.

Kelly, L. P., & Nolan, T. W. (1980). Identifying student paraprofessional training needs: An analytical approach. *Journal of College Student Personnel, 21,* 431–436.

Kerr, B. (1983). Alumni as peer advisers in a community college. *Journal of College Student Personnel, 24,* 366–367.

King, M. C. (1988). Advising delivery systems. In W. R. Habley (Ed.), *Status and future of academic advising* (pp. 142–149). Iowa City, IA: American College Testing Program.

King, M. C., Garing, M., Geisler, B., Mathieu, M., McKenna, K., & Terrell, J. A. (1987). *Two-year college advising model.* Columbus, OH: National Clearinghouse for Academic Advising.

Kramer, G. L., & Washburn, R. (1983). The perceived orientation needs of new students. *Journal of College Student Personnel, 24,* 311–319.

Kramer, G. L., Arrington, N. R., & Chynoweth, B. (1985). The academic advising center and faculty advising: A comparison. *NASPA Journal, 23,* 24–35.

Kramer, H. C. (1981). The advising coordinator: Managing from a one-down position. *NACADA Journal, 1,* 7–15.

Kramer, H. C., & Gardner, R. E. (1983). *Advising by faculty.* Washington, DC: National Education Association.

Larsen, M. D. (1983). Rewards for academic advising: An evaluation. *NACADA Journal, 3,* 53–60.

Levinson, J. H. (1976). *Peer academic advisement: The use of students as peer professional support staff.* Paper presented at the annual conference of NAWDAC, New Orleans. (ERIC Document Reproduction Service No. 136 159)

Lumpkins, B., & Hall, H. (1987). Advising college undergraduates—a neglected art. *College Student Journal, 21,* 98–100.

Lunsford, T. F. (1963). *The study of compus cultures.* Boulder, CO: Western Interstate Commission for Higher Education.

Mahoney, J., Borgard, J., & Hornbuckle, P. A. (1978). The relationship of faculty experience and advisee load to perceptions of academic advising. *Journal of College Student Personnel, 19,* 28–32.

McCoy, R. D. (1972). Academic self-counseling: Does it work? *Personnel and Guidance Journal, 50,* 834–835.

McCutchen, W. R. (1983). Computer-assisted advising for dental students. *Journal of Dental Education, 47,* 321–324.

McFarland, D., & Daniels, V. (1977). Academic advising with a personal plan and record book. *Journal of College Student Personnel, 18,* 243–244.

Meadows, M. E., & Higgins, E. B. (1976). Involving students in assessment of student development: A training modality. *Journal of College Student Personnel, 17,* 153–154.

Meskill, V. P., & Sheffield, W. (1970). A new specialty: Full-time academic counselors. *Personnel and Guidance Journal, 49,* 55–58.

Milheim, W. D., Bredemeier, N. I., & Clemente, R. (1989). A computer-based, student-operated advising system for educational majors. *NACADA Journal, 9,* 25–32.

Miller, M. J., & Springer, T. P. (1986). Perceived satisfaction of a computerized vocational counseling system as a function of monetary investment. *Journal of College Student Personnel, 27,* 142–145.

Moore, K. M. (1976). Faculty advising: Panacea or placebo? *Journal of College Student Personnel, 12,* 371–374.

Morstain, B. R. (1977). An analysis of students' satisfaction with their academic program. *Journal of Higher Education, 48,* 1–16.

Murry, J. P. (1972). The comparative effectiveness of student-to-student and faculty advising programs. *Journal of College Student Personnel, 13,* 562–566.

Noel, L., Levitz, R., & Saluri, D. (1985). *Increasing student retention.* San Francisco: Jossey-Bass.

O'Banion, T. (1972). An academic advising model. *Junior College Journal, 42,* 62–69.

O'Banion, T., Fordyce, J. W., & Goodwin, G. (1972). Academic advising in the two-year college: A national survey. *Journal of College Student Personnel, 22,* 483–488.

Olson, C. M. (1981). Professional academic advising and career planning: An integrated approach. *Journal of College Student Personnel, 22,* 483–488.

Pascarella, E. T., Duby, P. B., Terenzini, P. T., & Iverson, B. K. (1983). Student-faculty relationships and freshman year intellectual and personal growth in a non-residential setting. *Journal of College Student Personnel, 24,* 395–402.

Polson, C. J., & Jurich, A. P. (1979). The departmental academic advising center: An alternative to faculty advising. *Journal of College Student Personnel, 3,* 249–252.

Presser, N. R., Miller, T. B., & Rapin, L. S. (1984). Peer consultation: A new role for student paraprofessionals. *Journal of College Student Personnel, 25,* 321–326.

Rees, P. W., & Fischer, C. G. (1983). *Interactive computer advisement: Development of a model.* Paper presented at the NACADA National Conference, St. Louis, MO.

Roselle, B. E., & Hummel, T. J. (1988). Intellectual development and interaction effectiveness with DISCOVER. *Career Development Quarterly, 36,* 241–250.

Rossman, J. E. (1968). Released time for faculty advising: The impact on freshmen. *Personnel and Guidance Journal, 47,* 358–363.

Rudolph, F. (1962). *The American college and university.* New York: Vintage Books.

Sanborn, C. H., & Taylor, A. L. (1975). Predicting faculty interest in student advising in the community college. *Research in Higher Education, 3,* 67–75.

Sheffield, W., & Meskill, V. P. (1972). Faculty adviser and academic counselor: A pragmatic marriage. *Journal of College Student Personnel, 13,* 28–30.

Shell, D. F., Horn, C. A., & Severs, M. K. (1988). Effects of a computer-based educational center on disabled students' academic performance. *Journal of College Student Development, 29,* 432–440.

Spencer, R. W., Peterson, E. D., & Kramer, G. L. (1982). Utilizing college advising centers to facilitate and revitalize academic advisement. *NACADA Journal, 2,* 13–23.

Spencer, R. W., Peterson, E. D., & Kramer, G. L. (1983). Designing and implementing a computer-assisted academic advising program. *Journal of College Student Personnel, 24,* 513–518.

Stein, G. B., & Spille, H. A. (1974). Academic advising reaches out. *Personnel and Guidance Journal, 53,* 61–64.

Stickle, F. (1982). Faculty and student perceptions of faculty advising effectiveness. *Journal of College Student Personnel, 23,* 262–265.

Teague, G. V. (1977). Community college student satisfaction with four types of academic advisement. *Journal of College Student Personnel, 21,* 281–284.

Teague, G. V., & Grites, T. J. (1980). Faculty contracts and academic advising. *Journal of College Student Personnel, 21,* 40–44.

Thompson, R. G. (1980). Computer-assisted advising program. *Journal of College Student Personnel, 21,* 571–572.

Tinto, V. (1982). Limits of theory and practice in student attrition. *Journal of Higher Education, 53,* 687–700.

Trombley, T. B. (1984). An analysis of the complexity of academic advising tasks. *Journal of College Student Personnel, 25,* 234–239.

Upcraft, M. L. (1971). Undergraduate students as academic advisers. *Personnel and Guidance Journal, 49,* 827–831.

Vitulli, R. A., & Singleton, R. L. (1972). Computer-assisted advising and degree evaluation. *College and University, 47,* 492–502.

Vowell, F., & Karst, R. (1987). Student satisfaction with faculty advisers in an intrusive advising program. *NACADA Journal, 7,* 31–33.

Walsh, E. M. (1979). Revitalizing academic advisement. *Personnel and Guidance Journal, 57,* 446–449.

Wilder, J. R. (1981). A successful academic program: Essential ingredients. *Journal of College Student Personnel, 22,* 488–492.

Witters, L. A., & Miller, H. G. (1971). College advising: An analysis of adviser-advisee roles. *Journal of SPATE, 2,* 36–40.

Zultowski, W. H., & Catron, D. W. (1986). Students as curriculum advisers: Reinterpreted. *Journal of College Student Personnel, 27,* 199–204.

Zunker, V. G. (1975). Students as paraprofessionals in four-year colleges and universities. *Journal of College Student Personnel, 16,* 281–286.

Zwibelman, B. B. (1977). Differences in the utilization of professional and paraprofessional counseling services. *Journal of College Student Personnel, 18,* 358–361.

3

The Academic Advising Process

Adviser: "How may I help you?"

Student: "I need you to sign this form to drop a course."

or

"I don't know what I want to major in, and I'll be a sophomore."

or

"I'm not doing well in my chemistry course and it's required in my major. What should I do?"

The academic advising process consists of a complex set of variables that interact in many forms at many levels. What actually transpires during an advising contact depends on the presenting problems or needs students bring to the transaction, advisers' expertise and past experiences with the presenting problems, advisers' desire and ability to meet certain expectations for problem solving, and the type of history and relationship individual students and advisers have with each other.

This chapter discusses advising as a dynamic process that can have a significant impact on both student and institution. Immediate and long-term outcomes of this process will be determined by the institution's investment in advising in general and how these values have been integrated into the overall goals and objectives of the advising enterprise. Adviser commitment to student-centeredness is also a critical factor.

O'Banion (1972) claims that too often, advising programs have been planned on the basis of available personnel or a poorly thought-out philosophical rationale. The process or nature of academic advising has not been taken into account when programs have been initiated or reformulated. O'Banion describes the advising process in terms of the following steps: (1) exploration of life goals,

(2) exploration of vocational goals, (3) program choice, (4) course choice, and (5) scheduling courses. O'Banion views these dimensions as a necessary progression. Too often students and advisers start with course choice and scheduling before educational and vocational goals have been identified, clarified, and evaluated.

This chapter discusses the various ingredients of the advising process. Five basic components comprise the effectiveness of the advising exchange. An adviser must (1) understand the characteristics of the students to be advised, (2) be sensitive to the content and dynamics of what transpires in the advising interview, (3) acquire and use effectively the advising skills and techniques that are integral to the process, (4) use the most current and innovative advising materials available, and (5) adjust advising techniques and materials to the setting in which the advising takes place.

THE STUDENTS WE ADVISE

College students have probably been studied more than any other single population (Astin, 1977; Bowen, 1977; Feldman & Newcomb, 1969; Lenning et al., 1974). The decision to enter college profoundly influences one's life. It can affect one's personal, social, and career decisions. It can also have an impact on the rate and quality of individual development. Advisers' knowledge of the nonintellective as well as intellective characteristics of college students provides a foundation for the understanding and sensitivity essential to advising.

Collectively advisers see a tremendously heterogenous group. Students are from a wide variety of socioeconomic and cultural backgrounds and belong to many racial and age groups. Some students enter college with excellent academic preparation, while others present great academic deficiencies upon entrance. Individuals have certain attitudes, values, beliefs, aspirations, and other traits that make them unique. One of the most important tenets of academic advising is that advisers need to know their students from many perspectives. By understanding how students change over time, advisers become more sensitive to how individuals develop and grow and thus understand the needs of the individual type and level of students with whom they work.

In summarizing the effects of college on individuals, Astin (1977) demonstrates that students change in many way. A few of these changes are that many students

- develop a more positive self-image
- become more competent intellectually and interpersonally
- develop more liberal views and attitudes toward social issues
- may become less religious and altruistic
- as freshmen appear less studious and interact less with instructors; they become more studious and interact more with time in college

• generally get lower grades than they did in high school and are less involved in extra-curricular activities

The results of Astin's long-term studies of college students are published annually by the American Council on Education and the University of California at Los Angeles. Attitudes and characteristics of freshmen are assessed, including their reasons for attending college, their political views, what they think is important to accomplish during their lifetime, and their values and attitudes toward a variety of national and personal issues. As Levine (1989) suggests, we sometimes think of college students in generational stereotypes.

Undergraduates in the 20s were wet, wild and wicked. Students of the 1930s were somber and radical. Students of the 1940s were mature and "in a hurry." Students of the 1950s were silent. Students of the late 1960s and early 1970s were angry activists. More recently, students have been characterized as self-concerned and career oriented. (P. 15)

When college students in the 1930s were asked why they were in college, they said they wanted to learn a profession and improve themselves. Since many were first-generation college students, they saw a college education as a way to upward social mobility. They also wanted to increase their earning power. These were the children of the Great Depression.

In 1965 (over 30 years later) over 85 percent of entering freshmen said the major purpose of college for them was to "develop a philosophy of life." They wanted to help others, solve social problems, and learn about people who were culturally different from themselves. They were concerned about jobs and earning power, but these were not their highest priorities. In the late 1970s students indicated they were in college to find a career, but they were still interested in social and political issues (Astin, 1977).

When students in the late 1980s were asked why they were attending college, over 70 percent indicated "to get a better job" or "to make more money." About a third wanted to become a more cultured person or were in college because of parental wishes. Around 70 percent said that what was important to them was "to be very well-off financially," "to raise a family," or "to become an authority in their field." These students held a traditional interest in financial security and job opportunities and a declining tendency to view the college years as a time for learning and personal development. Green (1989) points out that the students of the 1980s experienced an economic upheaval, so it seems natural that they would be concerned about careers and jobs.

The shift to more conservative students in the 1980s was reflected in their dress, choice of academic major, personal values, professional aspirations, and political views. Many were serious, eager, and cooperative.

Schroeder, DiTiberio, and Kalsbeek (1989) discuss the gap between students and faculty in the 1980s. Many students wanted practical, job-related training; faculty, on the other hand, particularly those on liberal arts campuses, preferred that students encounter general education as a way of broadening their options, not narrowing them to one job. "Students want career advice about how to earn high salaries in secure positions; faculty are keenly, often painfully aware that their own career choices have led to compensation lower than that of the graduates who once sat in their classes" (p. 11).

Many adult students also seemed concerned about using college to improve their career options. Many young women, especially those who are the sole support of themselves and/or young children, view college as a path to a more secure future. Other adults value college as a place to develop personally and value learning for learning's sake.

Many of the changes at colleges and universities over the last 100 years have reflected changes in our larger society. These economic and social changes have important implications for advisers who are frequently involved in helping students identify and clarify their values and goals.

Students in the beginning of the twenty-first century will represent a dramatic change in the type of student we have traditionally seen (Hodgkinson, 1985). By the year 2000 one of every three Americans will be nonwhite. "Minorities will cover a broader socioeconomic range than ever before, making simplistic treatment of their needs even less useful" (p. 7). A declining overall pool of college-age youth into the last part of this century and the beginning of the next indicates that colleges and universities will need to enroll minority youth in order to maintain enrollments (Estrada, 1988). The impact of this ethnic and racial change in the student population may foretell a need for more remediation, greater emphasis on minority content in the curriculum, and competency testing, according to Estrada.

Hodgkinson (1985) predicts there will be a major increase in the number of college students who will need both financial and academic assistance. There will also be a major increase in the number of part-time college students and a decline of about one million full-time students.

This shift in the makeup of the college student population in the future will have a significant effect on the advising needs of students who will be approaching the college experience from many nontraditional perspectives. Advisers must have not only knowledge of the changing and developing college student in general, but specific knowledge of the unique characteristics of students on their campus as well. An adviser on a community campus with a majority of adult students will not only need to understand older students' developmental needs but also need to know about child care resources, math anxiety, and a host of other concerns unique to this population. Advisers on a four-year, traditional liberal arts campus will need to know about a very different set of developmental needs and resources. Chapters 5 and 6 detail the needs of special populations with whom many advisers work.

THE ADVISING EXCHANGE

The advising process is a complex set of interactions that identifies a problem, provides and evaluates information, produces a tangible solution, and implements the solution by taking action. Since most advising is done with individual students on an appointment basis, the problems students present usually become the immediate agenda. Experienced advisers, however, will use the opportunity to discuss other issues that seem relevant (or sometimes even urgent) to an individual student.

An understanding of the adviser-advisee relationship is at the heart of effective advising. Advisers make assumptions about college students in general and how they will assist them; students make assumptions about advisers and how they will help them with academic and career planning and decision making. If the adviser's and student's expectations of roles and responsibilities differ, effective communication may not take place. It is important, therefore, that these roles and responsibilities be identified, clarified, and agreed upon by both parties when the relationship begins.

Adviser Roles and Responsibilities

The role of adviser is clear in the context of advising about academic curricula and course requirements (information dissemination). In the area of interpersonal dynamics, the role of adviser is less clear. How advisers react in this area will depend on past training and experiences and how comfortable they feel in the role of adviser.

Advisers play many roles—expert, advocate, authority, rubber stamp, judge, teacher, and friend (Kramer & Gardner, 1983). When a student approaches an adviser with a specific concern, the student may assume that the adviser will play a specific role. For example, students may depend upon their advisers to tell them what courses to schedule; they see the adviser as an authority. Advisers, however, may reply from a teaching role, by teaching curricular information and procedures and expecting students to take responsibility for scheduling their own courses. Advisers, in this case, may expect students to play the role of responsible adult. When expectations are different and there is a confusion of roles, the advising experience may be unsatisfactory to both parties.

Different roles also imply different responsibilities. There are limits to an adviser's responsibility to the student, and students must learn what these limits are. How intrusive should an adviser be? At one extreme one might declare that students are adults who can read the catalog and therefore should take full responsibility for their own academic decisions. The other extreme is to be in constant contact with students about every detail of every decision they make. A middle path is needed. Advisers may need to take the initiative to contact the student under some circumstances, for example, when a scheduling error or procedural problem arises about which the student has no knowledge. Advisers should not control students but be prepared to serve as advocates when the situation indicates. Advisers may try to motivate students through encouragement and support, but the responsibility for taking action is the student's. When advisees feel the support of an adviser in their efforts to become successful students, a positive, productive relationship is more likely to develop.

Crookston's (1972) classic framework for academic advising offers an example of two advising approaches where adviser roles are well defined. Specific student characteristics, such as abilities, motivation, maturity, and responsibility, are viewed from two perspectives. The "prescriptive" adviser is one who focuses on student limitations. Students are assumed to be naturally immature and irresponsible and thus control and learning output are controlled by the adviser. "Developmental" advisers, on the other hand, concentrate on students' potentialities and view students as striving, responsible, and capable of self-direction. The adviser's role in the prescriptive approach is that of authority and judge. The developmental adviser's role is one of teacher where shared responsibility is assumed. While there may be situations where an adviser must be more prescriptive (e.g., interpreting a faculty rule), a developmental approach is more often seen as desirable.

Student Roles and Responsibilities

While it is possible to outline advisers' roles and responsibilities rather explicitly, it is more difficult to define these characteristics for students. Students give little thought to their responsibilities in the advising exchange unless this issue is discussed early in the relationship.

Some students may appear mature and sophisticated but in fact may be very unsure of themselves in a new situation. Others will want to become very dependent and expect their adviser to perform many tasks that they should be doing themselves. Still others may be perfectly capable of handling their own responsibilities. Each student brings to the advising situation a personal agenda that may or may not be apparent. Advisers' skill in responding to a student will depend on their ability to define the role the student has placed them in and how they communicate understanding and support for the student's concern.

Students expect advisers to provide reliable and current information about the academic program in which they are enrolled, to know how and where to refer them to proper campus resources to solve certain problems (e.g., financial or health concerns), to be an expert on the institution's procedures and policies, and to be an expert problem solver. Many younger students will be struggling with their own growing and changing self-concepts. Their discussion of academic major and career interests may reflect the "shoulds" and "oughts" of people whom they trust rather than their own desires. An awareness of the struggles and changes taking place in students may help advisers understand not only the surface problem that the student brings but the unspoken concerns as well. An important adviser role is to help students clarify their situation and assist them in taking responsibility for resolving it.

The Advising Interview

When an advising appointment is broken down into its components, the basic flow is established, whether it be for 20 minutes or an hour. A typical sequence is as follows:

1. *Opening the Interview*
- Opening question or lead, for example, "How can I help you?"
- Obtain student's folder or record so that relevant information is available during the interview and notes can be added later
- Openness, interest, concentrated attention are conveyed

2. *Identifying the Problem*
- Ask to state the problem; help student articulate if needed
- Help student state all relevant facts; gather as much information as needed to clarify situation for you and student
- Is presenting problem covering a real problem? Ask probing, open-ended questions
- Restate the problem in student's words; give student a chance to clarify, elaborate, or correct your interpretation, if needed

3. *Identifying Possible Solutions*
- Ask student for his or her ideas for solving problem
- Help student generate additional or alternative solutions
- What, how, when, who will solve the problem?
- What resources are needed?
- Discuss implications for each solution if two or more are identified

4. *Taking Action on the Solution*
- What specific action steps need to be taken? Is procedure, information, or referral needed?
- In what order do action steps need to be taken?
- In what time frame do they need to be taken?
- What follow-up is needed? By student? By adviser?

5. *Summarizing the Transaction*
- Review what has transpired, including restating action steps
- Encourage future contact; make a definite appointment time if referral or assignment has been made
- Summarize what has taken place in student's folder or record including follow-up steps or assignments if made

The initial contact with a student sets the tone for future interactions. Good communication skills are essential if the student is to feel comfortable. Positive verbal and nonverbal behaviors will suggest that the adviser is ready to concentrate on the student's concerns. Advisers who feel overwhelmed with large numbers of students and brief appointment times will find the need to focus especially challenging. Some simple modes of communication, such as concentrated listening, clarifying what students say, and reflecting back the meaning of their words, will assure students that their concerns are heard.

Student Problems

Students bring a plethora of problems to the advising exchange. Advisers need to take each concern seriously since it is important to the student who is experiencing it. Examples of academically related problems that students bring to advisers include choosing a major, academic planning and scheduling, negotiating the system, problems with administrators or faculty, difficulty with study habits or time management, and career decisions based on academic choices.

Some students have problems of a personal or social nature, including difficulties with personal relationships, anxiety, depression, physical health, finances, living conditions, employment, substance abuse, and a myriad of other concerns (Archer & Lamnin, 1985; Carney & Barak, 1976; Cook et al., 1984; Koplik & DeVito, 1986; Roberts & White, 1989; Roscoe, 1987; Shueman & Medvene, 1981). Since personal problems often affect academic progress, advisers need to provide an empathic ear and refer students to appropriate campus or community resources.

Hoffman and Weiss (1987) examined the influence of separation from parents and parental conflict and dominance on the common presenting problems of college students. A direct relationship was found between degree of family conflict and distress and the symptoms of personal distress students reported, both for themselves and their parents.

The type of student concerns may shift with changes in age, experiences, and campus or societal pressures. There is also evidence that students from different racial and cultural backgrounds have unique problems (Semmes & Makalani, 1985; Shang, 1989; Tomlinson & Cope, 1988; Tracey, Leong, & Glidden, 1986; Tyron, 1984). There are, however, common concerns that most college students experience regardless of age or type of institution. Most students are concerned about adjusting to a new environment, making friends, and doing well academically. Although experienced advisers have probably dealt with students' basic concerns many times, each student puts a different twist on the problem and makes each resolution unique. The solution to a given concern expressed by one student may not be the same for another.

Occasionally advisers will be in contact with students in crisis. Some students, especially on large campuses, may find their adviser the one adult to whom they can confide. There are many precipitating events—academic, career, or personal—that can initiate a crisis. Advisers may be able to help students resolve an academic crisis but must refer to appropriate resources on- or even off-campus when counseling or other resolutions are needed. Precipitating events may be either developmental in nature or situational, such as those caused by external events. Any event that the student considers a crisis should be treated as such by the adviser. Parental pressures, roommate conflicts, or failing grades may precipitate a crisis in a student's mind. More serious events such as rape, physical abuse, or an arrest can cause students severe problems, both emotional and physical. According to Taylor (1991) a crisis is a temporary state that is evidenced by an acute state of disorganization. Typical coping mechanisms break down. Advisers can help students examine the dimensions of the problem and explore specific solutions. Empathic and supportive listening, problem solving, and referral skills are critical in this situation. Sometimes advisers have an opportunity to make a difference in how students approach and resolve certain crises.

Advisers' responsibility in helping students identify and resolve their problems is not to solve them but to assist in generating and exploring alternatives. Some students need to be taught decision-making skills, and advisers can make them aware of these skills through modeling good decision-making practices. Advisers can often help students sort out the various aspects of a problem, offer relevant information, refer to specific resources, and provide support during the process. The student, however, is the ultimate decision maker and must take responsibility for whatever outcome the solution brings.

Advisers can also help students take action to implement a decision since they are often in a position to suggest ways to implement a choice. Actions may involve institutional procedures or steps that need to be initiated by the student. For example, students may want to declare a major but not know the official procedure; other students may find that family finances may force them to withdraw from school but do not know how to negotiate financial aid application procedures. Other students may simply need to confirm the direction they have chosen. When advisers summarize what has transpired at the end of each advising contact, students have the opportunity to confirm that their problem has been understood and that some reasonable solution has been found or is in the process of being found.

The summary can also review any assignments the student has been given, and a follow-up appointment can be made if needed. Recording briefly the important aspects of the conversation in the student's record is the final adviser responsibility.

ADVISING SKILLS

Advisers' repertoire of advising skills and techniques usually develops from their own personal style and experiences. An adviser's personality is bound to be reflected in the way advising is approached. An outgoing, extroverted adviser, for example, may convey a different demeanor in the advising exchange than a more introverted, quiet-mannered one. Both may be just as effective. Experienced advisers have had the time to develop and refine certain advising techniques through study and trial and error. In spite of varied personal approaches, there are basic skills that most advisers employ.

Information Dissemination

Providing information is central to most advising contacts. Students consider advisers authorities in providing institutional and academic information such as

curricular requirements, courses, institutional policies, academic majors, scheduling procedures, graduation requirements, and other aspects of the curriculum.

How one offers this information can be critical to the dissemination process.
Some students assimilate information better by reading printed materials while
others prefer to hear the information from the adviser. When information is
provided is also important. Some students can hear the same information two
or three times, but until they are ready to hear it, they will not internalize it.
The maturity and readiness of individual students will determine their ability to
understand and use information.

Advisers also need to be sensitive to information overload. Some students'
capacity for a great deal of information at one time is limited. When an adviser
senses that a student is confused and frustrated, it is time to back off and review
what has already been covered.

The type of material used in the information-giving aspect of advising is an
important component. Well-developed, up-to-date materials can provide a wealth
of information to students and save advisers considerable time. Advising materials may include catalogs, curriculum sheets, procedural forms, academic
planning guides, and other printed resources based on specific institutional needs.
Computer programs are another important resource for information dissemination. A more detailed discussion of advising materials is provided later in this
chapter.

Teaching Skills

Crookston (1972) regards advising as teaching, which is often called upon in
an advising exchange. Students may need to be taught institutional rules, the
rationale behind basic requirements, curricular structures, scheduling techniques,
and other methods for negotiating the system.

In the role of teacher, advisers can instruct students in certain essential knowledge and procedures so they are better able to take responsibility for their actions.

Counseling Skills

Although academic advisers are generally not trained counselors, there are
certain counseling techniques that can be used effectively in an advising exchange. Reflecting and clarifying what students say have already been mentioned
as techniques for assuring students they are heard accurately. The importance
of listening skills cannot be overemphasized.

Cook (1991) indicates that effective listening means that at least 51 percent
of the responsibility must be taken by the adviser (listener). He maintains that
listening is perhaps the single most important skill for successful advising. Examples of good listening techniques include concentrating on the message, not
the deliverer; eliminating distractions; not interrupting; and adopting good physical cues such as eye contact and posture. Effective relationships may be built

on several other core conditions. Establishing a sense of trust is imperative if students are to feel comfortable. Advisers cannot give the impression of being judgmental. Unconditional positive regard means communicating acceptance. Regardless of a student's past record, an adviser needs to concentrate on the student's potential rather than dwelling on past behavior.

A very important technique in advising is to help students look at their situation in concrete terms. Students often have a vague understanding of their problems and need help in clarifying them. For example, students who are having difficulty in certain courses may indicate that they are studying many hours a week on the subject but are doing poorly on exams. Asking specific questions, such as, "Describe the specific steps you take when outlining a chapter" or "How are you organizing the material covered in the exam?", may help students to think more concretely about their situation. Referrals for assistance will often emerge when concreteness is finally reached.

In certain situations confrontation techniques may be needed. Although this approach is used sparingly, some students may need to be challenged with uncomfortable questions. Some students perceive themselves to be externally controlled and blame their academic and other problems on instructors, roommates, the institutional bureaucracy, or any other source external to themselves. Unless students take responsibility for their own actions, their situation will probably not change. Confronting them will hopefully help them face the reality they refuse to acknowledge. Confrontation as a technique, however, is used sparingly and offered only in the spirit of acceptance and trust.

Mentoring Skills

Although mentoring is difficult to define (Gladstone, 1987), there are certain aspects of the mentoring process that may be adapted to the advising situation. Mentors have a real concern for students and concentrate on their potential. A mentoring relationship involves the sharing of common interests and goals. Both student and adviser are committed to the relationship, and the focus is on the student's growth and development. The mentoring skills of openness, trust, interest, and sincere concern for how students develop can be used to good advantage in the advising relationship. Bolles (1972) suggests that mentors are "the highest level of educators." When advisers have the opportunity to develop mentoring relationships with students, their influence can have a positive effect on students' lives.

Referral Skills

Being a referral agent is one of the most important roles an adviser plays. Advisers have the responsibility to know the campus and community resources available to students with any type of concern. Advisers need to listen carefully to students' expressed needs so that the best referral resource may be pinpointed.

Referrals made too quickly may suggest to students that the adviser is not interested in their problems. How and when an adviser refers must be carefully accomplished.

When referring, advisers need to make it clear to the student (1) why they are being referred, (2) where they are to go for help and whom to contact, (3) what questions to ask or what tasks need to be completed, and (4) how to provide feedback to the adviser about the outcome of the referral when it is appropriate.

Advising handbooks, training manuals, student handbooks, and other printed resources often contain information about various resources on campus. Sessions on resources may be included in adviser training activities or in updating sessions. Advisers, however, should feel responsible for learning about specific resources when they feel a void. Visiting the physical location of a resource on campus and talking with the people to whom students are referred will help advisers make more focused and well-informed referrals.

Monitoring

Intrusive advising involves an understanding of a student's academic goals and how those goals may be achieved. Monitoring a student's academic record is an essential aspect of advising. Monitoring may be accomplished by checking a student's record at regular time intervals such as scheduling periods or when grades are posted. Regular monitoring can often identify problems before they become too difficult to resolved. For example, when a student who is performing well academically suddenly has a poor showing or withdraws from courses, there may be extenuating conditions that need to be identified. For example, the student may be in financial difficulty, have family problems, or be physically ill. An intrusive adviser will contact the student and offer assistance if the student wishes to accept it.

Monitoring students in academic difficulty is especially important since their situation is precarious. Resources to help them with study skills, test anxiety, and other problems might be offered at strategic moments. Regular monitoring and contact with students with other known problems will often provide the type of support critical to their success and retention.

Advisers with large numbers of advisees may have more difficulty monitoring students because of the time involved. A quick review of advisees' progress once a term, however, can provide valuable insights into problems that may be confronted while help is still possible.

Decision-Making Skills

The content of almost every advising contract involves students in making decisions at many levels of importance and intensity. Most students do not approach problems systematically and often need to be educated in the process (Miller, Galanter, & Pribram, 1960). Advisers need to be aware of students' unique styles and approaches so that they may guide students to productive and realistic resolutions to their problems.

Advisers with effective decision-making skills will be able to recognize when students are moving in a realistic direction or are stuck in a particular aspect of the process. As indicated earlier, the advising interview itself can serve as a model for systematically identifying the problem, gathering relevant information, identifying certain alternatives, and finally deciding on the best solution, based on what is known at that particular time.

Experienced advisers are aware that sometimes their approach to decision making may be different from a particular student's and may need to adapt their own style in order to communicate effectively. There are also students with unique decision-making problems. Some students are indecisive and cannot make decisions in any situation. These students need to be referred to counselors who can deal with the psychological aspects of this problem. Other students may have problems with procrastination. Still others may have always had decisions made for them by others. Advisers need to be sensitive to the debilitating habits or attitudes of a small number of students who need help beyond the parameters of advising.

ADVISING MATERIALS AND RESOURCES

Advisers are only as effective as the materials and resources at their disposal. Most materials are locally developed because of the unique needs of institutions. Certain types of materials are common to most advising endeavors, however. These include college bulletins, handbooks, curriculum sheets, testing and placement materials, computer resources, and materials designed for student record keeping.

Catalogs or Bulletins

Smaller institutions will often publish one document to provide information about institutional policies, curricular requirements, and other important information. The catalog may also be used as the admissions bulletin. In some institutions this document serves as the bible for advising purposes. It is imperative that advisers are totally familiar with the content of the official documents of the institution. Advisers are in a position to suggest improvements about how the documents may be organized or changed to facilitate student use and the advising process.

Orientation Materials

After the official catalog, the first materials seen by students and parents are often orientation materials. These may include a copy of the students' handbook, parents' handbook, and scheduling or curricular materials. The quality of these materials is important since they offer a first impression of the institution's mission and administration. New students and parents will leave orientation with an impression of the campus based partially on the attractiveness and understandability of these materials.

Films, videos, speakers, and other aspects of orientation also present an image of the campus. Academic advisers need to be part of the planning of orientation, especially the parts that deal with academic sessions and materials used in those sessions.

Advising Handbooks

A comprehensive handbook for academic advisers is an indispensable tool for effective advising. Not only should careful planning be accomplished before writing, publishing, and disseminating the handbook, but responsibility for the updating and maintenance of the handbook should be determined.

Ford and Ford (1990) suggest the following content for an advising handbook: (1) philosophy and objectives of the advising program, (2) definitions of the adviser and the advising process, (3) general and specific responsibilities of the adviser, (4) characteristics of a good adviser and strategies for effective advising, (5) academic policies and procedures, (6) scheduling and registration procedures, (7) legal responsibilities of the adviser, (8) advising procedures for special populations (e.g., those on academic probation, undecided students), (9) listings of campus resources for referral purposes, (10) advising and scheduling calendar, (11) easily used table of contents, and (12) appendixes with test interpretation information, student assistance resources, and other pertinent material. A foreword written by the president or provost of the institution will emphasize the important role advising plays.

A loose-leaf notebook can make updating easier and more efficient. As indicated earlier, adviser handbooks need to be as current as possible, and appointing an individual or office to do this on a regular basis will ensure proper maintenance. Dissemination of the handbook needs to be addressed as well.

Advising Records

Every adviser should maintain a portfolio on each advisee so that each contact may be recorded, important information about the student may be readily available, and monitoring may be scheduled on a regular basis. Student folders are usually initiated during orientation. Although most institutions now have computer systems with immediate access to a student's record, recording in the student's folder what transpires in each contact will help maintain a personal relationship. Materials contained in the folder might include a paper record of the student's grades; degree audits, if available; the student's ACT or Scholastic Aptitude Test (SAT) scores and student profiles, if available; placement test results; procedural forms; and other relevant documents. Confidentiality of records must be maintained when working with students' records. Information on the record should never be communicated to another person unless permission has been granted by the student. The Family Educational Rights and Privacy Act of 1974 stipulates that written consent must be obtained before the release of education records or information. While there are exceptions to this (e.g., requests from faculty or staff who have a legitimate educational interest on a "need to know" basis; requests in compliance with a lawful subpoena or judicial order), the strictest adherence to this policy must be maintained.

Curricular Materials

One of the most useful documents in advising is the major curriculum sheet. Requirements for individual majors are often published in a catalog, but putting the information on a single sheet in the form of a checklist helps a student grasp the cohesiveness of the curriculum and provides a vehicle for monitoring progress. Curriculum sheets are also a help to undecided students or those who are in the process of changing majors since they can compare the requirements for several majors easily.

Advisers can use the sheets to demonstrate to a student how a baccalaureate degree is organized, the rationale for various requirements, and the number and type of electives and offer any other information about the major for which the student needs to be aware (e.g., selective admission, point hour restrictions, sequencing of requirements, prerequisite courses). Some campuses put occupational information on the reverse of the sheet to inform students about the types of career paths associated with that particular major.

Placement Testing Materials

An obvious advising task is to place students in courses that are appropriate for their level of familiarity with the subject. Placement test results are one vehicle for assuring that students are not bored in a course that repeats what they know but are placed in one that challenges them. These tests are particularly important for subjects like English, math, and foreign languages. Advisers need to understand the rationale for the local development of these tests, what they are measuring, and how to interpret the results in terms of proper course placement for individual students.

Advisers also need to understand national testing results, including the American College Test (ACT) or Scholastic Aptitude Test (SAT) and Advanced Placement Program (APP) instruments. While the use of these national tests in placement will vary with institutions, advisers need to be able to answer students' questions about them.

One danger in using and interpreting any test score is to place too much emphasis on literal translations. Students need to be aware that this is only one measure of past achievements. Although they are often used as entry assessments, they are not important once a student has established an academic record at the institution. As stated earlier, confidentiality must be adhered to while in possession of this information.

Computer Advising Programs

Computer programs have taken over many informational and procedural areas that were formerly performed on paper. This change has resulted in more efficient and thorough information resources available to advisers, such as student record keeping and curricular information. Advisers need to be proficient in accessing the student database and other systems operating on their campuses.

Some advantages of computer systems are that they provide information with speed and accuracy. Information becomes centralized and paperwork can be reduced. Errors in providing information about courses, curriculum, and graduation requirements are also reduced. The time eliminated in searching for information about a particular student can be cut substantially during an advising interview (Kramer & Megerian, 1985; Lowry & Grites, 1982; Peterson & Kramer, 1984; Spencer, Peterson, & Kramer, 1983). Computers allow advisers to be free from certain types of routine paperwork so that more quality time can be spent on the student's individual concerns. For example, scheduling information, academic and graduation requirements, placement test results, and other important information about the student can be contained in a database that is invaluable to advisers and allows them more time for students. The computer will never replace the relationship offered by a caring adviser. It is an important supplement to advising, however, because of the accuracy and speed with which information critical to the advising process can be accessed.

Student Handbooks

Although student handbooks are designed to provide students with important information about the institution and its resources, advisers can find the content of these handbooks useful in many ways. Many student handbooks provide information about topics that are quite relevant to the advising process, such as resources for study skills, scheduling techniques, or extracurricular activities. Pointing out to a student specific sections in the handbook that relate to a particular topic under discussion will show the student the value of the handbook and encourage its use.

Telephone

The telephone can be an effective advising tool when considered in this context. Students can often receive answers to questions or test ideas with an adviser about a variety of topics on the telephone when a personal contact is not needed or possible. Advising older or working students by phone may be the only method for exchanging much needed information.

The telephone may also be used as an intrusive advising tool when advisers need to make contact with students who need special attention. Calling a student who has not made contact for an extended period of time not only demonstrates a caring attitude on the part of the adviser, but may uncover problems that need to be resolved.

Many other excellent advising materials have been developed by individual institutions to fill a unique need on those campuses. Attractive, well-devised, current advising materials make a critical difference in advising. Training advisers to use the materials and resources on a campus is also part of a smoothly running program.

ADVISING SETTINGS

The advising skills and materials previously discussed in this chapter are used in many advising settings. Adviser and student contacts happen in as many settings as many times as the student's needs and the institution's calendar dictate. A different dynamic transpires in each of these times and settings. Other than individual contacts, these settings include (1) precollege contacts, (2) orientation, (3) freshman seminar courses, and (4) group advising. While parents or other significant family members may contact an adviser at any time during the student's college career, most contacts are made during the precollege and orientation periods.

Precollege Contacts

Admissions counselors are often involved in answering questions about academic majors and campus resources. Faculty advisers and professional advisers are more often involved with campus visitation programs. Prospective students and their parents are trying to size up an institution's academic and social climate when they arrive on campus. These contacts can be made through admissions or college-sponsored recruitment programs (e.g., Campus Days, Minority Recruitment program) or by individually initiated visits (Gass, 1990; Weigel & Smith, 1972). These programs often involve academic information sessions, campus tours, talks with currently enrolled students, visits to residences halls, and financial aid discussions.

Impressions about whether students feel they fit into an institution will often be determined by these visits. Faculty advisers who become personally involved with an individual student during these precollege experiences will often have great influence on the student's decision (Tinto, 1987). An advising session involving information about the curriculum and prospective majors is an important part of these visits. Follow-up contacts from faculty are also impressive signals to a prospective student.

Orientation

Orientation programs are increasingly seen as critical experiences for a successful transition from high school to college. While a few orientation programs emphasize personal and social adjustment to the college environment, most have a large academic information, planning, and scheduling component. Perigo and Upcraft (1989) discuss important goals of an orientation program, including familiarizing students with academic requirements and helping them make realistic assessments of their ability to meet them. The breadth and depth of academic offerings and a description of the academic resources on campus to help students succeed should also be included.

The National Orientation Directors Association's (NODA) data bank indicates that institutions hold a variety of orientation offerings. Some institutions hold one-day programs while others provide for two or more days. Brewer and Roller (1985) describe a four-week summer program that provides students with opportunities for individual advising and orients them to computerized registration. Retention data indicate that the longer students have to become familiar with their new environment, the likelier they are to stay during the first year (Bron & Gordon, 1986; Kramer & Washburn, 1983; Pascarella, Terenzini, & Wolfle, 1986).

Orientation activities are as varied as the times they are held. Examples of activities include workshops, small groups, programmed learning, simulation gaming, and short-term seminars (Howe & Perry, 1978; Klostermann & Merseal, 1978; Nelson & Toensing, 1976; Spooner & Paquini, 1981; Twale, 1989; Upcraft & Farnsworth, 1984). Banning (1989) describes a computer-assisted system to help incoming students learn about many facets of the campus.

Upcraft (1984) discusses the goals and characteristics of an effective orientation program, interventions and strategies that can be used, and orientation of students with special needs, such as minority, disabled, adult, and transfer students. Orientation programs can expose students to the new academic climate in a way that informs and encourages them to take advantage of the opportunities to help them grow intellectually.

Parent Orientation

Parents or other family members are often an important influence on students' choice of college and major (Boyer, 1987). These influences are especially strong during orientation and the freshman year. Including parents in the orientation program will help them feel a part of the transition that they and their child will be experiencing (Catron & Catron, 1989; Cohen, 1985; Cooper & Robinson, 1987; Harmon & Phatigan, 1990; Lollis & Eftink, 1990; Whitaker & Roberts, 1990). A wide variety of activities will expose them to the language and components of their son's or daughter's new environment.

Whitaker and Roberts (1990) suggest a shift from a student-centered orientation program to a parent-student-centered freshman orientation. They apply a psychographic typology to families so that activities may be tailored specifically to parents with different values and life-styles. They recommend such activities for parents as involvement in seminars on problem solving, computer simulations, language labs, placement tests, and mini-lectures by outstanding faculty. If parents are comfortable with the institution, generally their students will be also. A workshop for parents that addresses the developmental transition their children will experience is described by Treeger and Hammer (1985). Banning (1989) describes sessions where parents can discuss their concerns about their student's transition to college. Artman (1987) suggests using parents of upperclass students in a panel format during orientation to provide insights into parenting of college students. Parents' involvement in orientation not only helps them feel a part of the transition process but can involve them in the advising process as well. Understanding the academic aspects of their son's or daughter's curricular program can help make them critical allies. The institution also benefits from the public relations aspects of the orientation process.

Freshman Seminar Courses

Freshman seminar or orientation courses have been used as an advising tool for over a century. Although many topics making up the content of these courses have changed over the years, the similarities that have endured are striking (Gordon, 1989). While many of the traditional courses were concerned with adjustment concerns of new freshmen, the seminar course that is taught today is often more academically oriented.

As mentioned in Chapter 2, Gordon and Grites (1984) describe the various issues concerning freshman seminar courses. The content often relates directly to advising issues such as understanding the value of a college degree, an introduction to broad areas of study, academic major information, curricular requirements, graduation requirements, and course scheduling. Learning and study skills are often included, along with an exposure to the institution's policies and procedures relating to academic planning and scheduling. Knowledge of the institution's academic resources is usually provided so that students may become aware of available programs and services such as tutoring or test anxiety workshops. Freshman seminar courses have been shown to be an excellent vehicle for enhancing faculty-student relations (Pantages & Creedon, 1978; Terenzini & Pascarella, 1977; Tinto, 1985; Whitman, Spendlove, & Clark, 1984). Some courses are taught by faculty members who have been assigned the students in their section as advisees. There may be an emphasis on an academic theme along with advising issues (Jeweler, 1989).

Seminar courses have also been described as an effective retention strategy (Chapman & Reed, 1987; Fidler & Hunter, 1989; Gardner, 1986; Lenning, Beal, & Sauer, 1980; Tinto, 1987; Wilkie & Kuckuck, 1989). Participation in a freshman seminar has shown to improve academic performance, increase knowledge and use of campus resources, and influence personality development (Fidler & Hunter, 1989). There is no question that using a freshman course for advising is a strong vehicle for helping new students adjust to a new environment and learn a great deal of information that would be impossible to provide on an individual basis.

Group Advising

The last setting to discuss is the use of group approaches to advising. As indicated in Chapter 2, the use of groups has long been valued as an economical use of time as well as the method of choice in certain situations. The advantage to students is that they can hear other students expressing views on topics that are of concern to them. They can often obtain information in an organized way and gain insights into solutions to problems.

Advising groups can be used, for example, for information dissemination, scheduling, problem solving, teaching study skills for students in academic difficulty, and academic and career exploration. In some situations the freshman seminar is used as a group advising approach. The composition of the group will depend on the objectives of the group, the topic or topics covered, and the size of the group. A group for academic and career exploration, for example, will largely be made up of students who are needing to find or confirm a major or career choice. When large numbers of students are in the same academic major, group scheduling might be a more efficient use of adviser time.

Establishing group cohesiveness is important if there is to be the type of open communication and interaction that will benefit students. Students must know from the outset the purpose of the group and their role and responsibility. The adviser must create a comfortable and open atmosphere if students are to feel the group is worthwhile. Group advising can be an asset where the same information is needed by many students. After a group session, some individuals may need help in relating the information to a personal level. For most students, however, group advising can provide the type of setting that is effective for many types of information dissemination and processing.

SUMMARY

This chapter has discussed the elements that are critical to the academic advising process. What transpires between adviser and student is, in the end, at the heart of the enterprise. Advisers must be experts in knowing who their students are in many contexts. They must be concerned with students' growth and development as well as trends in demographic, personal, and social issues.

The advising interview is perhaps the most important component of the advising endeavor, and yet many advisers react to students' presenting problems in an ad hoc manner rather than analyzing their approaches. Each student is unique and brings to the advising exchange new twists to many old problems.

Advising skills and techniques are varied and complex. A conscientious adviser will always be trying to improve such skills as teaching, counseling, mentoring, referral, and information dissemination. The materials used in advising play a key role in assuring timeliness, accuracy, and efficiency. Catalogs, handbooks, curricular materials, student records, testing materials, and computer systems are only a few of the many materials indispensable to an adviser. Updating and maintaining materials are critical to their effectiveness.

How one advises, the skills needed, and the type of materials used will depend on the type of setting in which advising is provided. Precollege advising, orientation, freshman orientation courses, individual adviser contacts, and group advising are all vehicles in which advising takes place. Each setting dictates its own approaches and the type of student served.

Academic advising is seen as a complex process that requires a caring attitude toward students and a desire to help them solve complicated problems. Advising skills and techniques must be learned and refined on an ongoing basis. Many see advising as a teaching and learning endeavor where both student and adviser are constantly learning about each other and the academic enterprise.

REFERENCES

Archer, J., & Lamnin, A. (1985). An investigation of personal and academic stressors on college campuses. *Journal of College Student Personnel, 26*, 210–215.

Artman, R. (1987). Parents advising parents: An orientation program that works. *Journal of College Student Personnel, 28*, 179–180.

Astin, A. W. (1977). *Four critical years.* San Francisco: Jossey-Bass.

Banning, J. H. (1989). Impact of college environments on freshmen students. In M. L. & J. N. Gardner (Eds.), *The freshman year experience* (pp. 53–62). San Francisco: Jossey-Bass.

Bolles, R. N. (1972). *What color is your parachute?* Berkeley, CA: Ten Speed Press.

Bowen, H. R. (1977). *Investment in learning: The individual and social value of American higher education.* San Francisco: Jossey-Bass.

Boyer, E. L. (1987). *College: The undergraduate experience in America.* The Carnegie Foundation for the Advancement of Teaching. New York: Harper & Row.

Brewer, C. R., & Roller, J. M. (1985). Orienting new students to computerized registration: Providing opportunities for academic advising. *College and University, 60*, 180–184.

Bron, C. D., & Gordon, M. P. (1986). Impact of an orientation center on grade point average and attrition. *College Student Journal, 20*, 242–246.

Carney, C. G., & Barak, A. (1976). A survey of student needs and student personnel services. *Journal of College Student Personnel, 17*, 280–284.

Catron, D. W., & Catron, S. S. (1989). Helping parents let go: A program for the parents of college freshmen. *Journal of College Student Personnel, 30*, 463–464.

Chapman, L. C., & Reed, P. J. (1987). Evaluating the effectiveness of a freshman orientation course. *Journal of College Student Personnel, 28*, 178–179.

Cohen, R. D. (Ed.). (1985). *Working with parents of college students.* New Directions for Student Services, no. 32. San Francisco: Jossey-Bass.

Cook, E. P., et al. (1984). Students' perceptions of personal problems, appropriate help sources, and general attitudes about counseling. *Journal of College Student Personnel, 25*, 139–145.

Cook, H. B. (1991). Listening: The key to innovative academic advising. NACADA *Academic Advising Newsletter*. Vol. 13. Newark, DE: University of Delaware.

Cooper, S. E., & Robinson, D. (1987). Effectiveness of parental participation in freshman orientation programs on perceptions of the university. *Journal of College Student Personnel, 28*, 464–466.

Crookston, B. B. (1972). A developmental view of academic advising as teaching. *Journal of College Student Personnel, 13*, 12–17.

Estrada, L. F. (1988). Anticipating the demographic future. *Change, 20*, 14–19.

Feldman, K. A., & Newcomb, T. M. (1969). *The impact of college on students*. San Francisco: Jossey-Bass.

Fidler, P. P., & Hunter, M. S. (1989). How seminars enhance student success. In M. L. Upcraft & J. N. Gardner (Eds.), *The freshman year experience* (pp. 216–237). San Francisco: Jossey-Bass.

Ford, J., & Ford, S. S. (1990). *Producing a comprehensive academic advising handbook*. Columbus, OH: The National Clearinghouse for Academic Advising.

Friday, R. A. (1990). Faculty training: From group process to collaborative learning. *Journal of the Freshman Year Experience, 2*, 49–67.

Gardner, J. N. (1986). The freshman year experience. *College and University, 61*, 261–274.

Gass, M. A. (1990). The longitudinal effects of an adventure orientation program on the retention of students. *Journal of College Student Development, 31*, 33–38.

Gladstone, M. S. (1987). *Mentoring as an educational strategy*. Report of First International Conference on Mentoring, University of British Columbia, Vancouver, Canada.

Gordon, V. N. (1989). Origins and purposes of the freshman seminar. In M. L. Upcraft & J. N. Gardner (Eds.), *The freshman year experience* (pp. 183–197). San Francisco: Jossey-Bass.

Gordon, V. N., & Grites, T. J. (1984). The freshman seminar course: Helping students succeed. *Journal of College Student Personnel, 25*, 315–320.

Green, K. C. (1989). The children of the upheaval: A look at today's college freshmen. *Journal of the Freshman Year Experience, 1*, 20–42.

Harmon, W. W., & Phatigan, J. J. (1990). Academic course for parents of first-year students impacts favorably on student retention. *Journal of the Freshman Year Experience, 2*, 85–95.

Hodgkinson, H. L. (1985). *All one system: Demographics of education, kindergarten through graduate school*. Washington, DC: Institute for Educational Leadership.

Hoffman, J. A., & Weiss, B. (1987). Family dynamics and presenting problems in college students. *Journal of Counseling Psychology, 34*, 157–163.

Howe, C. G., & Perry, J. L. (1978). The evaluation of a participant-centered orientation program for incoming students. *College Student Journal, 12*, 248–250.

Jeweler, A. J. (1989). Elements of an effective seminar: The University 101 program. In M. L. Upcraft & J. N. Gardner (Eds.), *The freshman year experience* (pp. 198–215). San Francisco: Jossey-Bass.

Klostermann, L. R., & Merseal, J. (1978). Another view of orientation. *Journal of College Student Personnel, 19*, 286–287.

Koplik, E. K., & DeVito, A. J. (1986). Problems of freshman: Comparison of classes of 1976 and 1986. *Journal of College Student Personnel, 27*, 124–131.

Kramer, G. L., & Megerian, A. (1985). Using computer technology to aid faculty advising. *NACADA Journal, 5*, 51–61.

Kramer, G. L., & Washburn, R. (1983). The perceived orientation needs of new students. *Journal of College Student Personnel, 24*, 311–319.

Kramer, H., & Gardner, R. (1983). *Advising by faculty.* Washington, DC: National Education Association.

Lenning, O., Beal, P., & Sauer, K. (1980). *Student retention strategies.* Iowa City, IA: American College Testing Program. AAHE-ERIC Higher Education Research Report No. 8.

Lenning, O. T., Munday, L. A., Johnson, O. B., Vander Well, A. R., & Brue, E. J. (1974). *The many faces of college success and their nonintellective correlates: The published literature through the decade of the sixties.* Monograph 15. Iowa City, IA: American College Testing Program.

Levine, A. (1989). Who are today's freshmen? In M. L. Upcraft & J. N. Gardner, *The freshman year experience* (pp. 15–24). San Francisco: Jossey-Bass.

Lollis, T. J., & Eftink, S. (1990). Parent-student support program promotes academic success. *Journal of College Student Development, 31*, 377–379.

Lowry, G. R., and Grites, T. J. (1982). The classroom as an institutional resource: An example of computer-assisted advising. *NACADA Journal, 4*, 33–40.

Miller, G. A., Galanter, E., & Pribram, K. H. (1960). *Plans and the structure of behavior.* New York: Holt, Rinehart & Winston.

Nelson, N., & Toensing, J. (1976). A programmed learning approach to orientation. *Journal of College Student Personnel, 17*, 521–522.

O'Banion, T. (1972). An academic advising model. *Junior College Journal, 42*, 62–64.

Pantages, T. J., & Creedon, C. F. (1978). Studies of college attrition: 1950–1975. *Review of Educational Research, 48*, 489–501.

Pascarella, E. T., Terenzini, P. T., & Wolfle, L. M. (1986). Orientation to college and freshman year persistence/withdrawal decisions. *Journal of Higher Education, 57*, 155–175.

Perigo, D. J., & Upcraft, M. L. (1989). Orientation programs. In M. L. Upcraft & J. N. Gardner (Eds.), *The freshman year experience* (pp. 82–94). San Francisco: Jossey-Bass.

Peterson, E. D., & Kramer, G. L. (1984). Computer-assisted advising: The next agenda item for computer development. *NACADA Journal, 4*, 33–40.

Roberts, G. H., & White, W. G. (1989). Health and stress in developmental college students. *Journal of College Student Personnel, 30*, 515–521.

Roscoe, B. (1987). Concerns of college students: A report of self-disclosure. *College Student Journal, 21*, 158–161.

Schroeder, C. C., DiTiberio, J. K., & Kalsbeek, D. H. (1989). Bridging the gap between faculty and students: Opportunities and obligations of student affairs. *NASPA Journal, 26*, 14–20.

Semmes, C. E., & Makalani, J. K. (1985). Minority status and the problem of legitimacy. *Journal of Black Studies, 15*, 259–275.

Shang, P. (1989). Minority students and the AISP model. In U. Delworth (Ed.), *Dealing with the behavior and psychological problems of students* (pp. 67–73). New Directions for Student Services, no. 45. San Francisco: Jossey-Bass.

Shueman, S. A., & Medvene, A. M. (1981). Student perceptions of appropriateness of presenting problems: What's happened to attitudes in 20 years? *Journal of College Student Personnel, 22*, 264–269.

Spencer, R. W., Peterson, E. D., & Kramer, G. L. (1983). Designing and implementing a computer-assisted academic advisement program. *Journal of College Student Personnel, 24*, 513–518.

Spooner, S., & Paquini, L. (1981). Simulation gaming as an orientation tool. *Journal of College Student Personnel, 22*, 78–79.

Taylor, K. M. (1991). A crisis intervention perspective. Handout. Columbus: Ohio State University.

Terenzini, P. T., & Pascarella, E. T. (1977). Voluntary freshman attrition and patterns of social and academic integration in a university: A test of a conceptual model. *Research in Higher Education, 6*, 25–43.

Tinto, V. (1985). Dropping out and other forms of withdrawal from college. In L. Noel, R. Levitz, & D. Saluri (Eds.), *Increasing student retention: Effective programs and practices for reducing the dropout rate* (pp. 28–43). San Francisco: Jossey-Bass.

Tinto, V. (1987). *Leaving college*. Chicago: University of Chicago Press.

Tomlinson, S. M., & Cope, N. R. (1988). Characteristics of black students seeking help at a university counseling center. *Journal of College Student Development, 29*, 65–69.

Tracey, T. J., Leong, F.T.L., & Glidden, C. (1986). Help seeking and problem perception among Asian Americans. *Journal of Counseling Psychology, 33*, 331–336.

Treeger, M., & Hammer, A. L. (1985). Letting go: A developmental workshop for parents at orientation. *Journal of College Student Personnel, 26*, 364–365.

Twale, D. J. (1989). Social and academic development in freshman orientation: A time frame. *NASPA Journal, 27*, 160–167.

Tyron, G. S. (1984). Problems commuters, residence hall students, and students from different academic years bring to counseling. *College Student Journal, 18*, 215–221.

Upcraft, M. L. (Ed.). (1984). *Orienting students to college*. New Directions for Student Services, no. 25. San Francisco: Jossey-Bass.

Upcraft, M. L., & Farnsworth, W. M. (1984). Orientation programs and activities. In M. L. Upcraft (Eds.), *Orienting students to college*. San Francisco: Jossey-Bass.

Weigel, R. G., & Smith, T. T. (1972). The effects of pre-orientation information dissemination on academic choices and performances. *Journal of College Student Personnel, 13*, 452–455.

Whitaker, V. W., & Roberts, F. L. (1990). Applying values and lifestyles pscyhographics to parental involvement in college and university orientation. *NACADA Journal, 10*, 41–46.

Whitman, N., Spendlove, D., & Clark, C. (1984). *Student stress: Effects and solutions* (Higher Education Report No. 2). Washington, DC: Association for the Study of Higher Education.

Wilkie, C., & Kuckuck, S. (1989). A longitudinal study of the effects of a freshman seminar. *Journal of the Freshman Year Experience, 1*, 7–16.

4

Career Advising

Academic advising and career advising are so closely related in many students' minds that it is often difficult to separate them in an advising transaction. Some students equate a major decision with a career choice, and many base their initial major choice on the presumption they will automatically be assured of a job after graduation if a direct relationshiip is obvious. To counteract this narrow and often erroneous view, advisers may find themselves espousing the value of a liberal, broad-based education that prepares one for life, not just a vocation.

The current dilemma, according to Katchadourian and Boli (1985), is that the tradition of the liberal education is being replaced in some students' minds with vocationalism. The intent of a liberal education is to prepare one to be broadly educated in preparation for living one's life. As discussed in Chapter 1, many of the reasons students give for attending college are related to preparing for a career. Advisers may find themselves encouraging students to select general education courses wisely and with care so that a broad base of knowledge is acquired during the college years. Students attending technical colleges also need to be exposed to opportunities that can broaden their knowledge and experiential bases.

Career advising is an important part of academic advising because of students' concern about their work life after college. The responsibility advisers assume in career advising will vary with individual advisers' backgrounds and expertise, the occupational implications for the major(s) they advise, and the needs of the individual student. While most advisers are not considered counselors, they need to develop skills beyond the mere information-giving level. Helping students assess their needs and helping them understand the career decision-making process are important adviser responsibilities.

CAREER PLANNING PROCESS

College students are sometimes confused or uninformed about the career planning process in general and about specific aspects of it in particular. They may need to be guided through the questioning of how to start, where and how to obtain information, how to identify alternatives, how to make a choice from various options, and how to implement a decision once it is made. Career advising includes helping students explore or confirm academic choices and helping them understand the occupational implications (direct or indirect) of the academic decisions they are considering or have made. To accomplish this goal, advisers must be knowledgeable not only about the academic and occupational relationships within specialized areas but also about the career resources on campus so that appropriate referrals may be made.

Advisers can encourage academic and occupational exploration by helping students view this process as desirable and legitimate. Career exploration needs to be fostered in an atmosphere of encouragement and support. Students in different academic areas may present special types of career concerns. For example, engineering students may be concerned about their abilities to succeed in math and science, while students in health-related majors may be concerned with the stress and energy levels required in certain careers. Liberal arts students may be more concerned with finding occupational relationships with their majors than are physical therapy or education students.

There are also variations in the career decision-making concerns of different levels of students. Many freshmen may be more structured and narrow about career decisions than some sophomores, who may be more intuitive and questioning. Juniors may be more concerned about taking the right courses to fulfill requirements; seniors are more concerned about job-hunting skills and occupational entrance requirements. There are some important principles associated with effective career development:

1. Choosing a career is a lifelong process. Students should understand that they are at only one decision point in a long series of career choices.

2. The career decision-making process includes knowing facts about oneself and facts about the work world. Integrating these two areas of information in an organized way can help students identify realistic alternatives.

3. Choosing a career can be a complicated process that requires much study and thought. One has more control over one's life by learning how to make career decisions in an orderly, rational manner.

4. There are no right or wrong decisions—only satisfying and unsatisfying ones. Future events may affect a good decision in ways unforeseen at the time it was made.

5. Sex, race, or age should never be a barrier to exploring any and all possible career options.

Many myths are perpetuated in the minds of college students that impede their thinking about career planning. Some students think their major is their future job. Many students, particularly liberal arts majors, will not find direct vocational connections with their major but find employment in business, government, social service, and many other fields. Other students think they must have experience in a particular field before an employer will hire them. Employers who recruit on college campuses are looking for individuals who have the potential to learn, have developed good problem-solving skills, have excellent writing skills, and can communicate well verbally. Employers are looking for training potential.

ACADEMIC AND OCCUPATIONAL RELATIONSHIPS

In reviewing the literature on "job fit," Pascarella and Terenzini (1991) found that a student's choice of academic major influences his college experience. Some majors do prepare students for certain occupational "fits," while others, such as majors in the arts, social sciences, and humanities do not (Solomon, 1981). Pascarella and Terenzini summarize by indicating that skills learned in a major relate indirectly to job fit and satisfaction. Specific skills that are learned are most important in preparing students for entry jobs after graduation (Bisconti, 1987).

Some students believe their college major and their first job will determine their career path for life. The decision they make at graduation may influence certain career paths, but many workers' careers change dramatically over a lifetime. Exposure to certain types of work through part-time or summer jobs can also help them determine if their interests and capabilities are compatible with that field. Another myth that some students believe is that each job requires specific skills and expertise. Except for highly technical areas or occupations requiring specific preparation such as architecture or medicine, most jobs can be learned by a college graduate with the desire, interest, and motivation to master them.

When advisers hear students expressing views of the career planning process that are limiting or erroneous, they should help students rethink their approaches. Career can be defined as the sum of many vocational and a vocational activities over a lifetime. This is a much broader view of career than most college students possess, but one that suggests that college is a place to prepare for life rather than a job.

THE CHANGING WORKPLACE

Much has been written about the workplace of the future and the type of workers needed (Brown & Minor, 1989; Kutscher, 1987), In *Workforce 2000*, Johnston and Packer (1987) project that the work force in the twenty-first century will be composed of more women and minorities. Most new jobs will be in services and information areas and will require higher levels of skills. This development challenges institutions of higher education to produce a more flexible, broadly educated worker.

McKinley (1991) summarizes the important skills needed in the next decades for new workers and experienced ones who need to adapt. Examples include specialized analytical and strategic planning skills that go beyond the usual "number crunching" and skills possessed by those who can use numbers creatively to improve efficiency in operations and production. Smaller and emerging businesses will provide employment opportunities once offered by multinational corporations.

A recent Gallup Poll found that many college graduates do not feel their skills and abilities were being used "very well" in their current jobs. A policy implication for using this pool of talent is to find ways of increasing work motivation among college graduates who find themselves in jobs not requiring a college degree since this situation is not uncommon, particularly at the entry level (Brown & Minor, 1989).

Global competition, the decline in manufacturing, and the changing tastes of consumers are trends affecting the types of jobs available (Brown & Minor, 1989). Naisbitt (1982) points out that each new technological development is met with a compensatory human response. The material advances that technology brings must be balanced with a consideration of the human element. College graduates of the future must be prepared to live in a world demanding quantitative, analytical, and computer skills (McKinley, 1991). Those who have them will be the most competitive. Thus English and history majors, for example, will need to become familiar with computers if they are to open opportunities in the work world. While career decisions should not be based on job trends, helping students understand the demands of the workplace of the future will encourage them to prepare for it.

ELEMENTS IN CAREER PLANNING

Although academic advisers are not expected to be trained as career counselors, many are in a position to help students think about their strengths and limitations for certain fields as they explore a variety of occupational alternatives. Advisers are also in a position to determine if a student needs help with the career planning process. Referring individual students to the most relevant resources on campus in a timely way is an important aspect of career advising.

Advisers who have a basic understanding of career development and planning will be able to assist students through the complex maze of questions and answers involved in this process. A sampling of career development theories is outlined in Chapter 1. These are theoretical frameworks that help explain individual's approaches to career exploration and decision making. Specific knowledge is needed, however, by advisers helping students gather the kind of information needed to make realistic and satisfying choices at a most critical period in their

Figure 4.1
Making Satisfying Career Decisions—Where Do I Start?

<u>SELF-KNOWLEDGE</u>

Interests – What do I enjoy?
Aptitudes – What are my strengths? What skills do I have?
Values – What is important to me in a career? What do I believe in?
Goal–setting – Where am I going? How do I get there? What are my aspirations?

<u>OCCUPATIONAL KNOWLEDGE</u>

Nature of work – What tasks are involved?
Places of employment – Who will hire me?
Qualifications & advancement –   What entry level expertise is expected?
                                     What experiences do I need?
                                     What are the opportunities for promotion?
Employment outlook – What will the job market be like when I graduate?
Earning & working conditions –   What is the pay range? What are the physical
                                     demands of the job?
Job seeking skills – How do I write a resume? What job interview techniques are
                    desirable?

<u>EDUCATIONAL KNOWLEDGE</u>

What educational programs will provide the knowledge and skills I need?
What college majors interest me? What vocational programs interest me?
What courses will I need to take?
What degrees and/or credentials do I need?

<u>DECISION-MAKING KNOWLEDGE</u>

How can I link self–information with occupational information?
What kind of decision maker am I? What styles or strategies do I use?
What are the critical points in my life where I will make career decisions?
What kind of lifelong decision making skills do I need to learn?
How will do I integrate my values into my decisions?

lives. Among these areas are self, academic, and occupational knowledge as
well as an understanding of the decision-making process itself.

Self-knowledge

Some students, particularly traditional-age freshmen, are uncertain of their
interests and abilities for certain academic majors and/or occupations. Knowing
one's strengths and limitations is important in the educational and career decision-

making process. Some students make initial choices based on very little information about the course work required or the talents needed to succeed and be satisfied in certain fields. Although most academic advisers may not be trained to offer testing services, they should be able to recognize when students need help in assessing their personal characteristics in more depth so a proper referral may be made. Academic and career planning services need to work closely so that some continuity between these two functions is established. Developing materials relating to the integration of academic and career information for student use can be a cooperative effort.

Older students come to the career planning process from a very different perspective since they have had work and life experiences in which to test their values, interests, and skills. Some adults, however, may need to reevaluate what they know about themselves in terms of new opportunities and experiences. Advisers working with older students need to be aware of the very different issues they bring to the educational and career exploration process.

Academic advisers need to be sensitive to sex-role stereotyping on the part of students so that options are not limited because of preconceived or false assumptions about their ability to succeed in nontraditional career fields. Unfortunately many students do not consider occupational areas that have been traditionally identified with one sex or the other (Ellermann & Johnston, 1988; Gianakos & Subich, 1988). Advisers need to question the existence of their own stereotypes to make sure they are not unconsciously perpetuating old myths about career fields formerly associated with a certain gender.

Perhaps one of the most important aspects of advising is to draw students' attention to the value implications of their choices. Many students do not purposefully engage in evaluating what is important to them in terms of work values. Advisers might ask questions to help students ponder what is important in a major or career. Do they want economic rewards such as high salaries? (Most people-oriented jobs will not provide them.) Do they want a job that will continually challenge them intellectually? (What are the possibilities for such challenge in the careers they are considering?) Advisers can emphasize the importance of value clarification and challenge students' thinking as they identify specific alternatives.

Advisers can also help students realize the importance of goal setting. Goals can be conceived as short-term or long-range. Valuing is an integral part of goal setting since goals are values projected into the future. Advisers need to ask a series of questions to help students understand the importance of setting academic and vocational goals. What does the student want to accomplish during the next school term? What are some realistic goals to accomplish during the academic year? Advisers can help students realistically assess the personal characteristics that make them unique individuals by helping them question what they know about themselves and what further exploration in this area needs to be accomplished. Students should be encouraged to take time to confirm their interests and abilities in a variety of academic areas through course exploration, extracurricular activities, or work experiences while in college. Advisers are not only information sources for students but sources of support for them as they sometimes struggle through the exploration process.

Academic and Occupation Information

Advisers in specialized fields are often excellent sources of information about academic and occupational opportunities within that area. Students typically enter college with very little information about what is involved in a major. They need to understand how a degree is created through different layers of requirements. They also need to know how to read the catalog and other important printed resources furnished by the institution.

Advisers cannot possibly know the most updated and extensive information about occupations, trends, placement opportunities, and other data associated with career choices. They should, however, not only know where these information sources are but have personally experienced the resources to which they refer students. Working through a few modules of a computerized career information system or looking up the computer system's information in their field of specialization, for example, will provide firsthand knowledge when explaining to students what can be expected when using these resources.

Decision Making

Gathering information about one's interests, abilities, and values is an important step in the exploration process. Knowing what is involved in examining certain academic majors is also important. Relevant occupational information might include asking what tasks are involved in certain types of work; what kind of education or training is needed; what types of work environments are involved; what salary ranges are typical of a certain occupation; and what the future projections are for this type of work. If one cannot organize or make sense of all this information, however, it is not useful. Toffler (1981) emphasizes that many individuals are confused by the bits of information that are constantly offered us without being organized into a whole. He indicates that individuals must organize this information into a whole that makes sense for them. Teaching students how to make personal meaning out of fragmented pieces of information is teaching them a critical life skill.

Decision making encompasses the entire process of using the information in identifying alternatives, weighing the advantages and disadvantages of those alternatives, and eventually making a commitment to a specific choice. Advisers can often point out to students where they are in the decision-making process and help them question what the next logical step should be and help them ascertain where it can lead them.

There are many classification systems that can help students and advisers make connections among self, academic major, and occupational information. One

Table 4.1
Relationships Between Career Classification Systems

Worker Trait Group – Dept. of Labor	Harrington/O'Shea	Holland's Types	ACT's Job Families
CAREER AREA: 01. ARTISTIC WTG 01.01 Literary Arts WTG 01.02 Visual Arts WTG 01.03 Performing Arts: Drama WTG 01.04 Performing Arts: Music WTG 01.05 Performing Arts: Dance WTG 01.06 Technical Arts WTG 01.07 Amusement WTG 01.07 Modeling	ART WORK MUSIC WORK LITERARY WORK ENTERTAINMENT	ARTISTIC	Q. Applied Arts (Visual) R. Creative/Performing Arts S. Applied Arts (Written & Spoken)
CAREER AREA: 02. SCIENTIFIC WTG 02.01 Physical Sciences WTG 02.02 Life Sciences WTG 02.03 Medical Sciences WTG 02.04 Laboratory Technology	MATH– SCIENCE	INVESTIGATIVE	N. Medical Specialties & Technologies O. Natural Sciences & Mathematics
CAREER AREA: 03. NATURE WTG 03.01 Managerial Work: Nature WTG 03.02 General Supervision: Nature WTG 03.03 Animal Training and Care WTG 03.04 Elemental Work: Nature	MATH– SCIENCE TECHNICAL	REALISTIC	I. Agricultural & Natural Resources

Career Area	Work Type	Holland Type	Category
CAREER AREA: 04. AUTHORITY WTG 04.01 Safety and Law Enforcement WTG 04.02 Security Services	LEGAL WORK	REALISTIC	V. Social & Government Services
CAREER AREA: 05. MECHANICAL WTG 05.01 Engineering WTG 05.02 Managerial Work: Mechanical WTG 05.03 Engineering Technology WTG 05.04 Air & Water Vehicle Operation WTG 05.05 Craft Technology WTG 05.06 Systems Operation WTG 05.07 Quality Control WTG 05.08 Land Vehicle Operation WTG 05.09 Materials Control WTG 05.10 Skilled Hand & Machine Work WTG 05.11 Equipment Operation WTG 05.12 Elemental Work: Mechanical	MATH - SCIENCE TECHNICAL SKILLED CRAFTS	REALISTIC	G. Transportation Technologies H. Crafts & Industrial Technologies J. Crafts & Related Services K. Home/Business Equipment Repair L. Industrial Equipment Operation Repair M. Engineering & Related Technologies
CAREER ARE: 06. INDUSTRIAL WTG 06.01 Production Technology WTG 06.02 Production Work WTG 06.03 Production Control WTG 06.04 Elemental Work: Industrial	TECHNICAL SKILLED CRAFTS MANUAL WORK	REALISTIC	L. Industrial Equipment Operation & Repair
CAREER AREA: 07. BUSINESS DETAIL WTG 07.01 Administrative Detail WTG 07.02 Mathematical Detail WTG 07.03 Financial Detail WTG 07.04 Information Processing: Speaking WTG 07.05 Information Processing: Records WTG 07.06 Clerical Machine Operation	DATA ANALYSIS CLERICAL WORK MANAGEMENT	CONVENTIONAL	B. Management & Planning C. Records & Communications D. Financial Transactions E. Distribution & Dispatching F. Business Machine/Computer Operation
CAREER AREA: 08. PERSUASIVE WTG 08.01 Sales Technology WTG 08.02 General Sales WTG 08.03 Vending	SALES WORK	ENTERPRISING	A. Marketing & Sales

Table 4.1 (continued)

Worker Trait Group - Dept. of Labor	Harrington/O'Shea	Holland's Types	ACT's Job Families
CAREER AREA: 09. ACCOMMODATING WTG 09.01 Hospitality Services WTG 09.02 Barbering & Beauty Services WTG 09.03 Passenger Services WTG 09.04 Customer Services WTG 09.05 Attendant Services	PERSONAL SERVICES CUSTOMER SERVICES	CONVENTIONAL REALISTIC SOCIAL	W. Personal/Customer Services
CAREER AREA: 10. HUMANITARIAN WTG 10.01 Social Services WTG 10.02 Nursing & Therapy Services WTG 10.03 Child & Adult Care	SOCIAL SERVICE MEDICAL - DENTAL	SOCIAL	T. General Health Care V. Social & Government Services
CAREER AREA: 11. SOCIAL/BUSINESS WTG 11.01 Mathematical & Statistics WTG 11.02 Educational & Library Services WTG 11.03 Social Research WTG 11.04 Law WTG 11.05 Business Administration WTG 11.06 Finance WTG 11.07 Services Administration WTG 11.08 Communications WTG 11.09 Promotion WTG 11.10 Regulations Enforcement WTG 11.11 Business Management WTG 11.12 Contacts and Claims	MATH - SCIENCE EDUCATION WORK LEGAL WORK SALES WORK MANAGEMENT	INVESTIGATIVE SOCIAL ENTERPRISING	B. Management & Planning P. Social Sciences U. Education & Related Services V. Social & Government Services
CAREER AREA: 12. PHYSICAL PERFORMING WTG 12.01 Sports WTG 12.02 Physical Feats	PERSONAL SERVICES ENTERTAINMENT	REALISTIC SOCIAL	

example is that of Holland's notion of congruence between one's preferred life-style and a chosen work environment (see Chapter 1 for more detail). Other systems include the Department of Labor's *Worker Trait Group* system, which links an individual's personal characteristics with a cluster of occupations incorporating those traits. American College Testing's (ACT) *Job Family* system or Harrington-O'Shea's *Career Decision System* also make connections among self, academic, and career information. Any of these systems can help students bring together information in an organized manner so that alternatives may be narrowed and focused upon. Computerized career information programs use such classifications to help organize the mass of information available within their systems. Advisers will find two special groups of students who require more in-depth advising in the academic and career exploration process. These include undecided students and those who are in the process of changing majors. More specialized knowledge and skills are needed to advise these groups effectively, especially in the area of career advising.

UNDECIDED STUDENTS

Students who are uncertain of an educational or vocational direction upon entering college have been identified as a special population for over 50 years (Crites, 1969; Gordon, 1984). Some of the variables that have been studied in relation to undecided students include identity issues, locus of control, self-esteem, fear of commitment, and anxiety (Cooper, Fuqua, & Hartman, 1984; Hartman, Fuqua, & Blum, 1985; Ikenberry, 1987; Kimes & Troth, 1974; Salomone, 1982; Serling & Betz, 1990). Although a great deal of research has been performed on undecided students, most of it has shown the heterogeneity of this group.

Lucas and Epperson (1988) suggest that there are multiple subtypes among undecided students. One type is making progress in deciding on a major or vocation and needs additional information to finalize a decision. Another group displays high anxiety and low self-esteem that may indicate a perception of barriers and lack of clarity. Lucas and Epperson suggest this group may lack a sense of autonomy. A third group seems to lack motivation to enter the career decision-making process. This is attributed to the lack of competence felt by these students, who may not know how to begin the deciding process. The fourth group seems to lack the dedication or planning necessary, and students in this study scored low on career salience. The final group is relatively well adjusted and, although close to deciding, lacks the commitment to do so. Lucas and Epperson suggest that different types of undecided students need treatment strategies based on their particular needs and reasons for being undecided.

More recent research has concentrated on the indecisive student or one who is chronically unable to make decisions (Goodstein, 1965; Fuqua, Newman, & Seaworth, 1988; Mendonca & Seiss, 1976). The indecisive student needs extended, in depth counseling for debilitating anxiety and other symptoms that characterize indecisiveness.

Advisers who specialize in working with undecided students find that being a generalist in the academic offerings of their institution is required if students are to be exposed to all the alternative open to them. Not only is academic information important to them, but the ability to assess their personal characteristics and relate these to possible vocational areas is necessary if the total student is to be involved. This need requires an adviser who has or is willing to develop the expertise required of a generalist. It also indicates that different communication and counseling skills may be needed from those assumed in advising "decided" students.

Some research has indicated that undecided students are more anxious than those who are not undecided (Bradley & White, 1977; Brown & Strange, 1981; Fuqua, Newman & Seaworth, 1988). Anxiety may be a signal that indicates indecisiveness that requires in-depth counseling or may simply be the result of being uncomfortable with the undecided state. Advisers need to be sensitive to this anxiety when it seems to be impeding productive exploration. Mendonca and Seiss (1976) found that training in problem solving and anxiety management helped students proceed in the career exploration process.

A developmental perspective is perhaps the most reliable approach when working with undecided students (Crites, 1981; Gordon, 1981). Rather than viewing uncommitted students as having personality or ability problems, they may be acknowledged as expressing different levels in the developmental process (Gordon, 1981). Advisers need to be part of an overall environment that encourages undecided students to examine their strengths honestly, set goals, design plans of action, and continually evaluate their progress.

MAJOR-CHANGERS

A special type of undecided student but one who deserves special attention is the individual who is in the process of changing from one academic direction to another. Students who change majors do so for many reasons, such as changing interests or inability to perform in certain course work associated with a major (e.g., the hard sciences in premed or the math required for a business major). During the 1980s the number of oversubscribed majors increased substantially, particularly in business, computer science, engineering, journalism, and communication (Gordon & Polson, 1985). Students unable to access oversubscribed and selective majors are often left to find alternative academic and career directions on their own.

Theophilides, Terenzini, and Lorang (1984) classified major-changers into three groups: (1) those who change in their freshman year but not their sophomore year; (2) those who change in their sophomore year but not their freshman year; and (3) constant changers or those who change both in their freshman and sophomore years. Each group's reasons or motivations for change differ. For example, early changes may be the result of an unstimulating freshman year and may encourage a reconsideration of prior choices. Sophomore changes are more likely due to poor performance in required course work.

Gordon and Steele (1992) identify certain critical elements to be aware of when working with major-changers who are experiencing a sometimes traumatic transition. Timing is important since the motivation to change is often highest when students are feeling pressured to do so. If allowed to drift too long, students may become depressed or discouraged because of lack of direction. Help must be available when students decide they need it.

Intensity of need is also important. Students are often emotionally involved in the prospect of changing majors. They may feel they are letting someone down, or perhaps a lifelong dream has been shattered because of not being able to achieve a certain career goal. Academic progress may be impeded by unrecognized or unresolved emotional barriers. Advisers need to recognize and acknowledge this emotional content and help students resolve it.

Adviser accessibility, attitudes, and expertise are also important when working with major-changers. As mentioned above, timing of help is critical if it is to serve students when they are feeling pressured to change. Advisers need to project a positive attitude about the change process. Changing majors can be perceived as a natural, developmental phenomenon rather than a negative or punitive experience.

Advisers working with students in transition need to have special knowledge, skill, and patience. Theophilides, Terenzini, and Lorang (1984) noted that many influences causing change of major are not institutionally controlled. They are the result of student "interaction with institutional reality and the consequences of this interaction with one's self-image" (p. 277). Although "early" changers have time to make adjustments to their academic plans, the greatest need may be to find students with advanced hours who are drifting without assistance. Many are forced to change directions because of "institutional realities" and are not aware of the viable alternatives open to them (Gordon & Steele, 1992). For many of these students career advising and academic advising are critical if the students are to be retained and satisfied.

SUMMARY

In many students' minds the choice of major is closely associated with choice of career. Advisers can play a key role in helping students understand the value of career planning as it relates to academic choices and the decision-making process in general. Advisers who are specialized in certain fields can offer information about the career implications for the majors they are advising. Generalist advisers can also provide basic information about majors and the occupational relationships.

Advisers need to be knowledgeable about the career development process in general and the resources on campus to which students may be referred when testing and counseling in self-assessment, occupational information, decision-making techniques, and placement services are needed. Advisers are in an excellent position to help a student determine what career-related problems they are experiencing; referrals may then be made more effectively.

Although most advisers are not expected to be experts in career counseling and occupational information, they do have an obligation to help students clarify their values and set goals that may relate to career and life planning. Their knowledge of general academic and career information is even more important if they are working with undecided students or students who are in the process of changing from one major to another. A fundamental understanding of the career development process is essential if they are to be sensitive to each individual advisee's needs in the area of career exploration and planning.

REFERENCES

Bisconti, A. (1987). *Effective job performance: How does a college education contribute?* Paper presented at the meeting of the American Educational Research Association, Washington, DC.

Bradley, R. W., & White, G. W. (1977). Anxiety and the process of deciding about a major and vocation. *Journal of Counseling Psychology*, 5, 398–403.

Brown, D., & Minor, C. W. (1989). *Working in America: A status report on planning and problems*. Alexandria, VA: National Career Development Association.

Brown, G. S., & Strange, C. (1981). The relationship of academic major and career choice status to anxiety among college freshmen. *Journal of Vocational Behavior*, 19, 328–334.

Cooper, S. E., Fuqua, D. R., & Hartman, B. W. (1984). The relationship of trait indecisiveness to vocational uncertainty, career indecision, and interpersonal characteristics. *Journal of College Student Personnel*, 25, 353–356.

Crites, J. O. (1969). *Vocational psychology*. New York: McGraw-Hill.

Crites, J. O. (1981). *Career counseling: Models, methods, and materials*. New York: McGraw-Hill.

Ellermann, N. C., & Johnston, J. (1988). Perceived life roles and locus of control differences of women pursuing nontraditional and traditional academic majors. *Journal of College Student Development*, 29, 142–145.

Fuqua, D. R., Newman, J. L., & Seaworth, T. B. (1988). Relation of state and trait anxiety to different components of career indecision. *Journal of Counseling Psychology*, 35, 154–158.

Gianakos, I., & Subich, L. M. (1988). Student sex and sex role in relation to college major choice. *Career Development Quarterly*, 36, 259–268.

Goodstein, L. (1965). Behavior theoretical views of counseling. In B. Steffre (Ed.), *Theories of counseling* (pp. 140–192). New York: McGraw-Hill.

Gordon, V. N. (1981). The undecided student: A developmental perspective. *Personnel and Guidance Journal*, 59, 433–439.

Gordon, V. N. (1984). *The undecided college student*. Springfield, IL: Charles C. Thomas.

Gordon, V. N., & Polson, C. T. (1985). Students needing academic alternative advising: A national survey. *NACADA Journal*, 5, 77–84.

Gordon, V. N., & Steele, G. E. (1992). Advising major-changers: Students in transition. *NACADA Journal*, 12, 22–27.

Hartman, B. W., Fuqua, D. R., & Blum, C. R. (1985). A path-analytic model of career indecision. *Vocational Guidance Quarterly*, 33, 231–240.

Ikenberry, D. L. (1987). *A Study of the relationships among personality type, anxiety and career indecision*. Unpublished doctoral dissertation, Ohio State University, Columbus.

Johnston, W., & Packer, A. (1987). *Workforce 2000: Work and workers for the twenty-first century*. Indianapolis, IN: Hudson Institute.

Katchadourian, H. A., & Boli, J. (1985). *Careerism and intellectualism among college students*. San Francisco: Jossey-Bass.

Kimes, H., & Troth, W. (1974). Relationship of trait anxiety to career decisiveness. *Journal of Counseling Psychology*, 21, 277–280.

Kutscher, R. (September 1987). *Projections 2000: Overview and implications of the projections to 2000*. Monthly labor review. Washington, DC: U.S. Department of Labor.

Lucas, M., & Epperson, D. (1988). Personality types in vocationally undecided students. *Journal of College Student Development*, 29, 460–466.

McKinley, C. D. (July 1991). *What's hot, not next*. East Lansing, MI: CAM Report.

Mendonca, J. D., & Seiss, T. F. (1976). Counseling for indecisiveness: Problem-solving and anxiety management training. *Journal of Counseling Psychology*, 23, 339–347.

Naisbitt, J. (1982). *Megatrends*. New York: Warner Bros.

Pascarella, E. T., & Terenzini, P. T. (1991). *How college affects students*. San Francisco: Jossey-Bass.

Salomone, P. R. (1982). Difficult cases in career counseling II: The indecisive client. *Personnel and Guidance Journal*, 60, 496–500.

Serling, D. A., & Betz, N. E. (1990). Development and evaluation of a measure of fear of commitment. *Journal of Counseling Psychology*, 37, 91–97.

Solmon, L. (1981). New findings on the links between college education and work. *Higher Education*, 10, 615–648.

Theophilides, C., Terenzini, P. T., & Lorang, W. (1984). Freshman and sophomore experiences and changes in major field. *Review of Higher Education*, 7, 261–278.

Toffler, A. (1981). *The third wave*. New York: Bantam Books.

5

Advising Special Populations

For over 20 years the makeup of the college student population has been changing dramatically. What Cross (1971) called the ''new'' student of the 1970s and 1980s has become the regular students of the 1990s. Minorities, older adults, the academically underprepared, and other special populations attending college have increased dramatically and will continue to expand.

The trend toward specialized advising for these varied populations is already evident. Faculty advisers have always been specialists in their academic disciplines, but the complex needs of the populations described below require special advising approaches and a level of expertise that many advisers do not possess. It is increasingly evident that all advisers need a minimum level of knowledge and skills to work with the students for whom specialized services already exist on campus, since they will undoubtedly need to screen and refer to these resources. Training programs need to provide the information and the opportunity to develop the special skills required to advise these students in a sensitive and informed manner.

This chapter describes some of the characteristics of these special groups and suggests advising strategies tailored to be responsive to each individual's needs. The type and number of students in these special categories will vary widely on individual campuses. Advisers in community colleges, for example, may see more older adult students while institutions with well-known services for disabled students may find more of them in the general student population. Since minorities constitute an extremely diverse group of students with special needs, they are concentrated in Chapter 6.

ADULT STUDENTS

As the number of adult learners over the age of 25 increased in higher education during the past two decades, advisers were struck by the differences between them and traditional-age students. Adult students are a heterogeneous group. Their reasons for returning to school are varied (Aslanian & Brickell, 1980; Bers & Smith, 1987; Gordon, 1982; Graham, 1987; Smart & Pascarella, 1987). Houle (1961) identified three types of adult learners that still seem to exist today. The "goal-oriented" learner uses the educational experience to gain specific and practical objectives such as learning how to use computers. The "activity-oriented" learner participates primarily for the sake of the learning activity itself rather than to learn subject matter. The third type of learner identified by Houle is "learning-oriented." These adults enjoy and pursue learning for learning's sake. They have a fundamental desire to grow through learning activities. While academic advisers will be in contact with all these types of learners, goal-oriented and learning-oriented adults may be more inclined to matriculate in higher education. Continuing education advisers see the other types as well.

Morstain and Smart (1974) developed a scale to measure motivation for participating in education and found six related factors. Adults return to school for social relationships, external expectations, social welfare, professional advancement, escape/stimulation, and cognitive interest. Advisers often see adults who matriculate because of the desire for professional advancement and cognitive interest, but they may see older students return to college for any of Morstain and Smart's six motivational reasons. Many characteristics distinguish adult students from traditional ones (Ancheta, 1980; Etaugh & Claire, 1989; Freilino & Hummel, 1985; Richter-Antion, 1986; Von der Embse & Childs, 1979). They are more self-directed than younger students and use personal experiences as learning resources. Older students learn best when they can set their own pace. They are interested in immediate and practical uses of what they are learning. They have diverse learning styles and may prefer problem-centered learning.

There are many unique characteristics of adult students that have an impact on advising. Adult students often attend part-time because of work and family responsibilities. Some may have poor educational backgrounds and may lack self-confidence in the learning environment. Adult students may have unrealistic or inappropriate expectations about higher education that can create problems until they are oriented into the academic milieu. Some may perceive certain academic rules and requirements as irrelevant or repressive and react negatively to red tape. Many adults feel pressured to complete their education quickly since their life's "time clock" feels out of sync (Neugarten, 1977). Adult students may feel anxieties about their ability to perform in the academic environment. Some have concerns about relating to their younger classmates. These fears often evaporate, however, once classes actually begin (Rawlins, 1979).

The fear of failure is very real for many adults (Larkin, 1987; Roehl, 1980). Some put great pressures on themselves to perform exceptionally well. Rusty study habits and learning skills as well as distracting personal concerns may intrude until students realize that the expectation they place on themselves at first is unrealistic. Advisers can help returning students to enter the college experience with realistic expectations for themselves and what the institution can provide.

Adult students want and seek out professionals who understand the many roles and pressures impinging on their time and energy to attend school. Adults need placement in the proper level and sequences of courses as well as flexibility in curricular and scheduling options. They need information about majors and the rationale for curricular requirements. They are often concerned about the career implications of different educational options and worry about how their age will affect the job opportunities available to them (Perrone, Wollear, Lee, & Davis, 1977). Advising services must be available at nontraditional times of day and at convenient locations. Advisers also need to be aware of the career development needs of older students (Brown, 1981; Gerstein, 1982; Perrone et al., 1987; Stonewater, 1987). Griff (1987) describes some services that are needed to serve the diversity among older students. Included are self-exploration, topical workshops, support groups, academic advising, career counseling, and job placement services. Brown (1981) discusses several models of career development for adults, including self-help, informational, developmental, and structured group models. The developmental model can integrate life and career development since it incorporates decision making and future concerns.

A subpopulation that deserves special attention is the reentry woman (Badenhoop & Johansen, 1980; Brooks, 1976; Glass & Rose, 1987; Hooper & Traupmann, 1984). Women have, in addition to the special needs listed above, other concerns and problems unique to them (Brandenberg, 1974; Hooper, 1979; Roehl, 1980). A supportive family is perhaps the greatest asset to a returning woman student (Babier, 1971; Beutell & O'Hare, 1987; Roehl & Okun, 1984). Advisers can encourage orientation activities that include family members so that they can all feel part of the experience. A woman entering college will have less time for family responsibilities, and adjustments must be made accordingly. A working wife and mother can be especially at risk. Child care may be an issue for some older students. A class schedule that fits the student's life-style is important. Reentry women may also have concerns about finances when returning to college since this can be a severe drain on the family budget.

Career concerns are especially worrisome for women students who have never been in the work force or left some years before. They will need to identify resources to gather information and help in exploring occupational possibilities. Advisers need to be careful not to discourage a student from setting vocational goals because of sex or age stereotypes (Schlossberg, 1972).

Academic and personal support are extremely important to a returning adult. Advisers with some working knowledge of adult development theory are in a better position to understand the unique perspectives and motivations for returning to the classroom (Cross, 1981).

Academic advisers working with adult students should help them unleash their full potential and assist them with academic planning that is congruent with their personal interests, values, and goals. They can help them view learning as a lifelong process, support them as they enter a sometimes strange and confusing environment, and continue to encourage them as they proceed through the academic experience.

STUDENT ATHLETES

The initial concern of advisers when working with student athletes is to make sure they are academically "eligible" for participation in their sport. Many other issues must be considered, however. The student athlete has been the object of much controversy because of student exploitation and past breaches of academic integrity (Chu, Segrave, & Becker, 1985; Cramer, 1986; Hammel, 1980; Renick, 1974). Issues of educational value versus commercialism and the maintenance of institutional integrity have received a great deal of attention (Golden, 1984; Grant, 1979).

The Knight Foundation Commission on Intercollegiate Athletics examined management practices of intercollegiate athletics. The report, "Keeping Faith with the Student Athlete: A New Model for Intercollegiate Athletics" (1991), offered 30 recommendations to restore integrity to big-sports programs. In addition to recommending new models for sports governance, specific areas relate directly to academic advising. The commission urges that the academic performance of athletes be reviewed each semester (which is being done on many campuses currently) and that athletes should be declared ineligible if they are not making progress toward a specific degree. The commission also indicated that graduation rates of athletes should be the same as other students.

Gordon (1986) identified several issues that must be considered when advising the student athlete. The first issue questions the effect of athletic participation on academic performance. Both positive and negative influences have been identified (Dickason, 1979; Greendorfer & Blind, 1985; Higgins, 1976; Shapiro, 1984). Braddock (1981) showed significant positive association between sport participation and measures of academic achievement for both black and white student athletes. Purdy, Eitzen, and Hufnagel (1982) found in a study of 10,000 athletes that they were less prepared for college than the general population and achieved less academically. These findings were especially true for scholarship holders, blacks, and participants in football and basketball. Mayo (1980) found that female and male student athletes who participated in nonrevenue sports (e.g., track, swimming) performed better academically than their revenue-making counterparts (e.g., football, basketball).

Another issue involves the importance of recognizing individual differences among student athletes. Rehberg and Cohen (1975) found two distinct athlete populations: the pure athletes and scholar athletes. One of every six students was a scholar athlete and was able to balance both sports and academics and achieve well in both. In contrast, the pure athlete lagged behind on social and academic variables.

The individual needs of black student athletes are well documented (Daniels, 1987; Edwards, 1984; Henderson, 1986; Leach & Conners, 1984; Olsen, 1968; Welch, 1982). Some black athletes are not prepared for the academic rigor required in college and are sometimes overwhelmed by the pressures placed on them as student and athletes.

Lapchick (1989) discusses the ethical issues involved in the adjustment of black student athletes. Recommendations are made for helping black student athletes in the realm of coaching, recruiting practices, monitoring, special programs, conducive social environments, and posteligibility support.

Women athletes also have special needs and concerns, including health problems such as eating disorders, role conflict concerns, and overemphasis upon winning at the expense of educational values (Colker & Widom, 1980). Nixon, Maresca, and Silverman (1979) surveyed student attitudes toward females in sport and found college women feel comfortable in their involvement. Women's acceptance of females in sport was greater than male acceptance, however. Matross (1980) surveyed a large number of students at a large public university and found them to believe athletics (both women's and men's) helped the quality of life at the university, enhanced the personal development of athletics, and provided entertainment.

Women's problems receive less attention because of the lesser status of women's intercollegiate athletics and because they tend to do better academically. More recent data indicate that women athletes may be facing problems similar to those of men because of increasing extrinsic motivators (West, 1984).

Many studies have compared academic, personality, and other characteristics of athletes with nonathletes. Aamodt, Alexander, and Kimbrough (1982) found differences between athletes and nonathletes as well as between athletes who participated in various sports. Results indicated that overall, athletes were more dominant and active and less patient and calm than nonathletes at the college level. Personality characteristics of all athletic groups did differ, however. Baseball players were more similar to nonathletes, and track and field participants were most different from nonathletes in terms of high dominance and low steadiness. The role of sport in character building has been shown to be controversial (Stevensen, 1985).

A third issue in advising student athletes is acknowledging the conflict between student and athlete roles. Nixon (1982) found this conflict to be especially prevalent among student athletes who were academically deficient or those who did not look upon education in a favorable light. The student athletes themselves, according to Nixon, did not perceive a conflict in these roles.

Many developmental issues have been examined in exploring this role conflict (Chartrand & Lent, 1987; Kennedy & Dimick, 1987; Nelson, 1983; Sowa & Gressard, 1983). Where differences were found between athletes and nonathletes, athletes scored significantly lower on Chickerings' vectors of developing a career purpose, formulating educational goals, and developing mature relationships and, in some cases, autonomy. Blann (1985) posited that athletes from highly competitive programs may be experiencing environments that are detrimental to their personal development.

Several studies have examined sex role attitudes among athletes (Maier & Lavrakas, 1981; Wrisberg, Draper, & Everett, 1988). Hirt, Hoffman, and Sedlacek (1983) found there was a fairly consistent pattern among male varsity athletes in demonstrating more negative attitudes toward nontraditional sex role behaviors than did nonathletes. In a study conducted by Houseworth, Peplow, and Thirer (1989), athletes in contact sports held more traditional and conservative attitudes toward women than other athletes. No differences were found, however, in sex role orientation between athletes and nonathletes or between athletes in different sports.

Many special programming approaches have been designed for student athletes. All the factors in a student athlete's environment must be considered when advising this special group (Ender, 1983; Gibson & Creamer, 1987; Gurney & Johnson, 1986; Weber, Sherman, & Tegano, 1986; Zingg, 1982). The special counseling needs of student athletes have been described by Lanning (1982), who suggests that many athletic counselors are not trained to deal with issues regarding students' unrealistic goals of playing professional sports, self-image problems, and adjustments that become necessary because of injuries. Hurley and Cunningham (1984) discuss the counseling needed to address the pressures to achieve academic and athletic success.

A large group of sport psychologists offered their opinions about the most important life adjustment skills that should be incorporated into mental health programs for athletes (O'Block & Billimoria, 1988). They ranked stress management, coping with emotions, self-concept improvement, and developing a realistic self-image as the most important.

Many specific programs have been described to help student athletes succeed in the academic environment. Petitpas and Champagne (1988) propose a psychoeducational programming model that addresses developmental dynamics, a rationale for specific services, suggested psychoeducational programming, and implementation and evaluation considerations. Figler (1981) developed a program that included quality of life issues, establishment of academic, personal, and career goals, and the integration of institutional and expert resources.

There are obviously many complex issues involved in the advising of student athletes. Special skills and knowledge need to be refined as advisers serve this group's varied needs. Advisers need to be sensitive to the subpopulations within this special group and view each student individually when assessing potential for academic progress and success.

COMMUTER STUDENTS

A commuter student is defined as one who does not live in campus housing, in fraternity or sorority housing, or in the immediate area adjacent to campus

(Rhatigan, 1986). Commuter students comprise well over half of the under-graduate population and represent many different subgroups (Stewart, Merrill, & Saluri, 1985; Stewart & Rue, 1983). Since the types of commuter students are so varied, each campus may define them within its own context. Compared with residential students, the age range among commuters is broader, more commuters are employed, and work or home commitments may hold a higher priority than a commitment to school (Chickering, 1974; Schuchman, 1974).

The commuter student profile might include a traditional-age full-time student who lives with parents because of financial constraints; an adult student with a spouse and children who attends day classes; a traditional-age student who shares an apartment with other students off-campus; and an adult who works full-time in the day and attends evening classes. Since the needs of this heterogeneous group are so complex, advisers need to develop the skills and knowledge to accommodate a wide variety of individuals.

Some authors have challenged the myths or biases associated with commuter students from earlier research. They were described as less able academically, less committed to education, and not having an interest in the campus beyond their classes (Foster, Sedlacek, & Hardwick, 1977; Knefelkamp & Stewart, 1983; Rhatigan, 1986; Rice, 1989). The older adult student in particular sometimes finds it difficult to adjust to a campus where the majority of students are of traditional age and residentially based. As Andreas (1983) points out, the present-day commuter's college experience may revolve around food service facilities, library stacks, parking lots, and administrative offices in addition to the class-room. Since commuter students represent the majority of college students, they must be acknowledged as important when supportive campus environments are being created (Knefelkamp & Stewart, 1983).

Pascarella and Terenzini (1991) discuss retention of students living on campus versus those who are commuting. The academic, social, and personal integration of a student into the campus milieu has a positive effect on persistence. The social-psychological environment of commuter campuses is generally not as conducive to integration as are residential ones. There is a need to bring the educational experiences of commuters closer to those of residential students if this positive integration is to be realized (Rice, 1989). Some vehicles for ac-complishing this goal are redesigning admissions practices, offering specialized orientation programs (including parents and spouses), providing short residential experiences, initiating activities that promote faculty-student interactions, and even redesigning curricula to acknowledge student differences and needs.

Some campuses have established commuter student offices that provide fa-cilities for students to relax, store their belongings, and have access to com-fortable surroundings where they can study or meet with friends. The National Clearinghouse for Commuter Programs (1978) conducted a survey to collect information abut programs and services for commuter students. The services most frequently provided were information centers, off-campus housing referrals, and car pooling services. Many campuses provided special programs that included activities to promote faculty and student interaction, specialized counseling, tutorial services, and workshops on relevant topics. Commuter students often need opportunities for more intensive peer interaction as well (Knefelkamp & Stewart, 1983). Advisers are often in a position to encourage commuter students to become more involved in campus activities such as concerts, lectures by guest speakers, interest groups, career- or major-related clubs, or social activities.

Commuter students may not use advising services as frequently as they should because of time and other constraints. An intrusive advising approach may be necessary with students who drive to campus, attend class, and then drive home or to work.

Advisers on predominantly commuter campuses are familiar with the multiple roles many commuter students play; advisers on campuses where commuter students are the minority need to make a special effort to identify them and ensure that adequate, specialized advising services are available.

DISABLED STUDENTS

Disabled students represent many categories of disabilities, including the orthopedically handicapped, visual- and hearing-impaired, emotionally disturbed, learning disabled, and other health impaired groups (Beiber et al., 1987; Geist & Calzaretta, 1982; Hippolitus, 1987). With the passing of the Rehabilitation Act of 1973, Section 504, students with disabilities have been guaranteed the right of access to higher education. The number of students with disabilities attending college has increased dramatically since that time (Hoy & Gregg, 1986).

Some campuses have specially trained professionals who work with disabled students on a daily basis. It is imperative that advisers work closely with these services when they are available. A student's disability may have an effect on that individual's daily living, academic progress, social development, and educational and career decision making (Saunders & Ervin, 1984). Lombana (1989) claims that few advisers and counselors have received the training required to work effectively with this population. Advisers must become familiar with the various barriers and problems these students experience (Greenwood, 1987; Humes, Szymanski, & Hohenshil, 1989) so that an effective advising relationship can be established.

There are many specific issues that students with physical disabilities experience. Accessibility is especially important to the mobility-impaired student. An advising office must accommodate these students with parking facilities, automatic doorways, elevators, and other physical structures to make offices accessible. While advisers are not usually responsible for these accommodations, they do need to be aware of the structural barriers that might prevent a student from accessing advising services.

Course scheduling and planning may pose difficulties for disabled students.

Some may not have been prepared for the rigors of academic work and may need access to remedial services in addition to disability support services. When these offices are separate on a campus, coordination of services is critical if individuals are to receive the type of help their disability requires.

Some institutions grant priority scheduling to disabled students so that accessibility to classrooms and buildings is assured and enough time is available to move from one class to another. Careful scheduling is important since some mobility-impaired students expend a great deal of time and energy in each class to compensate for their disability.

Hameister (1984) identified six developmental issues that are important to disabled students: (1) developing intellectual and academic competence, (2) establishing and maintaining interpersonal relationships, (3) developing sex role identity and sexuality, (4) deciding on a career and life-style, (5) formulating an integrated philosophy of life, and (6) maintaining health and wellness. The issues of developing intellectual and academic competence and deciding on a career and life-style have special significance for academic advising. Academic competence signifies that students are able to succeed in the academic milieu. Unfortunately, some disabled students may have unrealistic expectations of the effort it will take to meet course requirements. Some are reluctant to mention their disabling conditions to instructors. Many need tutoring, study skills improvement, time management, and microcomputer use. Many physically impaired students are especially in need of career planning services that are tailored to their particular situation (Humes & Hohenshil, 1985; Kirchner, Simon, & Stern, 1985; Sampson, 1984). Levinson (1986) observed that handicapped students often leave school without marketable skills and are unable to function independently in the community. He describes a vocational evaluation program that incorporates a two-phase, multidisciplinary team approach. The vocational aspects of the program included recommendations from the professional evaluation team for vocational exploration activities (e.g., work adjustment activities, vocational counseling, remedial academic programming, or a referral for further evaluation). Although this program was designed for middle and high school students, its evaluation framework is relevant to college students as well.

Many disabled students lack work experience and the accompanying social experience that are important in learning job skills and employer expectations. It is important for disabled students to have access to work-study jobs, internships, and other types of work experiences. Roessler (1987) suggests that unless there are changes in public policies, rehabilitation practices, and employer benefits, future economic prospects for disabled individuals are not as positive as they should be.

Learning Disabled Students

An understanding of learning disabilities is extremely important for academic advisers since they are in a position to suspect a learning disability that has not been diagnosed previously. When advisers sense that individuals with whom they are working have difficulty in understanding abstract concepts, reasoning in a deductive manner, remembering, sustaining attention to task, or organizing ideas and information, a learning disorder might be suspected.

There are many types of learning disabilities, including auditory perceptual, memory, motor, visual perceptual, dyslexia (difficulty with reading), dyscalculia (difficulty with mathematics), dysgraphic (difficulty with writing), and cognitive complexity (Block, 1991; Hartman & Krulwich, 1984). Hoy and Gregg (1986) indicate that learning disabilities interfere with a student's ability to perceive, process, sort, store, or retrieve information.

Learning disabled students sometimes enroll in courses too difficult for them, underestimate the reading and writing requirements of courses, do not report accurately on how they are progressing in courses, do not seek out the services they need, have difficulty concentrating, and may have social adaptation difficulties (Mangrum & Strichard, 1988). Block (1991) suggests that advisers look for students whose verbal expression far surpasses their written work. Poor spelling and handwriting may indicate an inability to make words flow or sequence ideas. Sequencing problems can interfere with learning in math, science, history, or English. A problem with concentrating may be resolved by permitting students to take examinations in distraction-free environments (Lazarus, 1989). Poor performance in multiple-choice tests, especially those that are computer-scored, may indicate an inability to put the right answers in the right place.

Lutwak and Fine (1983) discuss countertherapeutic counseling styles that advisers may inadvertently employ when working with learning disabled students. Some of the behaviors they identify include limiting options, fostering pseudo-autonomy, negative dependency, avoidance, pigeonholing, and encouraging premature termination from school. Becoming more informed and sensitized to the unique characteristics of these special students will help to eliminate negative approaches.

When advisers work with students with any type of disability, they need to encourage independence, recognize them as individuals, and help them honestly evaluate their performance (Hartman, 1986). It is also important for advisers to work closely with disability services so that the student receives a unified approach to academic and other problems. In this way a successful experience is more likely to be realized.

GRADUATE STUDENTS

Graduate student advising is under the purview of faculty, and the demands and responsibilities of such a role are critical to the admission, program planning, and retention of these special students. Faculty have great influence on students' educational aspirations, particularly the decision to enter graduate school (Hearn, 1987; Pascarella & Terenzini, 1991). For many faculty, however, the time and energy involved in the adviser-student relationship are demanding (Kammerer,

1986). The quality of the graduate student's performance and persistence to the final degree depends largely on this relationship (Kowalik, 1989; Malany, 1987; Pascarella & Terenzini, 1991; Smith & Valentine, 1987).

The graduate student adviser's role may be viewed from two perspectives. The first includes the faculty adviser's academic responsibilities; the second, the personal and supportive role that the relationship requires. Winston and Polkosnik (1984) describe the adviser as a reliable information source. This includes helping the student understand the institutional requirements for deadlines, procedures, and other policies. Since these rules are often not conveyed in an orderly manner, many graduate students need to be guided by their faculty adviser through a bureaucratic maze.

Helping students build a program of study is one of the most important faculty adviser's functions. Some curricula are highly structured, while others allow for a great deal of flexibility. A careful assessment of the student's interests and past academic experiences is obviously a first step. Advisers also need to prepare students for the general examinations that are required in the department. Winston and Polkosnik (1984) recommend that advisers outline the examination process so that students will know exactly what is expected of them. Feelings of anxiety about the process can be abated if the process is understood beforehand (Carmel & Berstein, 1989). For doctoral students, surmounting the hurdles of writing a dissertation will be made easier by close attention and support from their adviser (Bargar & Duncan, 1990; Beatty & Stamatakos, 1990; Connell, 1985; Sternberg, 1981).

An orientation program designed to introduce graduate students to their new academic and institutional roles is recommended by Vickio and Tack (1989). The authors created a program to help new graduate students become acquainted with their department, faculty, administrative personnel, and university services. It also introduced them to their responsibilities as research or teaching assistants.

In addition to the academic responsibilities, advisers of graduate students need to assume a more personal or mentoring role. In graduate education, a positive personal relationship with faculty members can predict the completion of the graduate degree (Pascarella & Terenzini, 1991; Smith & Valentine, 1987).

Students must make a tremendous commitment to graduate education, which often calls for personal and financial sacrifice. Tuckman, Coyle, & Bae (1989) studied the time it took to complete the doctoral degree and found a 20 percent increase between 1967 and 1986. Advisers need to be sensitive to the pressures their advisees are experiencing during this lengthy commitment and maintain an open, caring relationship.

Winston and Polkosnik (1984) outline some excellent recommendations for an effective graduate student adviser to incorporate. Included are holding seminars to promote interaction between the students and faculty in the field; modeling the role of researcher by writing and publishing with students; giving students specific feedback about their performance as often as possible; and making sure their students are not discriminated against based on gender or racial background. They also suggest confronting students directly who do not have the ability, attitude, or personality for graduate study so that alternative directions may be identified.

While faculty advising at the undergraduate level is extremely important, the graduate student adviser must assume more responsibility for the student's course of study because of its complexity and adaptation to the personal and professional interests of the advisee. For the experience to be successful and the goal of obtaining a degree to reach fruition, advisers need to see the importance of their involvement in the process. Great satisfaction can be derived from seeing a former student become a recognized and contributing member of one's academic field.

HIGH-ABILITY STUDENTS

High-ability students may be described as those who performed well in high school and are recognized as potential scholars upon entry into college or those who perform extremely well in academic work after they are enrolled. Students with excellent high school records and high achievement scores are often recruited for the honors opportunities established on many campuses (Douglas, Powers, & Choroszy, 1983). Although the majority of these students fulfill their potential during college, some may not perform as predicted. Students who achieve well after matriculation are often identified during, or at the end of, the freshman year and invited to participate in an honors program.

Jenkins-Friedman (1986) discusses the recruitment and selection of honors students based on criteria beyond grades and test scores. Although many students have above average ability, the interaction among intellectual ability, creativity, and task commitment is a better indicator of "giftedness" (Renzulli, 1978). Jenkins-Friedman advocates broadening the selection of honors students to include creativity and the ability to persevere in a task.

Several studies have tried to find factors that can predict high academic achievement in colleges as students enter. McDonald and Gawkoski (1979) found that high school grade point average was the strongest predictor of success in the university's honors program. SAT mathematics and verbal scores were also related to success for women. Other studies (Centra & Rock, 1971; Coursol & Wagner, 1986) also found high school grades to be the best predictor of high academic success.

High-achieving students have been found to possess certain characteristics that may be important in the adviser-advisee relationship. Advisers must be sensitive to issues of conformity, status, sociability, self-concept, flexibility, and leadership (Colangelo, Kelly, & Schrepfer, 1987; Holland & Astin, 1962; Karnes, Chauvin, & Trant, 1984b; Kodman, 1984; Mason, Adams, & Blood, 1965; Ory & Braskamp, 1988; Tomlinson-Keasey & Smith-Winberry, 1983). Karnes, Chauvin, and Trant (1984a) compared personality factors with American College Testing scores and found high math, social studies, and composite scores were related to such positive factors as enthusiasm, emotional stability, trust, assertiveness, and astuteness.

Many high-achieving students are not exempt from academic concerns. Although they perform well, they do not always possess good study habits or time management skills. Lack of motivation may also be a debilitating factor. A few high-ability students may simply be "burned out" from the intensity of performing in high school and may want to pull back from too much involvement when they enter college. Sensitive advisers will recognize the need to focus on students' feelings in this regard and, while being supportive, will encourage them to become involved in honors opportunities and campus life.

High-ability students have career issues that may be different from those of regular students (Gordon, 1983). They are often dealing with issues of multipotentiality, identity concerns, clarifying values, and pressures to choose a major or career area. Some students may narrow their choices prematurely because of pressures to become decided. Talented women students may not be considering the many options open to them because of sex role stereotyping. Academic advisers need to be aware of these issues and listen for attitudes and beliefs that might be counterproductive as students make important educational and occupational decisions.

Although the entry of high school students concurrently into college is not a new phenomenon, early entry programs are becoming more prevalent with the passing of state laws mandating the opportunity to enter college courses. Alexakos and Rothney (1967) found that students who had participated in college while in high school exceeded a similar group without the college experience by the amount of scholarship aid they received later, held more academic honors in college, and earned a higher grade point average in college. Students with the same ability who had not attended college while in high school had higher college attrition rates. Janos et al. (1988) found that early entrants supported each other during the first two years of college and used these relationships as a base for developing relationships with older students as upperclass persons and as graduates. Stanley and McGill (1986) studied students who entered college two or more years earlier than the traditional-age student and found that they were able to make good grades, win honors, and graduate promptly.

Advising early entrants often requires advising skills that incorporate closer contacts with parents and other family members. While these students are gifted intellectually, they may need closer monitoring than older students. A mentoring relationship is often desirable since some of these students may find the transition to college more difficult personally and socially.

Many types of honors opportunities have been described (Austin, 1986; Clark, 1965; Cohen, 1966; Cummings, 1986; Danzig, 1982; Friedman & Jenkins-Friedman, 1986). Gabelnick (1986) describes some creative curriculum designs for honors programs. According to Gabelnick, honors curricula reflect the often conflicting values and philosophies of American society and put students in touch with enduring intellectual debates in higher education.

Day (1989) outlines many approaches to challenging high-achieving students through honors programs. These include general honors programs, departmental courses, clusters or groups of students who study a given theme, interdisciplinary general education courses, and colloquia. Honor societies provide increased contact with faculty and peers and can provide incentives for achievement. Gabelnick (1986) also discusses models of instruction. She advocates team teaching, interdisciplinary seminars, and the establishment of "learning communities" that allow for innovative experiential opportunities.

Community colleges have found honors programs to be beneficial (Heck, 1985; Jackson, 1986; Piland, McKeague, & Montgomery, 1987). Todd (1988) suggests that creating an honors program will help community colleges attract and retain high-achieving students. Other positive effects include encouraging better faculty-student relations and enhancing entry opportunities to four-year colleges and into the job force. A successful honors program, according to Todd, must have clearly defined goals and be tailored to the individual community, students, faculty members, and administrators. The program could offer special sections of classes, seminars, or individualized or independent study. Piland and Azbell (1984) also suggest broad-based course topics and encouragement of self-directed study at the community college level.

Some honors programs offer residentially based opportunities. De Coster (1966) describes a living unit that encouraged interaction among the students themselves. It was found that the students had better grades than high-ability students not living in the residence hall. Stewart (1980), on the other hand, did not find any differences in achievement between those in honors-designated housing and those in nonhonors residential housing. The advantages of honors housing, however, are that high-ability students may be intellectually stimulated by peers, programming opportunities can exist, faculty involvement can be expanded, and computer and other resources may be easily accessible to high-achieving students. In some honors programs special sections of honors courses are taught in the living unit, and faculty have their offices in the building as well.

If any group of students needs close and frequent contact with faculty advisers, it is the student with the potential to achieve at high levels. Tacha (1986) advocates developing intellectually challenging and personally supportive faculty-student relationships outside of the classroom for high-ability students. Advising can become the critical vehicle for a great deal of this personal interaction. Hickerson (1982) describes a contract advising program for highly motivated students that helps them set goals and plan academic programs. Since many of these students will continue into graduate programs (Malaney & Isaac, 1988; Parker & Karnes, 1987; Thistlethwaite & Wheeler, 1966), they need to be encouraged and given accurate information about opportunities for advanced degrees.

Gamson (1967) found some variance with faculty attitudes and behaviors in grading, interactions with students outside of class, and faculty styles between natural science and social science departments. The contrasting ways of relating to students led to different kinds of problems for each department and different resolutions. The author found these differences in faculty style consistent with the differences in beliefs and values within the disciplines. Since close and positive faculty relationships have been shown to be a critical link to retention (Noel, Levitz, & Saluri, 1985; Tinto, 1987), the role faculty play in advising high-ability, honors students cannot be overstated.

Advisers of high-ability students may want to keep the following in mind as they work with individual students:

- Although traditional-age students demonstrate the potential for exceptional scholarship, they are still involved in transition issues such as adjusting to academic demands, residence hall living, and other personal-social concerns.

- The development tasks associated with their age group will include issues of autonomy, developing social and physical competencies, and managing emotions.

- High-ability students may be dealing with issues of fear of success or failure.

- Choosing a major and/or career field may be especially difficult for them since they have the potential to succeed in many areas.

- Clarifying personal and work values may be an important task when working with students who may already have an idea of their interests and abilities.

- They may be trying to please significant others rather than exploring alternatives and taking responsibility for educational and vocational decisions that appeal to them.

Most advisers find working with these students to be extremely challenging and pleasurable. Assuming a mentoring role may prove to be as rewarding for the adviser as it is for the student.

TRANSFER STUDENTS

One of every five students who attend a two-year college transfers into a four-year institution (Adelman, 1988). Fifteen percent of all four-year students also transfer at least once during their first two years (Tinto, 1987). Transfer students, thus, comprise a significantly large segment of the overall college population. Transfer students are often faced with unique problems involving articulation, including credit evaluation, course placement, and barriers that are institution-specific. Tinto (1987) contends that transfer students experience many difficulties in adjusting to a new campus because they are rarely given an orientation to academic programs and services.

Donovan and Schaier-Peleg (1988) studied the transfer problems of urban minority students. They maintain that too few two- and four-year colleges have communicated effectively about transfer issues. Discussions about curriculum, teaching strategies, and outcomes may not occur often enough. Recommendations from their report for improving the transfer process include productive collaboration between two- and four-year institutions with better articulation agreements; better data collection so that the characteristics of the students transferring may be known; improved academic environments within the two-year colleges; and responsive support services to anticipate non-academic needs.

One of the most difficult problems transfer students experience is the evaluation of prior credit (Fleck & Shirley, 1990; Ford, 1986). The whole process of credit evaluation has been facilitated within recent years by computer-based articulation systems that help to standardize information and provide it to the student more efficiently (Schinoff & Kelly, 1982; Stones, 1987; Waggaman, 1982).

Transfer students are less likely to complete a degree (Pascarella, 1986; Trent & Medsker, 1968). Johnson (1987) found that transfer student persistence was strongly associated with perceptions of the work-relatedness of their degree, their integration, performance, and satisfaction with their academic program, and their intent to continue in college. Educational attainment is affected by the continuity of experiences in one campus. An interruption in this continuity tends to inhibit the attainment of a degree (Pascarella & Terenzini, 1991). Kocher and Pascarella (1988) also found that transferring had a negative impact on job status because of this lack of educational attainment.

While most transfers occur from two-year to four-year colleges, Hogan (1986) examined reverse transfers, that is, from four-year to two-year institutions. The reverse transfer student was more likely to be older, married, employed, and enrolled part-time. The reverse transfers earned higher grades than native students and were planning to earn credits toward a four-year degree. Pascarella and Terenzini (1991) suggest that to ease the transition of transfer students, more flexible admissions procedures, greater flexibility in transfer credit policies, easier access to financial aid, and more equitable opportunities for on-campus housing need to be established. Advising and other support services must be sensitized to the unique needs of transfer students if they are to experience a successful transition. Advisers on the sending end must prepare students for the types of problems they will encounter and provide information about resources to assist them. Advisers on the receiving end cannot assume that because students have had college experience they will be able to function optimally in their new environment. In institutions where great numbers of transfer students matriculate, the creation of special services for transfers, the establishment of orientation programs, and the specialization of advisers for transfer students can offer the type of help these students require and deserve.

ACADEMICALLY-AT-RISK STUDENTS

Some students who enter college can be identified as academically high risk from the outset. These are often students underprepared for college work because of poor high school preparation. Some of these students come from low socioeconomic backgrounds where there was little support for schools. Others may not have considered a college education a goal during their elementary and high school years and did not engage in a college preparatory curriculum (Jones & Watson, 1990). Many special programs and support services have been developed to help underprepared students, particularly minorities, to acquire the skills and knowledge they need to succeed in higher education (Ahrendt, 1987).

As Groves and Groves (1981) point out, it is inaccurate to assume that academically underprepared students are of lower intelligence and development. Low academic self-concept, lack of direction and goal setting, and poor educational skills are typical of these students (Pollard, Benton, & Hinz, 1983). Another group of academically-at-risk students includes those who by all predictions should succeed in college but who do not perform up to standards and are placed on probation or academic jeopardy by the institution (Cocher, 1989). Graham and Dallam (1986) found that transfer students were more likely to be placed on academic probation than students native to the institution. Some students do poorly their freshman year because they are not expecting the rigors or discipline that the academic work requires. Poorly developed study habits in high school are carried over into college and may establish a pattern that is difficult to overcome.

Although advisers encounter both types of academically-at-risk students, advising approaches may be different since the students arrive at their difficulties from different perspectives. Underprepared students are often identified prior to enrollment and scheduled into special services, usually during their freshman year, which assist them with remediation in academic subjects, study skills, mentoring, and special monitoring. Advisers working with these students are often specialists, trained to recognize the needs and concerns of this special population. Developmental education programs have played an important role in the successful transition of many students into the academic and social life of an institution (Sharma, 1977).

As Jones and Watson (1990) point out, supplementing the academic curriculum with remedial courses and nonacademic courses designed to help students improve their academic performance is not enough. Courses and activities to integrate these students into the college environment are essential. Curricular and noncurricular activities need to be incorporated into a holistic approach.

Many advisers find themselves in contact with the second type of academically-at-risk student, that is, those who are not performing well in the classroom and are in danger of being dismissed. These students are particularly challenging since the causes of their poor performance can be complex. Lack of maturity, poor motivation, personal or family problems, adjustment concerns, or low academic self-concept are just a few of the causes advisers have observed. Some working students consider school a second priority and thus do not give the optimal time and energy to that endeavor. A few students will not face the difficulties that are leading them into academic jeopardy and dig themselves into an academic black hole.

Some students in academic difficulty may have an undiagnosed learning disability. Advisers need to be aware of the types and symptoms of learning disorders since they may be the only professional to see the total academic record and discuss the students' perceptions of their difficulties.

Many studies have examined students who are in academic difficulty from a retention perspective. Anderson (1985) analyzed the internal and external forces influencing student persistence and achievement. Financial problems, housing or roommate problems, and work demands often distract students and lead to poor performance. Internal forces include self-management problems, fear of failure, value conflicts, and other personal concerns. Daubman et al. (1985) found that students who voluntarily withdrew were more often on academic probation, withdrew because of academic difficulty, and had a pattern of withdrawals for this reason. Brown (1989) proposes a model for retention for academically-at-risk students that coordinates curricula, instructional accommodation strategies, and support systems.

Unfortunately, some students in academic difficulty use poor judgment in trying to extract themselves from their situation. They schedule an overload of courses to make up for the credit lost by the failed ones. They may use the course withdrawal option frequently as a way to avoid failure. They may take courses where they feel comfortable and avoid requirements they perceive to be too difficult. Advisers need to be especially alert for any counterproductive behavior on the part of students in academic difficulty.

Many services, programs, and techniques have been devised to assist the student who is academically-at-risk (Hunt & Germinaro, 1988; Lupack, 1983; Lyons, 1985; Noel & Levitz, 1982). Friedlander (1982) identified successful support services for underprepared students. Some of these included interventions during the early and middle part of the term, use of faculty referral slips, coordination of support services with content courses, monitoring student progress, block programming, and supplemental support instruction. Many support services may exist on a campus, but one of the most important is advising since this is where a personal, supportive relationship can help students identify the forces that are causing their academic difficulties and find the type of help that is tailored to the individual student's situation and circumstance. Very few students in academic trouble are there because of lack of ability. Advisers need to help them understand and overcome the causes of their academic failure.

SUMMARY

The makeup of the college population has changed dramatically over the past 20 years. The special types of students described in this chapter bear witness to the need for academic advisers to be knowledgeable and skilled in working with a broad spectrum of students. The concerns that a transfer student brings to the advising exchange may be very different from those of someone with a learning disability. Advisers in certain types of institutions may see a predominance of certain types (such as adult students in a community college or a continuing education unit) and become experts in the needs of that group.

The need for adviser training is obvious. Learning about the characteristics of certain types of students and how to advise them will become increasingly important as the numbers of these special students increase. The trend toward training specialists to work with certain types of students in specially created programs and services will also remain.

Advisers need to approach each student with whom they are in contact with the sensitivity to understand each student's unique perspectives. A caring, open attitude will help set the tone for productive advising relationships, regardless of the student's special needs or circumstances.

REFERENCES

Aamodt, M. G., Alexander, C. J., & Kimbrough, W. W. (1982). Personality characteristics of college non-athletes and baseball, football, and track team members. *Perceptual and Motor Skills*, 55, 327–330.

Adelman, C. (1988). Transfer rates and the going mythologies. *Change*, 20, 38–41.

Ahrendt, K. M. (Ed.). (1987). *Teaching the developmental education student*. New Directions for Community Colleges. Issue 57. (ERIC Document Reproduction Service No. ED 280 519)

Alexakos, C. E., & Rothney, J. W. (1967). Post-high school performance of superior students. *Personnel and Guidance Journal*, 46, 150–155.

Ancheta, B. (1980). Counseling needs of traditional and non-traditional community college students. *Journal of College Student Personnel*, 21, 564–567.

Anderson, E. (1985). Forces influencing student persistence and achievement. In L. Noel, R. Levitz, & D. Saluri (Eds.), *Increasing student retention* (pp. 44–61). San Francisco: Jossey-Bass.

Andreas, R. E. (1983). Institutional self-study: Serving commuter students. In S. S. Stewart (Ed.), *Commuter students: Enhancing their educational experiences* (pp. 9–24). New Directions for Student Services, no. 24. San Francisco: Jossey-Bass.

Aslanian, C. B., & Brickell, H. M. (1980). *Americans in transition: Life changes as reasons for adult learning*. New York: College Board.

Austin, C. G. (1986). Orientation to honors education. In. P. G. Friedman & R. C. Jenkins-Friedman (Eds.), *Fostering excellence through honors programs* (pp. 5–16). New Directions for Teaching Learning, no. 25. San Francisco: Jossey-Bass.

Babier, M. (1971). Counseling the mature woman. *Adult Leadership 20*, 187–189.

Badenhoop, M. S., & Johansen, M. K. (1980). Do reentry women have special needs? *Psychology of Women Quarterly*, 4, 591–595.

Bargar, R. R., & Duncan, J. K. (1990). Creative endeavor in Ph.D. research: Principles, contexts, and conceptions. *Journal of Creative Behavior*, 24, 59–71.

Bargar, R. R., & Mayo-Chamberlain, J. (1983). Adviser and advisee issues in doctoral education. *Journal of Higher Education*, 54, 407–432.

Beatty, D. L., & Stamatakos, L. C. (1990). Faculty and administration perceptors of knowledge, skills, and competencies as standards for doctoral preparation programs in student affairs administration. *Journal of College Student Development*, 31, 221–229.

Beiber, T., Kay, C., Kerkstra, P., & Ratcliff, J. (1987). *Community colleges and students with disabilities: A directory of services and programs.* (ERIC Document Reproduction Service No. ED 300 069)

Bers, T. H., & Smith, K. (1987). College choice and the nontraditional student. *Community College Review*, 15, 39–45.

Beutell, N. J., & O'Hare, M. M. (1987). Coping role conflict among returning students: Professional versus nonprofessional women. *Journal of College Student personnel*, 28, 141–145.

Blann, F. W. (1985). Intercollegiate athletic competition and students' educational and career plans. *Journal of College Student Personnel*, 26, 115–118.

Block, L. (1991). Points to consider when working with a student with a learning disability. Handout, Office for Disability Services, Ohio State university, Columbus.

Braddock, J. H. (1981). Race, athletics, and educational attainment: Dispelling the myths. *Youth and Society*, 12, 335–350.

Brandenberg, J. B. (1974). The needs of women returning to school. *Personnel and Guidance Journal*, 53, 11–18.

Brooks, L. (1976). Supermoms shift gears: Re-entry women. *Counseling Psychologist*, 6, 33–37.

Brown, D. (1981). Emerging models of career development groups for persons at midlife. *Vocational Guidance Quarterly*, 29, 332–340.

Brown, J. M. (1989). A comprehensive retention system for at-risk learners in a post-secondary vocational education program. *Journal of Reading, Writing, and Learning Disability International*, 5, 141–156.

Carmel, S., & Berstein, J. (1989). Trait-anxiety and sense of coherence: A longitudinal study. *Psychological Reports*, 65, 221–222.

Centra, J. A., & Rock, D. (1971). College environments and student academic achievement. *American Educational Research Journal*, 8, 623–634.

Chartrand, J. M., & Lent, R. W. (1987). Sports counseling: Enhancing the development of the student-athlete. *Journal of Counseling and Development*, 66, 164–167.

Chickering, A. W. (1969). *Education and identity.* San Francisco: Jossey-Bass.

Chickering, A. W. (1974). *Commuting versus resident students: Overcoming educational inequities of living off campus.* San Francisco: Jossey-Bass.

Chu, C., Segrave, J. O., & Becker, B. J. (1985). *Sport and higher education.* Champaign, IL: Human Kinetics.

Clark, R. D. (1965). The organization of an honors college: An adventure in cooperation. *Journal of Higher Education*, 26, 313–321.

Cocher, N. C. (1989). Academic standing: Its definition and implementation at 25 small liberal arts institutions. *College and University*, 64, 246–259.

Cohen, J. W. (Ed.). (1966). *The superior student in American higher education.* New York: McGraw-Hill.

Colangelo, N., Kelly, K. R., & Schrepfer, R. M. (1987). A comparison of gifted, general, and special learning needs students on academic and self-concept. *Journal of Counseling and Development*, 66, 73–77.

Colker, R., & Widom, C. S. (1980). Correlates of female athletic participation: Masculinity, femininity, self-esteem, and attitudes toward women. *Sex Roles*, 6, 47–58.

Connell, R. W. (1985). How to supervise a Ph.D. *Vestes*, 28, 38–42.

Coursol, D. H., & Wagner, E. E. (1986). Prediction of academic success in a university honors program. *Psychological Reports*, 58, 139–142.

Cramer, J. (1986). Winning or learning? Athletics and academics in America. *Phi Delta Kappan*, 67, 1–8.

Cross, K. P. (1971). *Beyond the open door: New students to higher education*. San Francisco: Jossey-Bass.

Cross, K. P. (1981). *Adults as learners*. San Francisco: Jossey-Bass.

Cummings, R. J. (1986). Exploring values, issues, and controversies. In P. G. Friedman & R. C. Jenkins-Friedman (Eds.), *Fostering academic excellence through honors programs* (pp. 17–27). New Directions for Teaching and Learning, no. 25. San Francisco: Jossey-Bass.

Daniels, O. C. (1987). Perceiving and nurturing the intellectual development of black student athletes: A case for institutional integrity. *Western Journal of Black Studies*, 11, 155–163.

Danzig, A. (1982). *Honors at the University of Maryland: A status report on programs for talented students*. College Park: University of Maryland. (ERIC Document Reproduction Service No. ED 243 358)

Daubman, K. A., Williams, V. G., Johnson, D. H., & Crump, D. (1985). Time of withdrawal and academic performance: Implication for withdrawal policies. *Journal of College Student Personnel*, 26, 518–534.

Day, A. L. (1989). Honors students. In M. L. Upcraft & J. N. Gardner (Eds.), *The freshman year experience* (pp. 352–362). San Francisco: Jossey-Bass.

De Coster, D. A. (1966). Housing assignments for high ability students. *Journal of College Student Personnel*, 7, 19–22.

Dickason, D. G. (1979). The future of collegiate athletics. *Educational Record*, 60, 499–509.

Donovan, R. A., & Schaier-Peleg, B. (1988). Making transfer work: A practical blueprint for colleges. *Change*, 20, 33–37.

Douglas, P., Powers, S., & Choroszy, M. (1983). Factors in the choice of higher educational institutions by academically gifted seniors. *Journal of College Student Personnel*, 24, 540–544.

Edwards, H. (1984). The black "dumb jock": An American sports tragedy. *College Board Review*, 131, 8–12.

Ender, S. C. (1983). Assisting high academic risk athletes: Recommendations for the academic adviser. *NACADA Journal*, 3, 1–10.

Etaugh, C., & Claire, B. (1989). Attitudes toward men: Comparison of traditional-aged and older college students. *Journal of College Student Development*, 30, 41–46.

Figler, S. K. (1981). *Sport and play in American life: A textbook in the sociology of sport*. New York: Saunders College.

Fleck, R. A., & Shirley, B. M. (1990). Expert systems for transfer credit evaluation: Problems and prospects. *College and University*, 65, 78–83.

Ford, J. (1986). Promoting advising and course articulation between a university and community colleges. *NACADA Journal*, 6, 93–98.

Foster, M. E., Sedlacek, W. E., & Hardwick, M. W. (1977). The student affairs staff attitudes towards students living off campus. *Journal of College Student Personnel*, 18, 291–296.

Freilino, M. K., & Hummel, R. (1985). Achievement and identity in college-age vs. adult women students. *Journal of Youth and Adolescence*, 14, 1–10.

Friedlander, J. (1982). *Innovative approaches to delivering academic assistance to students*. (ERIC Document Reproduction Service No. ED 220 172)

Friedman, P. G., & Jenkins-Friedman, R. C. (1986). Implications for fostering excellence. In P. G. Friedman & R. C. Jenkins-Friedman (Eds.), *Fostering academic excellence through honors programs* (pp. 109–113). New Directions for Teaching and Learning, no. 25. San Francisco: Jossey-Bass.

Gabelnick, F. (1986). Curriculum designs: The medium is the message. In P. G. Friedman & R. C. Jenkins-Friedman (Eds.), *Fostering academic excellence through honors programs* (pp. 75–86). New Directions for Teaching and Learning, no. 25. San Francisco: Jossey-Bass.

Gamson, Z. (1967). Performance and personalism in student-faculty relations. *Sociology of Education*, 40, 279–301.

Geist, C. S., & Calzaretta, W. A. (1982). *Placement handbook for counseling disabled persons*. Springfield, IL: Charles C. Thomas.

Gerstein, M. (1982). Vocational counseling for adults in varied settings: A comprehensive view. *Vocational Guidance Quarterly*, 30, 315–322.

Gibson, D. E., & Creamer, D. G. (1987). Perceptions of academic support by student athletes. *College Student Affairs Journal*, 7, 43–49.

Glass, J. C., & Rose, A. R. (1987). Reentry women: A growing and unique college population. *NASPA Journal*, 25, 110–119.

Golden, D. C. (1984). Supervising college athletes: The role of chief student affairs officer. In A. Shribert & F. R. Brodzinski (Eds.), *Rethinking services for college athletes* (pp. 59–69). New Directions for Student Services, no. 28. San Francisco: Jossey-Bass.

Gordon, R. L. (1986). Issues in advising student-athletes. *NACADA Journal*, 6, 81–86.

Gordon, V. N. (1982). Reasons for entering college and academic and vocational preferences. *Journal of College Student Personnel*, 23, 371–377.

Gordon, V. N. (1983). Meeting the career development needs of undecided honor students. *Journal of College Student Personnel*, 24, 82–83.

Graham, S. W. (1987). The needs and learning preferences of community college adults: Implications for program planning and marketing. *Community College Review*, 15, 41–47.

Graham, S., & Dallam, J. (1986). Academic probation as a measure of performance: Contrasting transfer students to native students. *Community/Junior College Quarterly of Research and Practice*, 10, 23–33.

Grant, C.H.B. (1979). Institutional autonomy and intercollegiate athletics. *Educational Record*, 60, 409–419.

Greendorfer, S. L., & Blind, E. M. (1985). "Retirement" from intercollegiate sport: Theoretical and empirical considerations. *Sociology of Sport Journal*, 2, 101–110.

Greenwood, R. (1987). Expanding community participation by people with disabilities: Implications for counselors. *Journal of Counseling and Development*, 66, 185–187.

Griff, N. (1987). Meeting the career development needs of returning students. *Journal of College Student Personnel*, 28, 469–470.

Groves, S. L., & Groves, D. L. (1981). The academic assistance advisor program. *College Student Journal*, 15, 309–314.

Gurney, G. S., & Johnson, S. P. (1986). Advising the student-athlete. *NACADA Journal*, 6, 27–29.

Hameister, B. G. (1984). Orienting disabled students. In M. L. Upcraft (Ed.), *Orienting students to college* (pp. 67–79). New Directions for Student Services, no. 25. San Francisco: Jossey-Bass.

Hammel, B. (1980). Student-athletes: Tackling the problem. *Phi Delta Kappan*, 62, 7–15.

Hartman, R. C. (1986). *Strategies for advising disabled students for postsecondary education*. Washington, DC: American Council on Education.

Hartman, R. C., & Krulwich, M. T. (1984). *Learning disabled adults in postsecondary education*. Department of Education, Washington, DC (ERIC Document Reproduction Service No. ED 264 685)

Hearn, J. C. (1987). Impacts of undergraduate experiences on aspirations and plans for graduate and professional education. *Research in Higher Education*, 27, 119–141.

Heck, J. (1985). Model for community college honors programs. *Community College Review*, 13, 46–49.

Henderson, G. (1986). Advising black student-athletes. *NACADA Journal*, 6, 3–11.

Hickerson, J. H. (1982). A model of advising in an individualized undergraduate college. *NACADA Journal*, 2, 90–96.

Higgins, R. J. (1976). American athletic mentality: Identities and conflict. *Sport Sociology Bulletin*, 5, 14–24.

Hippolitus, P. (1987). *College freshmen with disabilities preparing for employment: A statistical profile*. Research report, Presidents' Committee on Employment of the Handicapped/American Council on Education.

Hirt, J., Hoffman, M. A., & Sedlacek, W. E. (1983). Attitudes toward changing sex roles of male varsity athletes versus nonathletes: Developmental perspectives. *Journal of College Student Personnel*, 24, 33–38.

Hogan, R. R. (1986). An update on reverse transfers to two-year colleges. *Community/Junior College Quarterly of Research and Practice*, 10, 295–306.

Holland, J. A., & Astin, A. W. (1962). The prediction of the academic, artistic, scientific, and social achievement of undergraduates of superior scholastic aptitude. *Journal of Educational Psychology*, 53, 132–143.

Hooper, J. O. (1979). Returning women and their families. *Journal of College Student Personnel*, 20, 145–152.

Hooper, J. O., & Traupmann, J. (1984). Women students over 50: Why do they do it? *Journal of College Student Personnel*, 25, 171–172.

Houle, C. O. (1961). *The inquiring mind*. Madison: University of Wisconsin Press.

Houseworth, S., Peplow, K., & Thirer, J. (1989). Influence of sport participation upon sex role orientation of Caucasian males and their attitudes toward women. *Sex Roles*, 20, 317–325.

Hoy, C., & Gregg, N. (1986). Learning disabled students: An emerging population on college campuses. *Journal of College Admissions*, 112, 10–14.

Humes, C. W., & Hohenshil, T. A. (1985). Career development and career education for handicapped students: A reexamination. *Vocational Guidance Quarterly*, 34, 31–40.

Humes, C. W., Szymanski, E. M., & Hohenshil, T. H. (1989). Roles of counseling in enabling persons with disabilities. *Journal of Counseling and Development*, 68, 145–150.

Hunt, E., & Germinaro, V. (1988). *The at-risk student: Answers for educators*. Lancaster, PA: Technomic.

Hurley, R. B., & Cunningham, R. L. (1984). Providing academic psychological services for the college athlete. In A. Shriberg & F. R. Brodzinski (Eds.), *Rethinking services for college athletes* (pp. 51–58). New Directions for Student Services, no. 28. San Francisco: Jossey-Bass.

Jackson, J. W. (1986). The growth of honors programs in small community colleges. In P. G. Friedman & R. C. Jenkins-Friedman (Eds.), *Fostering academic excellence through honors programs.* New Directions for Teaching and Learning, no. 25. San Francisco: Jossey Bass.

Janos, P. M., et al. (1988). A cross-sectional development study of the social relations of students who enter college early. *Gifted Child Quarterly*, 32, 210–215.

Jenkins-Friedman, R. C. (1986). Identifying honors students. In P. G. Friedman & R. C. Jenkins-Friedman (Eds.), *Fostering academic excellence through honors programs* (pp. 29–40). New Directions for Teaching and Learning, no. 25. San Francisco: Jossey-Bass.

Johnson, N. T. (1987). Academic factors that affect transfer student persistence. *Journal of College Student Personnel*, 28, 323–329.

Jones, D. J., & Watson, B. C. (1990). *"High risk" student in higher education.* ASHE-ERIC Higher Education Report No. 3. Washington, DC: George Washington University, School of Education and Human Development.

Kammerer, D. (1986). *Adviser's perceptions of their advising experiences with their doctoral students during the dissertation.* Unpublished doctoral dissertation, Ohio State University, Columbus.

Karnes, F. A., Chauvin, J. C., & Trant, T. J. (1984a). Comparisons of the personality factors and American college test scores for university honors students. *Educational and Psychological Research*, 4, 111–114.

Karnes, F. A., Chauvin, J. C., & Trant, T. J. (1984b). Leadership profiles as determined by the 16 PF scores of honors college students. *Psychological Reports*, 55, 615–616.

Kennedy, S. R., & Dimick, K. M. (1987). Career maturity and professional sports expectations of college football and basketball players. *Journal of College Student Personnel*, 28, 293–297.

Kirchner, C., Simon, Z., & Stern, H. B. (1985). Career planning and visually impaired students: How it's being handled—what needs to be done. *Journal of College Placement*, 45, 53–56.

Knefelkamp, L. L., & Stewart, S. S. (1983). Toward a new conceptualization of commuter students: The developmental perspective. In S. S. Stewart (Ed.), *Commuter students: Enhancing their educational experiences* (pp. 61–69). New Directions for Student Services, no. 24. San Francisco: Jossey-Bass.

Knight Foundation Commission on Intercollegiate Athletics (1991). Keeping faith with the student athlete: A New model for Intercollegiate athletics. *Chronicle of Higher Education*, 37, 1.

Kocher, E., & Pascarelli, E. (1988). *The effects of institutional transfer on status attainment.* Paper presented at the meeting of the American Educational Research Association, New Orleans.

Kodman, F. (1984). Some personality traits of superior university students. *Social Behavior and Personality*, 12, 135–138.

Kowalik, T. F. (1989). What we know about doctoral student persistence. *Innovative Higher Education*, 13, 163–171.

Lanning, W. (1982). The privileged few: Special counseling needs for athletes. *Journal of Sport Psychology*, 4, 19–23.

Lapchick, R. E. (1989). The student athlete. *New Perspectives*, 19, 35–45.

Larkin, L. (1987). Identity and fear of success. *Journal of Counseling Psychology*, 34, 38–45.

Lazarus, B. D. (1989). Serving learning disabled students in postsecondary settings. *Journal of Developmental Education*, 12, 2–4.

Leach, B., & Conners, B. (1984). Pygmalion on the gridiron: The black student athlete at a white university. In A. Shriberg & F. R. Brodzinski (Eds.), *Rethinking services for college athletes* (31–49). New Directions for Student Services, no. 28. San Francisco: Jossey-Bass.

Levinson, E. M. (1986). A vocational evaluation program for handicapped students: Focus on the counselor's role. *Journal of Counseling and Development*, 65, 105–106.

Lombana, J. H. (1989). Counseling persons with disabilities: Summary projections. *Journal of Counseling and Development*, 68, 177–179.

Lupack, B. T. (1983). *Early alert: Reaching students in time*. (ERIC Document Reproduction Service No. ED 239 568).

Lutwak, N., & Fine, E. (1983). Countertherapeutic styles when counseling the learning disabled college student. *Journal of College Student Personnel*, 24, 320–324.

Lyons, A. W. (1985). *Applying humanistic and behavioral principles to assist high-risk freshmen*. (ERIC Document Reproduction Service No. ED 262 692)

Maier, L. A., & Lavrakas, P. J. (1981). Some personality correlates of attitudes about sports. *International Journal of Sports Psychology*, 12, 19–22.

Malaney, G. D. (1987). *A decade of research on graduate students: A review of the literature in academic journals*. Paper presented at the meeting of the Association for the Study of Higher Education. (ERIC Document Reproduction Service No. ED 292 383)

Malaney, G. D., & Isaac, P. D. (1988). The immediate post-baccalaureat educational plans of outstanding undergraduates. *College and University*, 63, 148–161.

Mangrum, C. T., & Strichard, S. S. (1988). *College and the learning disabled student*. New York: Grune & Stratton.

Mason, E. P., Adams, H. L., & Blood, D. F. (1965). Personality characteristics of gifted college freshmen. *Proceedings of the 73rd Annual Convention of the American Psychological Association*. Washington, DC: The Association, 301–302.

Matross, R. P. (1980). Student attitudes toward intercollegiate athletes. *Journal of College Student Personnel*, 21, 299–304.

Mayo, A. M. (1980). *The relationship between athletic participation and the academic aptitude, achievement and progress of male and female athletes in revenue and non-revenue sports at the Ohio State University*. Unpublished doctoral dissertation, Ohio State University, Columbus.

McDonald, R. T., & Gawkoski, R. S. (1979). Predictive value of SAT scores and high achievement for success in a college honors program. *Educational and Psychological Measurement*, 39, 411–414.

Mingle, J. R. (1987). *A focus on minorities: Trends in higher education-participation and success*. (ERIC Documentation Reproduction Service No. ED 287 404)

Morstain, B. R., & Smart, S. C. (1974). Reasons for participation in adult education courses: A multivariate analysis of group differences. *Adult Education*, 24, 83–98.

National Clearinghouse for Commuter Programs. (1978). *Index of Commuting Programs*. College Park: University of Maryland.

Nelson, E. S. (1983). How the myth of the dumb jock becomes fact: A developmental view for counselors. *Counseling and Values*, 29, 176–185.

Neugarten, B. L. (1977). Adaptation of the life cycle. In N. K. Schlossberg & A. D. Entine (Eds.), *Counseling adults* (pp. 34–36). Monterey, CA: Brooks-Cole.

Nixon, H. (1982). The athlete as scholar in college: An exploratory test of four models. In A. O. Dunleavy, A. W. Miracle, & C. R. Rees (Eds.), *Studies in sociology of sport* (pp. 239–256). Ft. Worth: Texas Christian University Press.

Nixon, H. L., Maresca, P. J., & Silverman, M. A. (1979). Sex differences in college students' acceptance of females in sport. *Adolescence*, 14, 755–764.

Noel, L., & Levitz, R. (1982). *How to succeed with academically underprepared students: A catalog of successful practices*. (ERIC Document Reproduction Service No. ED 227 804)

Noel, L., Levitz, R., & Saluri, D. (1985). *Increasing student retention*. San Francisco: Jossey-Bass.

O'Block, F. R., & Billimoria, A. (1988, August). *College athletes' mental health needs: A national survey of sports psychologists*. Paper presented at the meeting of the American Psychological Association, Atlanta, GA.

Olsen, J. (1968). *The black athlete: A shameful story*. New York: Time-Life Books.

Ory, J. C., & Braskamp, L. A. (1988). Involvement and growth of students in three academic programs. *Research in Higher Education*, 28, 116–129.

Parker, J. P., & Karnes, F. A. (1987). A current report on graduate degree programs in gifted and talented education. *Gifted Child Quarterly*, 31, 116–117.

Pascarella, E. T. (1986). *Are value-added analyses valuable?* Paper presented at the Educational Testing Service Invitational Conference on Assessment in Higher Education, New York.

Pascarella, E. T., & Terenzini, P. T. (1991). *How college affects students*. San Francisco: Jossey-Bass.

Perrone, P., Wollear, P., Lee, J., & Davis, S. (1977). Counseling needs of adult students. *Vocational Guidance Quarterly*, 26, 27–35.

Petitpas, A., & Champagne, D. E. (1988). Developmental programming for intercollegiate athletes. *Journal of College Student Development*, 29, 454–459.

Piland, W. E., & Azbell, J. (1984). A typical profile: The honors program student. *Community and Junior College Journal*, 54, 45–47.

Piland, W. E., McKeague, P., & Montgomery, W. (1987). Serving academically gifted students in community colleges. *College Board Review*, 143, 20–23.

Pollard, K., Benton, S., & Hinz, K. (1983). The assessment of developmental tasks of students in remedial and required programs. *Journal of College Student Personnel*, 24, 20–28.

Purdy, D. A., Eitzen, D. S., & Hufnagel, R. (1982). Are athletes also students: The educational attainment of college athletes. *Social Problems*, 29, 439–448.

Rawlins, M. (1979). Life made easier for the over-thirty undergrads. *Personnel and Guidance Journal*, 58, 139–142.

Rawlins, M. E., & Lenihan, G. O. (1982). A cooperative endeavor for integrating adults in a 4-year university. *Journal of College Student Personnel*, 23, 531–537.

Rehberg, R. A., & Cohen, J. (1975). Athletes and scholars: An analysis of the compositional characteristics and images of these two youth culture categories. *International Review of Sport Sociology*, 63, 91–106.

Renick, J. (1974). The use and misuse of college athletes. *Journal of Higher Education*, 45, 545–552.

Renzulli, J. S. (1978). What makes giftedness? Reexamining a definition. *Phi Delta Kappan*, 60, 180–184.

Rhatigan, J. J. (1986). Developing a campus profile of commuting students. *NASPA Journal*, 24, 4–10.

Rice, R. L. (1989). Commuter students. In M. L. Upcraft & J. N. Gardner (Eds.), *The freshman year experience* (pp. 316–326). San Francisco: Jossey-Bass.

Richter-Antion, D. (1986). Qualitative differences between adult and younger students. *NASPA Journal*, 23, 58–62.

Roehl, J. (1980). Self-concept and the re-entry woman student. *Lifelong Learning*, 3, 12–13.

Roehl, J. E., & Okun, M. A. (1984). Depression symptoms among women reentering college: The role of negative life events and family social support. *Journal of College Student Personnel*, 25, 251–254.

Roessler, R. T. (1987). Work, disability, and the future: Promoting employment for people with disabilities. *Journal of Counseling and Development*, 66, 188–190.

Sampson, D. (1984). Specialized career services: An AHSSPPE survey. *Bulletin of the AHSSPPE*, 2, 12–20.

Saunders, S. A., & Ervin, L. (1984). Meeting the special advising needs of students. In. R. B. Winston, T. K. Miler, S. C. Ender, and T. J. Grites (Eds.), *Developmental academic advising* (250–286). San Francisco: Jossey-Bass.

Schinoff, R. B., & Kelly, J. T. (1982). *Improving academic advising and transfer articulation through technology. New Directions for Community Colleges*, 10, 71–82.

Schlossberg, N. (1972). A framework for counseling women. *Personnel and Guidance Journal*, 51, 137–143.

Schuchman, H. (1974). Special tasks of commuter students. *Personnel and Guidance Journal*, 52, 465–470.

Shapiro, B. J. (1984). Intercollegiate athletic participation and academic achievement: A case study of Michigan State University student athletes, 1950–1980. *Sociology of Sport Journal*, 1, 46–51.

Sharma, S. C. (1977). *Academic support services programs in higher education*. (ERIC Document Reproduction Service No. ED 221 079)

Smart, J. C., & Pascarella, E. T. (1987). Influences on the intention to reenter higher education. *Journal of Higher Education*, 58, 306–321.

Smith, E. R., & Valentine, N. (1987, May). *Factors related to attrition from doctor of education programs*. Paper presented at the meeting of the Association for Institutional Research, Kansas City, MO.

Sowa, C. J., & Gressard, C. F. (1983). Athletic participation: Its relationship to student development. *Journal of College Student Personnel*, 24, 236–239.

Stanley, J. C., & McGill, A. M. (1986). More about young entrants to college: How did they fare? *Gifted Child Quarterly*, 30, 70–73.

Sternberg, D. (1981). *How to complete and survive a doctoral dissertation*. New York: St. Martin's Press.

Stevensen, C. L. (1985). College athletics and character: The decline and fall of social-ization research. In D. Chu, J. O. Segrave, and B. J. Becker (Eds.), *Sport and higher education* (pp. 249–266). Champaign, IL: Human Kinetics.

Stewart, G. M. (1980). How honors students' academic achievement relates to housing. *Journal of College and University Student Housing*, 10, 26–28.

Stewart, S., Merrill, M., & Saluri, D. (1985). Students who commute, In L. Noel, R. Levitz, & D. Saluri (Eds.), *Increasing student retention* (pp. 162–182). San Francisco: Jossey-Bass.

Stewart, S. S., & Rue, P. (1983). Commuter students: Definition and distribution. In S. S. Stewart (Ed.), *Commuter students: Enhancing their educational experiences* (pp. 3–8). New Directions for Student Services, no. 24. San Francisco: Jossey-Bass.

Stones, D. H. (1987). The how's and why's of automated transfer equivalency systems. *College and University*, 63, 5–22.

Stonewater, B. B. (1987). Career traits, decision style, and Gilligan: Implications for counseling women. *Journal of NAWDAC*, 50, 17–26.

Tacha, D. R. (1986). Advising and interacting outside the classroom. In P. G. Friedman & R. C. Jenkins-Friedman (Eds.), *Fostering excellence through honors programs* (pp. 53–63). New Directions for Student Services, no. 25. San Francisco: Jossey-Bass.

Thistlethwaite, D. L., & Wheeler, N. (1966). Effects of teacher and peer subcultures upon student aspirations. *Journal of Educational Psychology*, 57, 35–47.

Tinto, V. (1987). *Leaving college*. Chicago: University of Chicago Press.

Todd, F. J., Terrell, G., & Frank, C. E. (1962). Differences between normal and un-derachievers of superior ability. *Journal of Applied Psychology*, 46, 183–190.

Todd, S. M. (1988). Scholars and strategies: Honors programs in community colleges. *Community College Review*, 16, 18–29.

Tomlinson-Keasey, C., & Smith-Wineberry, C. (1983). Educational strategies and per-sonality outcomes of gifted and nongifted college students. *Gifted Child Quarterly*, 27, 35–41.

Trent, J., & Medsker, L. (1968). *Beyond high school: A psychological study of 10,000 high school graduates*. San Francisco: Jossey-Bass.

Tuckman, H. P., Coyle, S., & Bae, Y. (1989). The lengthening of time to completion of the doctoral degree. *Research in Higher Education*, 30, 503–516.

Vickio, C. J., & Tack, M. W. (1989). Orientation programming for graduate students: An institutional imperative. *NACADA Journal*, 9, 37–42.

Von der Embse, T. J., & Childs, J. M. (1979). Adults in transition: A profile of the older college student. *Journal of College Student Personnel*, 20, 475–479.

Waggaman, J. S. (1982). *Articulation outcomes from use of the products and services of the Florida statewide course numbering system*. Paper presented at the 15th Annual Florida Statewide Conference on Institutional Research, Orlando. (ERIC Document Service No. Ed 248 819)

Weber, L. J., Sherman, T. M., & Tegano, C. (1986, April). *An investigation of the influence of academic assistance programs on the graduation rates of scholarship football athletes at Division I-A colleges*. Paper presented at the meeting of the American Educational Research Association, San Francisco.

Welch, H. (1982). The exploitation of the black athlete: A proposal for change. *NASPA Journal*, 19, 10–14.

West, C. (1984). The female athlete: Who will direct her destiny? In A. Shriberg &
    F. R. Brodzinski (Eds.), *Rethinking services for college athletes* (pp. 21–30).
    New Directions for Student Services, no. 28. San Francisco: Jossey-Bass.
Winston, R. B., & Polkosnik, M. C. (1984). Advising graduate and professional students.
    In R. B. Winston, T. K. Miller, S. C. Ender, & T. J. Grites (Eds.), *Develop-
    mental academic advising* (pp. 289–314). San Francisco: Jossey-Bass.
Wrisberg, C. A., Draper, M. V., & Everett, J. J. (1988). Sex role orientations of male
    and female collegiate athletes from selected individual and team sports. *Sex Roles*,
    19, 81–90.
Zingg, P. J. (1982). Advising the student athlete. *Educational Record*, 63, 16–19.

6

Advising Culturally Diverse
Students

Perhaps one of the most striking characteristics of culturally diverse students is
their heterogeneity. There is great diversity not only between racial and ethnic
groups but within the groups themselves. Each minority group springs from a
community that has its own customs, traditions, and values. The immediate and
extended family provides a support system that has great influence on minority
students' lives. Many minority students are the first in their family to attend
college, and this fact places enormous pressures on them to succeed. These and
many other issues are the key to responsive advising. As the proportion of
minority students increases dramatically in the future, identifying and dealing
with the issues and characteristics of these students will take on special significance.

Advisers need to be especially sensitive to the developmental needs of culturally diverse students. Wright (1987) suggests that the current theories of
student development do not take into account culture-specific influences that
affect specific minority groups. Cultural identity development can be enhanced
by providing programs, services, and activities designed to help students manage
the campus environment effectively.

Sedlacek (1981) recommends that when working with culturally diverse students, advisers be aware of and tap into, other types of abilities beyond those
analytical abilities measured by standardized tests. These students tend to use
''synthetic and systematic'' abilities more than traditional students. Synthetic
abilities are related to interpreting information in changing contexts while systematic abilities help students interpret their environment to their advantage.
Sedlacek suggests that being aware of noncognitive variables can help an adviser
assess a nontraditional student's problems more effectively. He lists eight noncognitive abilities that advisers can listen for: (1) has positive self-concept or

confidence, (2) has realistic self-appraisal, (3) understands and deals with racism, (4) prefers long-range goals to short-term or immediate needs, (5) has available a strong support person, (6) has successful leadership experience, (7) has demonstrated community services, and (8) has knowledge acquired in a field.

Sedlacek translates these noncognitive variables into principles for interviewing in the advising process. During the interview, advisers can listen for comments pertaining to the above and probe further those that seem most relevant. Through this vehicle, a very practical application of advising techniques may be tailored to each culturally diverse student.

Advising students from a culture different from one's own can be challenging since it requires a great deal of knowledge about other cultures and a sensitivity to individual students' perceptions of who they are and want to become. It also requires an honest appraisal of one's own racial biases. As Bynum (1991) points out, when advisers understand and appreciate the "cultural and historical social sciences" of their advisees, better communication can take place and students will perceive advisers as being genuinely interested in them as persons.

A profile of some culturally diverse populations is provided below, with suggestions for advising practices. These special groups include African American, Asian American, Hispanic, and Native American students. International students also represent a population with special advising needs because of their extremely diverse cultural and racial backgrounds.

AFRICAN AMERICAN STUDENTS

Many complex issues are involved in black students' participation in higher education. Fleming's (1984) classic study of black students in white institutions and in traditional black institutions (TBI) points out the issues involves in black education: (1) the debate about the necessity for the existence of black colleges, (2) the social adjustment crisis of black students attending white colleges, and (3) the challenges that black students face as they try to resolve developmental tasks, including finding their identity.

Black students attending black colleges are offered a more supportive community, which seems to encourage cognitive growth and facilitates a positive self-image and a clearer sense of purpose (Fleming, 1984; Gurin & Epps, 1975). Fleming found that black students on black campuses had more positive feelings about college and their peers and made a more positive adjustment to social and academic life than black students on white campuses.

The psychosocial well-being of black students is enhanced on black campuses because of the numbers of black students attending and the black faculty and staff available to them (Allen, 1986; McBay, 1985). In contrast, black students at predominantly white colleges have greater social adjustments to make, often with accompanying feelings of role confusion, anxiety, and depression (Fleming, 1984; Schaefer, 1987).

Gibbs (1974) outlines four responses that black students demonstrate as they try to cope with identity conflicts within a white setting: withdrawal, separation, assimilation, and affirmation. In Gibbs's study withdrawal was the predominant mode with 51 percent of students in this category. Withdrawal is categorized by feelings of helplessness, apathy, depression, and depersonalization. The 33 percent of students who exhibited affirmation, on the other hand, felt acceptance, a positive ethnic identity, and high achievement motivation.

In a review of the literature during the past 20 years on black students in white institutions, Sedlacek (1987) found that blacks seem to have difficulties with self-concept, racism, developing a community, and other noncognitive variables. Minority groups tend to have more socialization problems than nonminorities, and minority females tend to have greater problems than males (Guloyan, 1986; Mallinckrodt, 1988). Washington (1989) indicates these socialization problems may be the result of a conflict between the school's culture and the student's racial identity that causes a disequilibrium. Black students often come to white colleges expecting less prejudice and more social integration than they find. As a consequence they turn to other blacks for social life and mutual validation (Willie & McCord, 1972).

Davis and Borders-Patterson (1973) describe black students at white schools as having sharpened perceptions of themselves as a minority and the ability to identify unique characteristics of their own cultural heritage that may not have crystallized as quickly in black colleges.

A developmental perspective of advising demands that a holistic approach be implemented. Black students' personal, social, and vocational development is critical in identity formation. Hughes (1987) outlines the most relevant approaches to understanding black students' development in higher education. The sociopolitical approach identifies external societal variables that impede students' progress. The interpersonal approach examines the interactive social factors that exist among individuals and groups. The campus ecological model identifies elements in the campus environment that affect students' adjustment. Finally, the intrapsychic dimension focuses on the inner experience of the student in the campus environment. Hughes maintains that neither predominantly white nor black institutions are providing purposeful student development programming for black students.

Pounds (1987) suggests that professionals working with black students determine if they are the first in their families to attend college. This will suggest the type of transition and adjustment the student will need to make. The student's prior background will influence learning, developmental needs, and expectations of the college experience. To become successful, first-generation students need to develop appropriate interpersonal skills, acquire educational beliefs and values, and become responsible individuals. Pound indicates that faculty, advisers, and other college personnel need to develop a new understanding of black students, especially first-generation students. They can thus have a positive impact on the student's social adjustment and learning potential.

A great deal has been researched and written about the effectiveness of coun-

selors with the same or different racial background of their clients (Bishop &
Richards, 1987; Burrell & Trombley, 1983; Sattler, 1977). Although in a review
of this literature Atkinson (1987) found conflicting results, there was consistent
evidence that black clients preferred black counselors. Carroll (1988) found black
freshmen's perceptions of counselor effectiveness the best predictor of persistence
at a black college.

Trippi and Cheatham (1991) support the contention that students in their first
year are more likely to initiate contact with a professional for academic concerns
rather than personal ones. They suggest that sophomores are more likely to need
assistance in making academic major and career choices. Graduation rates for
the black students in their study were directly related to exposure to special
counseling and advising programs.

Watkins and Terrell (1988) found that some black students expect a white
counselor to be less accepting and genuine and expect a more negative outcome.
Black students may prefer black counselors because of this expectation, but
research has shown that white counselors are not systematically biased in favor
of or against black clients (Atkinson, 1987).

Help-seeking behaviors of black students have also been examined. Cheatham,
Shelton, and Ray (1987) found that black students reported a higher number of
problems than did white students, but whites reported more problems as severe
than blacks. There was a tendency for black students to make external attributions
while white made internal attributions. Blacks were three times more likely to
seek help from a professor or an academic adviser than were whites. The results
of this study indicated that blacks and whites were more similar than different
in their experiencing of personal problems and in help-seeking behaviors. Gibbs
(1974) suggests that blacks tend to use formal help sources in their freshman
year but later turn to peers and other informal sources.

Advising Implications

Academic advisers who work with students from another race and culture
must honestly appraise their own prejudices and biases. While they are never
totally absent, just being aware of these biases will help advisers become more
sensitive to how they might be perceived by students. Advisers also need to be
a force on campus for recognizing and eliminating racial injustices in any campus
policy or practice.

Fleming (1984) identifies developmental pressures black students encounter.
Advisers can acknowledge these pressures and try to guide their advisees into
becoming involved in campus life. Good adjustment to the campus environment
can be facilitated if students take leadership roles in campus organizations, work
in campus jobs (rather than off-campus), and interact with faculty and peers.
Students who become involved are better time managers and active learners
(Fleming, 1984). This is especially true of black students on white campuses,

where becoming involved is more difficult but more essential to social adjust-ment.

Helping students become competent is one of the most important develop-mental tasks during the college years (Chickering, 1969). Special services to help students acquire the academic skills necessary for academic competence should be available to all students, but especially to black students, who may enter college underprepared for the rigors of academic demands.

Another critical developmental task is developing a career purpose and an appropriate life-style (Chickering, 1969). Although some studies have indicated black students tend to choose careers in education and the social sciences (Post, Stewart, & Smith, 1991; Sewell & Martin, 1976; Smith, 1980), Arbona and Novy (1991a) did not find significant differences in the scope of career choices when black students were compared to white or Mexican-American students. Gender seemed to be more highly associated with career choice than was eth-nicity. Advisers can broaden students' information base about careers associated with academic programs and encourage exploration at an earlier stage before a student forecloses on a career direction.

Black students need to form positive attachments to adults during their college years. Their strong attachment to family leads to a need for strong adult approval. Fleming (1984) found that freshmen were less likely than seniors to attach to faculty and staff members and less likely than seniors to express admiration of faculty and staff. She also found that black students at white colleges felt their teachers were unfair in grading, lacked interest in them, and did not encourage them. These perceptions make mentoring relationships difficult to establish.

Fleming (1984) indicates that black students may feel threatened in some situations, especially in predominantly white institutions. Threatening situations are defined by Fleming as physical attacks, violation of the law, legal difficulties, and changes in beliefs. Personal threats were a major concern to black students in white colleges. Advisers must help create an environment that is conducive to student growth and development and free from threatening situations. Advisers can serve as student advocates when advisees report incidents they feel are threatening.

Bynum (1991) suggests that advisers begin to change by acknowledging they are capable of "harboring racist attitudes." He recommends that counselors who work with black students learn about African American history, experiences, and life-styles. He recommends, for example, reading black newspapers for insights into the black experience.

Conscientious advisers will want to establish a productive and positive rela-tionship with each African American advisee. Recognizing students' feelings and behavior within the context of the students' milieu is a first step. Advisers can help them understand their values and how these influence their setting of life goals. Advisers need to provide information about academic majors and occupations that goes beyond their own stereotypes and encourage students to consider alternatives that are realistic yet challenging. Providing the support they need while they engage in the decision-making process is essential.

Advisers need to understand that black students constitute a heterogeneous group. They differ in social class, economic status, values, customs, and family background (Pounds, 1987). Approaching each student as an individual will assure that preconceived ideas of who the student is and can become will give way to working with each student's unique qualities and strengths.

Burrell and Trombley (1983) found that minority students perceived academic advising as their most important support resource. If the advising challenges of each black student are to be met, we must be ready to prepare ourselves in the knowledge and skills required to help them through the mazes of their academic life.

ASIAN AMERICAN STUDENTS

Asian American students are the fastest growing minority group in higher education (Hsia, 1988). Although Asian Americans make up over 2 percent of the U.S. population, 10 percent to 20 percent comprise the entering classes of colleges and universities (Hsia, 1988). Since there are over 20 Asian subgroups within the Asian American population, it is important to be aware of the differences among ethnic groups, native-born, and recent immigrants when working with them.

Studies on Asian students' values and personality characteristics indicate that they differ from Western values and characteristics. For example, Asians traditionally have valued inconspicuousness, accommodation to a group, deference, and self-sacrifice, while Western culture values independence, assertiveness, and autonomy (Fernandez, 1988; Kitano, 1976; Sue & Kirk, 1972). Thus, Asian American students are often nonvocal or nonassertive about their problems and concerns (Minatoya & Sedlacek, 1981).

Chew and Ogi (1987) discuss the role of family in an Asian American student's perceptions. The individual is subsumed under the family structure, and individual worth is based on this interdependence and the worth of the family as a whole. This reliance on family may prove incongruent with the educational goal of learning how to think independently and critically as well as team building. Chew and Ogi suggest developing programs in which families may participate so that they may understand what their students are experiencing.

Asian values and characteristics affect the type of academic programs and career fields Asian American students select. Their top choices are in applied fields such as science, math, engineering, premedicine, and computer science (Bagasao, 1983; Hsia, 1988; Sue & Kirk, 1972). Leong (1985) studied the three personality variables that seemed relevant to career development of Asian American students: locus of control, society anxiety, and intolerance of ambiguity. These traits seemed to reinforce occupational choices and interest in science and technical fields. Many possess an external locus of control, suffer from greater

social anxiety, and dislike ambiguity. These choices are moderated by acculturation, however, and Leong warns that overgeneralizing to all Asian American
students may be misleading.

Asian American women students who are recent immigrants are not as acculturated and may face special adjustment problems. Their cultural background
has historically perpetuated sexual and occupational segregation (Yang, 1991).
They may feel torn between the values of their native culture and the values of
American society, where self-expression and recognition are often enhanced in
a career.

When the abilities of Asian American students are assessed, verbal abilities
are generally lower and mathematical ability higher. Hsia (1988) found that
students from higher-income families have higher verbal abilities. Lower-income
students' math abilities are the same, but their verbal abilities are lower. Asian
American students prepare for college early by taking more academic courses,
especially higher-level math and science courses and college prep programs.

After two years in college, some students change their major to business,
health areas, and life sciences. They are more likely to persist, to stay in the
same institution they initially entered, and to graduate (J. Carroll, 1988; Peng,
1985).

Equality of access has become an issue for some Asian American students.
Although the numbers do not imply overall barriers to access, they are the only
group not to be considered for admission to selective universities because too
many want to major in premed, engineering, science, and math (Li, 1988;
Nakanishi, 1988).

Asian values and personality traits may influence the use of counseling and
advising services. Gim, Atkinson, and Soo (1991) indicate that underuse and
high drop-out rates in counseling may reflect a conflict between Asian American
culture and the values associated with the counseling process. It could also be
accounted for by the lack of culturally sensitive counselors (Sue & Morishima,
1982). Gim, Atkinson, and Soo also found that the degree of acculturation
affected students' perceptions of the value of counseling. Low-acculturated students consistently gave their lowest credibility ratings to culture-blind Caucasian-
American counselors. Atkinson and Gim (1989) found that the most acculturated
students were the most tolerant of the stigma associated with psychological help,
the most likely to recognize the need for help, and the most open to discuss
problems with a psychologist.

Advising Implications

Asian Americans have been described as the ''model minority'' (Change,
1989; Hsia, 1988) because of their cultural values relating to educational achievement, diligence, and cooperation. This myth, however, has masked some Asian
American college students' experiences with tension, apprehension, and social
introversion (Minatoya & Sedlacek, 1981; Sue & Sue, 1991). The myth of the

super Asian may work against them in admissions to selective institutions but may also exacerbate divisiveness among ethnic groups (Hsia, 1988). Asian American students, like other minorities, may harbor feelings of alienation, powerlessness, and social isolation (Asamen & Berry, 1987).

As Minatoya and Sedlacek (1981) found, Asian American undergraduates "share some perceptions common to all students, some that are similar to other minority groups, and some that seem unique" (p. 336). The unique qualities of being nonvocal and nonassertive may make it more difficult for Asian American students to identify and discuss their problems. Advisers must acquire a working knowledge of the Asian American heritage, which emphasizes a respect for family members and the role expectations of different members of the family (Lee, Juan, & Hom, 1984). Advisers must make a special effort to understand the unique cultural environment in which the student is operating and try to develop a level of trust so that these highly motivated students may feel more comfortable sharing their advising-related concerns.

HISPANIC STUDENTS

U.S. citizens whose heritage includes countries colonized by Spain and are Spanish-speaking are grouped as Hispanics by the U.S. government. (The term *Latino* may be used in certain parts of the country as well.) This group includes 61 percent Mexican-Chicanos, 15 percent Puerto Ricans, 6 percent Cuban Americans, and 18 percent other Hispanics (U.S. Bureau of Census, 1985). Although diversity among Hispanics is evidenced in their political and economic backgrounds, demographic patterns, and language variations, Ruiz and Padilla (1977) suggest they have many historical similarities in common, such as language and values. Most Hispanic students use their specific nationalities when identifying themselves (Ethier & Deaux, 1990; Quevedo-Garcia, 1987).

Nielsen (1986) points out that when Hispanics are compared to non-Hispanic whites, their enrollment numbers in college are similar. Nielsen suggests that the major educational barrier for Hispanics is not the transition from high school to college but high school graduation. If Hispanic students can graduate from high school, they have an equal chance of going on to college. That many Hispanics are from disadvantaged families and tend to be recent immigrants tends to have implications for their educational attainment (Ortiz, 1986).

Arbona and Novy (1991b) categorize Hispanic college students into two groups. In the first group are those who were born in the United States of Puerto Rican or Mexican descent or who came to this country at an early age. The students in this group often come from working-class families. Students in the second group may have come from other countries to attend college or have immigrated legally with their families. This second group tends to belong to middle- and upper-class families. Arbona and Novy contend that when distinctions among Hispanic subgroups are ignored, research results may be distorted. When Arbona and Novy (1991b) compared Mexican American students with

Hispanic, non-Mexican American students, they found that Mexican American students reported considerably lower levels of parental socioeconomic status and educational attainment than did the non-Mexican American students. Although they expressed high educational aspirations, a large percentage felt uncertain about obtaining a college degree. The subgroups differed in the barriers they expected to encounter in the process of pursuing a college degree. More Mexican American than non-Mexican American students expected to have financial and academic difficulties. A larger proportion of the non-Mexican American men indicated they would leave the university if offered a good job. Contrary to other findings, the two Hispanic subgroups in this study were similar in terms of academic performance and retention rates, even though they differed considerably in terms of socioeconomic background.

Quevedo-Garcia (1987) outlines some of the issues pertinent to working with Hispanic students. These include (1) assimilation versus integration, (2) family and community ties, (3) choice of college, and (4) the precollege experience. As students enter college, they need to integrate into the larger academic and social environment while maintaining their own cultural identity. Providing opportunities to understand the Anglo culture as well as their own is essential.

Anglos value openness, frankness, and directedness. Hispanics may view this less formal approach to interpersonal relationships as a sign of disrespect (Grossman, 1984). The Hispanic culture values diplomacy and tactfulness when communicating with another individual and has great respect for authority. Children are taught respect for their parents, teachers, and other persons they consider in authority. Students may seemingly agree out of respect for an adviser rather than expressing their true disagreement in certain situations. Quevedo-Garcia (1987) suggests that Hispanic students need to develop assertiveness skills if they are to compete in an Anglo-dominated college environment.

As with many other minorities, the family is the most valued institution in the Hispanic culture. Male and female roles are distinct, with the father as authority and decision maker and the mother as nurturer and comforter (Grossman, 1984). Students may view themselves as representatives of their family and community first and themselves as individuals second (Quevedo-Garcia, 1987). Understanding the student's home environment may be important in problem solving, since a family-oriented student may seek help from this quarter rather than using advising and counseling services (Caraveo-Ramos, Francis, & Odgers, 1985; Keefe, Padilla, & Carlos, 1978; Sanchez & King, 1986).

In certain situations there may be a need to enlist the family's help and involvement (Ruiz & Padilla, 1977). Grossman (1984) recommends that when working with Hispanic parents, an adviser should establish a more formal relationship until the parents indicate otherwise. More time may be needed to accomplish the agenda since parents may need to be encouraged to ask questions and express their opinions when they disagree.

Hispanics often attend college close to their homes (Burgos-Sasscer, 1987). This is frequently the result of lack of financial support as well as family ties.

Family responsibilities and finances are also among the reasons many Hispanic students attend community colleges (Chacon, Cohen, & Strover, 1986). The quality of students' precollege work is important to their success (Rendon & Nora, 1989). Quevedo-Garcia (1987) indicates that sound academic preparation in language, math, and science is essential. The knowledge of career options must be provided at an early age. Dillard and Perrin (1980) found that career aspirations of males correlated highly with ethnic group membership. Puerto Rican and black male adolescents aspired to enter higher-level careers. No relationships were found for females. Adolescents' career development varied as their social class position and grade level increased.

Advising Implications

According to Grossman (1984), Hispanics believe there is a unique Hispanic culture within the United States, and he encourages professionals to take these cultural factors into consideration when working with Hispanics students. Advisers need to take into account the effects of living in two different cultures and need to tailor their advising approaches to the "cultural realities" of the student. Ruiz and Padilla (1977) suggest that knowledge of the importance of *personalismo* among Latinos should influence the way advisers greet advisees for the first time and thereafter. To establish and maintain rapport, small talk at the the initial meeting and at subsequent sessions is important. They also point out that cultural differences in temporal perspective are normal. Caraveo-Ramos, Francis, and Odgers (1985) suggest that in referring students for counseling, the ethnic gap may be bridged by referring Hispanics to clergy, in keeping with their cultural and religious experiences. More Hispanic professionals need to be available in the areas of teaching, administration, and student affairs, and existing staff need to be trained in the characteristics and culture of the Hispanic student (Quevedo-Garcia, 1987). Hispanic role models should be available to students both in the college environment through exposure to currently enrolled students and outside through Hispanic alumni. Tutoring and mentoring programs are productive ways to increase this interaction. Pinkney and Ramirez (1985) found Hispanic students less realistic in their career planning attitudes than white students. Advisers need to be sensitive to Hispanic students' approach to choosing a major since these students' perceptions of possible alternatives might be limited. Academic and career choices also might involve identity issues. Advisers need to be aware of the effect of culture on students' career planning beliefs and attitudes.

Because of cultural conflicts and other barriers for Hispanic women, advisers' awareness of these barriers is especially important. Keefe, Padilla, and Carlos (1978) found Mexican American women often experienced role conflict when wanting an education or career as opposed to the more traditional stereotypic role of wife and mother. Arredondo (1991) outlines some of the issues Latinas face. Just a few are stress reactions to trying to manage work and home life, first-generation women's desire to attend college away from home and the ensuing guilt feelings of disloyalty to the family and adjustment to new surroundings, and professional women's balancing of carer goals with cultural values and roles.

Fewer Mexican American women (15 percent) complete a college degree than Mexican American men (32 percent) (U.S. Commission on Civil Rights, 1978). Relevant support services for women, however, have been shown to increase Hispanic women's success (Quezada & Jones, 1984).

Munoz (1986) indicates that Hispanic students feel a great deal of stress while in college. The main stress-producing problem is financial. They perceive themselves as not being as well prepared academically, and family responsibilities contribute to the pressures they feel. Munoz also points out that for some, adjusting to a new culture with different values and expectations contributes to their stress.

Understanding the cultural milieu of each Hispanic student is essential if good advising is to take place. Being aware of within- and between-group differences will help to approach the Hispanic student in the most personalized way. While some writers are of the opinion that Hispanic advisers and counselors are the best role models, advisers from other cultures who are willing to learn about their Hispanic students can be effective. Ongoing staff development programs on Hispanic culture, Hispanic student development theory, and advising techniques will help to make advisers more sensitive to the issues and concerns that Hispanic college students face (Quevedo-Garcia, 1987).

NATIVE AMERICAN STUDENTS

Native Americans make up less than 1 percent of the U.S. population, but the 500 tribes, bands, and Native groups in the United States represent 50 percent of the diversity (Hodgkinson, Outtz, & Obarakpor, 1990). The latest U.S. census figure shows a great increase in the numbers of American Indians. Some of this increase can be attributed to the fact that people who did not call themselves Indians in an earlier census are doing so now (New York Times National, 1991).

To understand the background and culture of Native American students, advisers must be aware of the complexity of tribal differences. Students, for example, will differ if they come from cities or reservations; speak a native language; participate in ceremonies; or attended all-Indian schools (Tierney, 1991). Regional differences also have a great impact. Sage (1991) suggests, for example, that an Eastern Woodlands tribal member has different worldviews, cultural beliefs, language, and eating and clothing habits from a Northern or even Southern Plains tribal members.

Enrollment in college is frequently the first concentrated exposure to a non-Indian environment for the many Indian students who attended high school on the reservation (LaCounte, 1987). Because of the rural nature and other features of most reservations, the Indian student usually encounters a foreign environment upon entering college and experiences great culture shock. La Counte indicates that only a termendous desire for learning and personal growth motivates a Native American to enter and remain in college.

Tribal colleges evolved during the 1970s in response to the lack of success of Indian students in mainstream colleges. Wright and LaSalle (1991) found that attending a tribally controlled community college enhanced the academic performance of Native American students when they transferred to a four-year institution. Tribal colleges today serve about 10,000 American Indians. The 24 tribal colleges in 11 states are controlled by the Indian people (Wright & Tierney, 1991). According to Wright and Tierney, less than 60 percent of Native American high school students graduate, and less than 40 percent go on to college. Only a fifth will receive a college degree. Upon leaving the reservation for college, some Native American college students lose their tribal role models and sense of security. This loss may lead to feelings of isolation and depression. The sense of obligation that Native American students feel for their family is paramount (Tierney, 1991), and many will leave school if the family needs them.

Many Native Americans, like other minorities, do not often use counseling services. According to Sue, Allen, and Conaway (1981), of those who do, few return for a second session. Johnson and Lashley (1989) found that Indians with a strong commitment to Native American culture showed a preference for an Indian counselor. Dauphinais, Dauphinais, and Rowe (1981) also found that Native American high school students perceived a Native American counselor as more effective than a non-Native American.

Native American students expect nurturance and facilitative conditions in the counseling process, expect a high degree of competency from their counselor, and prefer a more directive approach (Johnson & Lashley, 1989). Johnson and Lashley suggest that the traditional respect that Native Americans have for those in authority might carry over into the counseling situation.

In a precollege intervention program (Hill, 1991), success is based on the value placed on American Indian culture. High expectations are emphasized, and tribal needs and college achievement are stressed. Learning takes place within the cultural context, and teachers and mentors are Native Americans.

Beaulieu (1991) found differences at the elementary and secondary levels in academic achievement between Indian students on reservations and those living in urban communities. The withdrawal rates for students in tribally controlled schools are less than for urban ones. In general, public schools do not adequately prepare students for college work (Huffman, Sill, & Brokenleg, 1986). Postsecondary preparation programs are critical to some Indian students' entry and retention. In addition to financial aid, students must have help in acquiring the academic skills necessary for success. According to Beaulieu, support services need to be ''sensitive to the difference between academic skills and preparation and the unique learning styles and needs of Indian students'' (p. 34).

Advising Implications

Beaulieu (1991) contends that individuals who serve as advisers to Native American students need to have a knowledge and understanding of American

Indian language, history, and culture. Their unique and special needs require that advising services be sensitized to their way of learning. An important area that is often difficult for Native American students in a dominant college environment is the difference in communication styles between Indians and non-Indians. Traditionally the history of American Indians' identity is maintained through oral tradition, which means words are "powerful and value-laden" (Sage, 1991). Making small talk, using words casually, or talking loudly should be avoided in the advising session, according to Sage. Advisers also need to be sensitive to Native Americans who are uncomfortable about discussing their Indian identity. Advisers need to recognize the conflicts that many students experience when trying to survive in a foreign culture. To help Native American students who feel caught between two cultures, advisers can acknowledge and support the importance of their history, tribe, and family while helping them adapt to the essential aspects of the college culture. Tierney (1991) indicates that instead of changing the student to fit the college environment, there is a need to reorient the environment to make the student feel welcome and comfortable. When students feel their advisers are aware of their unique background and prior experiences and convey high expectations for their success, adjustment to a strange environment will be facilitated.

INTERNATIONAL STUDENTS

International students represent a complex array of cultural, ethnic, and personal characteristics. An estimated 342,000 students come from more than 150 countries to attend about 3,000 colleges and universities in the United States (Barber, 1985; Bulthuis, 1986). According to Barber (1985), 15 countries account for 60 percent of foreign students. Bulthuis (1986) predicts that this percentage will shift as some institutions reach their capacity and move to balance their undergraduate and graduate enrollment.

On campuses with large numbers of international students, advising specialists work closely with them. International student counselors need to be familiar with immigration regulations, political changes, fluctuations in international currency rates, and other specialized knowledge (Cadieux & Wehrly, 1986). The National Association for Foreign Student Affairs (NAFSA) recommends that there be one foreign student adviser per 250 international students.

Many nonspecialized undergraduate and graduate academic advisers will be assigned to foreign students, however. Understanding such a complex group requires special efforts to learn about their adjustment concerns, linguistic problems, and other unique characteristics these students bring to advising sessions. Problems, for example, may develop in adjusting to a different educational system, financial concerns, problems with social interaction, and even dietary concerns (Bulthuis, 1986; Cadieux & Wehrly, 1986; Heikinheimo & Shute, 1986; Schram & Lauver, 1988). International students may also experience homesickness and loneliness. Some have a fear of failure since they are often sponsored by governments or families at great expense and feel enormous pressures to succeed. Depression is common among international students, but its etiology and severity is culture-related (Cadieux & Wehrly, 1986; Kleinman & Good, 1985). How well foreign students accept and adjust to the U.S. culture will often depend on the culture they represent and how different it is from their new one. European and Latin American students are more positive about their new environment than Asian or African students (Marion, 1986).

Altscher (1976) insists special counseling and advising programs need to be established for international students who are confronted with communication difficulties, unfamiliar customs, and lack of knowledge about social and student etiquette on American campuses. Loneliness and isolation are often felt by foreign students as they struggle to adapt socially and personally, not to mention academically. Foreign students come to the United States with different values and principles. Cultural problems may arise from many sources. For example, a student may have a different concept of time and may have difficulty in adapting to and even understanding the importance we place on the clock. Classroom behavior may be difficult for a student whose culture places value on silence but who is expected to speak up in class (Spees & Spees, 1986).

Some students may come from cultures where male and female roles are rigid and specific. Some studies have shown that females report more problems in adjusting than their male counterparts (Pruitt, 1978). Some women students may find it difficult to readjust upon returning home if their home culture does not allow as much freedom as they had in the United States (Marion, 1986).

One advantage of having international students on a campus is the opportunity it affords American students to broaden their worldview and appreciation of different cultures and to provide a more diverse student body (Thackaberry & Liston, 1986). Spaulding and Flack (1976) suggest that American students need to become more open and sensitive to different cultures. In examining several studies on the interaction between American and international students, Marion (1986) found that the best opportunity for interaction seemed to be in small colleges in small towns. Large universities in large cities offered the least potential for this interaction.

Boyer and Sedlacek (1988) found that different non-cognitive variables could be used as predictors of academic success and persistence among international students. Positive adjustment to the educational system and their external environment was significantly related to persistence.

Advising Implications

According to Cadieux and Wehrly (1986), international students place achieving academic goals as their highest priority. Relevance of their academic program is related to its applicability in the context of their home country. Advisers can help students relate the value and relevance of their education to the realities they will face upon returning home.

Althen (1981) suggests that cross-cultural counseling depends on the level of awareness of how one's culture influences how one thinks and feels. Knowing something of the student's country and customs will help develop rapport. An understanding of the type of educational system the student comes from will ensure advisers are working within the student's educational context and experience. This is important when helping students schedule appropriate and realistic courses. Some students may have unrealistic ideas of what it takes to succeed in certain courses and may overload or overestimate their English language facility.

One area of concern may be offenses dealing with the honor code. Some foreign students may have experienced only the lecture method of teaching and their cultural perspective on working with fellow students may lead to cheating and plagiarism. Since they have had memorization and factual content stressed, they may not understand that copying from a published text is an offense. It is critical that definitions of plagiarism and what constitutes cheating be made clear by instructors and advisers so that these offenses may be avoided (Bulthuis, 1986).

Heikinheimo and Shute (1986) studied how international students interacted with others. They found that as English skills improved, social and academic adjustment improved. International students are more apt to be academically and personally satisfied when the environment in which they operate becomes more congenial. They also found that students from African and Southeast Asian countries felt racial discrimination, which could cause insecurity and create barriers for social interaction with American students. The highest-risk student in their study was the non-European undergraduate who spent little time with others. They suggest that "informal channels" within the student's own ethnic or national group would help with adjustment concerns, but these must be established as soon as the student arrives.

Schram and Lauver (1988) recommend the establishment of a peer advising system to help alleviate alienation and feelings of aloneness. Marion (1986) urges each institution to research how the climate of the campus affects its international students and develop programs and resources to assure it is providing a reinforcing and positive learning environment.

Reiff and Kidd (1986) suggest that good orientation programs can help international students adjust more quickly and smoothly. Programs need to take into account the English proficiency of the student and the degree of culture shock, provide information about campus resources, and offer an introduction to the U.S. educational system. Implementing a buddy system with experienced students from their home country or a mentoring program will provide the kind of immediate contact these students need as they enter a strange and often difficult new environment.

When Leong and Sedlacek (1986) studied where international students went for help, they found that these students are more prone to use the formal resources provided by the institutions than American students. Foreign students indicated they would go to faculty advisers and counselors for help whereas American students would use informal resources such as parents and friends. This finding emphasizes the need to establish special advising and counseling programs for foreign students as well as special training for faculty advisers.

Advisers can help international students understand the value of being open and receptive to the new culture in which they are now living and encourage personal contact with them when problems arise. Students from different countries and cultures have little in common so it is difficult to generalize about them. Advisers, therefore, need to learn some of the important differences among their students from different cultures in the areas of communication (including important nonverbal differences), manners, and customs. Heikinheimo and Shute (1986) emphasize the need for in-service training for advisers to learn about these areas and the unique adjustment concerns their advisees face so they can be alert to problems before they become severe.

Advisers will find that international students will probably require more time since information may need to be given and repeated in a careful manner depending on the student's English skills (Weill, 1982). Advising international students needs to be highly individualized since so many complicating variables impinge on the communication patterns that need to be established. Although this may take time and energy, the rewards of knowing and helping this special group of students is well worth the effort.

SUMMARY

Many recurring themes can be recognized when discussing culturally diverse students who will appear in the advising setting. Not only must each culturally different group be recognized, but important differences within each group must be acknowledged. Most of these students will have difficult adjustment concerns that are unique to each population and yet common to all. Many students may feel a sense of being different and alone. Advisers can make a difference in how these students perceive themselves and others in relation to the campus environment.

Each student represents a unique cultural background, including language, customs, manners, values, and attitudes. Some may be open to absorbing the new culture before them, while others will want to withdraw into their academic work. Advisers who are sensitive to each student's particular situation can offer the type of help and personalization required to help them adjust successfully. Faculty and staff development programs that teach the important aspects of different cultures and help advisers become aware of the differences among these special populations will provide the specialized knowledge and skills needed. The personal and professional growth that comes from working with culturally diverse students is a reward that cannot be overestimated.

REFERENCES

Allen, W. (1986). *Gender and campus race differences in black student academic performance, racial attitudes, and college satisfaction.* Atlanta, GA: Southern Education Foundation.

Althen, G. (Ed.). (1981). *Learning across cultures: Intercultural communication and international educational exchange.* Washington, DC: National Association for Foreign Student Affairs.

Altscher, D. C. (1976). A rationale for a counseling program designed uniquely for international students. (ERIC Reproduction Document Service No. ED 134 888)

Arbona, C. A., & Novy, D. M. (1991a). Career aspirations and expectations of black, Mexican American, and white students. *Career Development Quarterly*, 39, 231–239.

Arbona, C. A., & Novy, D. M. (1991b). Hispanic college students: Are there within-group differences? *Journal of College Student Development*, 32, 335–341.

Arredondo, P. (1991). Counseling Latinas. In C. L. Courtland & B. L. Richardson (Eds.), *Multicultural issues in counseling* (pp. 143–156). Alexandria, VA: American Association for Counseling and Development.

Asamen, J. K., & Berry, G. L. (1987). Self-concept, alienation, and perceived prejudice: Implications for counseling Asian Americans. *Journal of Multicultural Counseling and Development*, 15, 146–160.

Atkinson, D. R. (1987). Counseling blacks: A review of relevant research. *Journal of College Student Personnel*, 28, 552–558.

Atkinson, D. R., & Gim, R. H. (1989). Asian American cultural identity and attitudes toward mental health services. *Journal of Counseling Psychology*, 36, 209–212.

Bagasao, P. Y. (1983, September). Factors related to science-career planning among Asian and Pacific American college-bound high school seniors. *Clippings.* New Orleans: National Association for Asian and Pacific Students.

Barber, E. G. (Ed.). (1985). *Foreign student flows.* New York: Institute of International Education.

Beaulieu, D. (1991). The state of the art. *Change*, 23, 31–35.

Bishop, J. B., & Richards, T. F. (1987). Counselor intake judgments about white and black clients in a university counseling center. *Journal of Counseling Psychology*, 34, 96–98.

Boyer, S. P., & Sedlacek, W. E. (1988). Noncognitive predictors of academic success for international students: A longitudinal study. *Journal of College Student Development*, 29, 218–222.

Bulthuis, J. D. (1986). The foreign student today: A profile. In K. R. Pyle (Ed.), *Guiding the development of foreign students* (pp. 19–27). New Directions for Student Services, no. 36. San Francisco: Jossey-Bass.

Burgos-Sasscer, R. (1987). Empowering Hispanic students: A prerequisite is adequate data. *Journal of Educational Equity and Leadership*, 7, 21–36.

Burrell, L. F., & Trombley, T. B. (1983). Academic advising with minority students on predominantly white campuses. *Journal of College Student Personnel*, 24, 121–126.

Bynum, A. S. (1991). *Black student/white counselor* (2nd ed.). Indianapolis, IN: Alexandria Books.

Cadieux, R.A.J., & Wehrly, B. (1986). Advising and counseling the international student. In K. R. Pyle (Ed.), *Guiding the development of foreign students* (pp. 51–63). New Directions for Student Services, no. 36. San Francisco: Jossey-Bass.

Caraveo-Ramos, L. E., Francis, R. W., & Odgers, R. P. (1985). Attitudes of Mexican-American and Anglo-American college students toward psychologists and psychiatrists. *Journal of College Student Personnel*, 26, 134–137.

Carroll, C. D. (1988, April). *College access and persistence among Asian Americans: Findings from the high school and beyond study*. Paper presented at the meeting of the American Educational Research Association, Division J, New Orleans.

Carroll, J. (1988). Freshman retention and attrition factors at a predominantly white university. *Journal of College Student Development*, 29, 52–59.

Chacon, M. A., Cohen, E. G., & Strover, S. (1986). Chicas and Chicanos: Barriers to progress in higher education. In M. A. Olivas (Ed.), *Latino college students* (pp. 296–324). New York: Teachers College, Columbia University.

Change Magazine. (1989). *Asian and Pacific Americans: Behind the myths*, 22, 12–63.

Cheatham, H. E., Shelton, T. O., & Ray, W. J. (1987). Race, sex, causal attribution, and help-seeking behavior. *Journal of College Student Personnel*, 28, 559–568.

Chew, C. A., & Ogi, A. Y. (1987). Asian American college student perspectives. In D. J. Wright (Ed.), *Responding to the needs of today's minority students* (pp. 39–48). New Directions for Student Services, no. 38. San Francisco: Jossey-Bass.

Chickering, A. W. (1969). *Education and identity*. San Francisco: Jossey-Bass.

Dauphinais, P., Dauphinais, L., & Rowe, W. (1981). Effects of race and communication style on Indian perceptions of counselor effectiveness. *Counselor Education and Supervision*, 21, 72–80.

Davis, J. A., & Borders-Patterson, A. (1973). *Black students in predominantly white North Carolina colleges and universities. Research Report No. 2*. New York: College Entrance Examination Board.

Dillard, J. M., & Perrin, D. W. (1980). Puerto Rican, Black, and Anglo adolescents' career aspirations, expectations, and maturity. *Vocational Guidance Quarterly*, 28, 313–321.

Ethier, K., & Deaux, K. (1990). Hispanics in Ivy: Assessing identity and perceived threat. *Sex Roles*, 22, 427–440.

Fernandez, M. S. (1988). Issues in counseling Southeast Asian students. *Journal of Multicultural Counseling and Development*, 16, 157–166.

Fleming, J. (1984). *Blacks in college*. San Francisco: Jossey-Bass.

Gibbs, J. T. (1974). Patterns of adaptation among black students at a predominantly white university. *American Journal of Orthopsychiatry*, 44, 728–740.

Gim, R. H., Atkinson, D. R., & Soo, J. K. (1991). Asian American acculturation, counselor ethnicity and cultural sensitivity, and ratings of counselors. *Journal of Counseling Psychology*, 38, 57–62.

Grossman, H. (1984). *Educating Hispanic students: Cultural implications for instruction, classroom management, counseling and assessment*. Springfield, IL: Charles C. Thomas.

Guloyan, E. V. (1986). An examination of white and non-white attitudes of university freshmen as they relate to attrition. *College Student Journal*, 20, 396–402.

Gurin, P., & Epps, E. G. (1975). *Black consciousness, identity and achievement*. New York: Wiley.

Heikinheimo, P. S., & Shute, J.C.M. (1986). The adaptation of foreign students: Students' views and institutional implications. *Journal of College Student Personnel*, 27, 399–406.

Hills, N. (1991). AISES: A college intervention program that works. *Change*, 23, 24–30.

Hodgkinson, H. L., Outtz, J. H., & Obarakpor, A. M. (1990). *The demographics of American Indians: One percent of the people; fifty percent of the diversity*. Washington, DC: Institute for Educational Leadership, Center for Demographic Policy.

Hsia, J. (1988). *Asian Americans in higher education and at work*. Hillsdale, NJ: Lawrence Erlbauam.

Huffman, T. E., Sill, M. L., & Brokenleg, M. (1986). College achievement among Sioux and white South Dakota students. *Journal of American Indian Education*, 25, 32–38.

Hughes, M. S. (1987). Black students' participation in higher education. *Journal of College Student Personnel*, 28, 532–545.

Johnson, M. E., & Lashley, K. H. (1989). Influence of Native Americans' cultural commitment on preferences for counselor ethnicity and expectations about counseling. *Journal of Multicultural Counseling and Development*, 17, 115–122.

Keefe, S. E., Padilla, A. M., & Carlos, M. L. (1978). The Mexican-American extended family as an emotional support system. In J. M. Casas & S. E. Keefe (Eds.), *Family and mental health in the Mexican American community*, Monograph 7 (pp. 49–69). Los Angeles: Spanish-Speaking Mental Health Research Center.

Kitano, H.H.L. (1976). *Japanese Americans: The evolution of a subculture* (2nd ed.). Englewood Cliffs, NJ: Prentice-Hall.

Kleinman, A., & Good, B. (1985). *Culture and depression*. Berkeley: University of California Press.

LaCounte, D. W. (1987). American Indian students in college. In D. J. Wright (Ed.), *Responding to the needs of today's minority students* (pp. 65–79). New Directions for Student Services, no. 38. San Francisco: Jossey-Bass.

Lee, P., Juan, G., & Hom, A. (1984). Groupwork practice with Asians: A sociocultural approach. *Social Work with Groups*, 7, 37–48.

Leong, F.T.L. (1985). Career development of Asian Americans. *Journal of College Student Personnel*, 26, 539–546.

Leong, F.T.L., & Sedlacek, W. E. (1986). A comparison of international and U.S. students' preferences for help sources. *Journal of College Student Personnel*, 27, 426–430.

Li, V. H. (1988). Asian discrimination: Fact or fiction? *College Board Review*, 149, 20.

Mallinckrodt, B. (1988). Student retention, social support, and dropout intention: Comparison of black and white students. *Journal of College Student Development*, 29, 60–64.

Marion, P. B. (1986). Research on foreign students at colleges and universities in the United States. In K. R. Pyle (Ed.), *Guiding the development of foreign students* (65–82). New Directions for Student Services, no. 36. San Francisco: Jossey-Bass.

McBay, S. (1985). *The racial climate on the MIT campus*. Cambridge, MA: Minority Student Issues Group.

Minatoya, L. Y., & Sedlacek, W. E. (1981). Another look at the melting pot: Perceptions of Asian-American undergraduates. *Journal of College Student Personnel*, 22, 328–336.

Munoz, D. G. (1986). Hispanic high school students: Making choices. In M. A. Olivas (Ed.), *Latino college students* (pp. 131–156). New York: Teachers College, Columbia University.

Nakanishi, D. T. (1988). Asian Pacific Americans and selective undergraduate admissions. *Journal of College Admissions*, 118, 17–26.

New York Times National. (March 5, 1991). *Census finds many claiming new identity: Indian*, pp. A 1, A 10.

Nielsen, F. (1986). Hispanics in high school and beyond. In M. A. Olivas (Eds.), *Latino college students* (pp. 71–103). New York: Teachers College Press, Columbia University.

Olivas, M. A. (1986). *Latino college students*. New York: Teachers College Press, Columbia University.

Ortiz, V. (1986). The transition from high school to college. In M. A. Olivas (Ed.), *Latino college students* (pp. 29–46). New York: Teachers College Press, Columbia University.

Peng, S. S. (1985, April). *Enrollment patterns of Asian American students in postsecondary education*. Paper presented at the Annual Meeting of the American Educational Research Association, New Orleans.

Pinkney, J. W., & Ramirez, M. (1985). Career-planning myths of Chicano students. *Journal of College Student Personnel*, 26, 300–305.

Post, P., Stewart, M. A., & Smith, P. L. (1991). Self-efficacy, interest, and consideration of math/science and non-math/science occupations among black freshmen. *Journal of Vocational Behavior*, 38, 179–186.

Pounds, A. W. (1987). Black students' needs on predominantly white campuses. In D. J. Wright (Ed.), *Responding to the needs of today's minority students* (pp. 23–38). New Directions for Student Services, no. 38. San Francisco: Jossey-Bass.

Pruitt, F. J. (1978). The adaptation of foreign students on American campuses. *Journal of NAWDAC*, 41, 144–147.

Quevedo-Garcia, E. L. (1987). Facilitating the development of Hispanic college students. In D. J. Wright (Ed.) *Responding to the needs of today's minority students* (pp. 49–63). New Directions for Student Services, no. 38. San Francisco: Jossey-Bass.

Quezada, R., & Jones, L. K. (1984). Hispanic women: Academic advisees of high potential. *Improving College and University Teaching*, 32, 95–98.

Reiff, R. F., & Kidd, M. A. (1986). The foreign student and student life. In K. R. Pyle (Ed.), *Guiding the development of foreign students* (pp. 39–49). New Directions for Student Services, no. 38. San Francisco: Jossey-Bass.

Rendon, L. I., & Nora, A. (1989). A synthesis and application of research on Hispanic students in community colleges. *Community College Review*, 17, 17–24.

Ruiz, R. A., & Padilla, A. M. (1977). Counseling Latinos. *Personnel and Guidance Journal*, 55, 401–408.

Sage, G. P. (1991). Counseling American Indian adults. In C. C. Lee & B. L. Richardson (Eds.), *Multicultural issues in counseling* (pp. 23–35). Alexandria, VA: American Association for Counseling and Development.

Sanchez, A. R., & King, M. (1986). Mexican Americans' use of counseling services: Cultural and institutional factors. *Journal of College Student Personnel*, 27, 344–349.

Sattler, J. M. (1977). The effects of therapist-client racial similarity. In A. S. Gurman

& A. M. Razin (Eds.), *Effective psychotherapy: A handbook of research* (pp. 252–290). New York: Pergamon Press.

Schaefer, R. T. (1987). Social distance of black college students at a predominantly white university. *Sociology and Social Research*, 72, 30–32.

Schram, J. L., & Lauver, P. J. (1988). Alienation in international students. *Journal of College Student Development*, 29, 146–150.

Sedlacek, W. E. (1987). Black students on white campuses: 209 years of research. *Journal of College Student Personnel*, 28, 484–495.

Sedlacek, W. E. (1991). Using noncognitive variables in advising nontraditional students. *NACADA Journal*, 11, 75–82.

Sewell, T. E., & Martin, R. P. (1976). Racial differences in patterns of occupational choice in adolescents. *Psychology in the Schools*, 13, 326–333.

Smith, E. J. (1980). Career development of minorities in non-traditional fields. *Journal of Non-White Concerns in Personnel and Guidance*, 8, 141–156.

Spaulding, S., & Flack, M. (1976). *The world's students in the United States*. New York: Praeger.

Spees, E. C., & Spees, E. R. (1986). Internationalizing the campus: Questions and concerns. In K. R. Pyle (Ed.), *Guiding the development of foreign students* (pp. 5–18). New Directions for Student Services, no. 36. San Francisco: Jossey-Bass.

Sue, S., Allen, D. B., & Conaway, L. (1981). The responsiveness and equality of mental health care to Chicanos and Native Americans. *American Journal of Community Psychology*, 6, 137–146.

Sue, D. W., & Kirk, B. A. (1972). Psychological characteristics of Chinese American students. *Journal of Counseling Psychology*, 19, 471–478.

Sue, D. W., & Kirk, B. A. (1973). Differential characteristics of Japanese American and Chinese American college students. *Journal of Counseling Psychology*, 20, 142–148.

Sue, D. W., & Morishima, J. K. (1982). *The mental health of Asian Americans*. San Francisco: Jossey-Bass.

Sue, S., & Sue, D. W. (1991). Counseling strategies for Chinese Americans. In C. C. Lee & B. L. Richardson (Eds.), *Multicultural issues in counseling* (pp. 79–90). Alexandria, VA: American Association for Counseling and Development.

Thackaberry, M. D., & Liston, A. (1986). Recruitment and admissions: Special issues and ethical considerations. In K. R. Pyle (Eds.), *Guiding and development of foreign students* (pp. 29–37). New Directions for Student Services, no. 36. San Francisco: Jossey-Bass.

Tierney, W. G. (1991). Native voices in academe. *Change*, 23, 36–44.

Trippi, J., & Cheatham, H. E. (1991). Counseling effects on African American college student graduation. *Journal of College Student Development*, 32, 342–349.

U.S. Bureau of Census (1985). *Persons of Spanish origin in the United States: March, 1985* (Advanced Report, Current Population Reports, Series P–20, No. 403). Washington, DC: U.S. Government Printing Office.

U.S. Commission on Civil Rights. (1978). *Improving Hispanic unemployment data*. Washington, DC: USCCR.

Washington, E. D. (1989). A componential theory of culture and its implications for African American identity. *Equity and Excellence*, 24, 24–30.

Watkins, C. E., & Terrell, F. (1988). Mistrust level and its effects on counseling expectations in black client-white counselor relationships: An analogue study. *Journal of Counseling Psychology*, 35, 194–197.

Weill, L. V. (1982). Advising international students at small colleges. *NACADA Journal*, 2, 52–56.

Willie, C. V., & McCord, A. (Eds.). (1972). *Black students in white colleges*. New York: Praeger.

Wright, B., & LaSalle, L. (1991, April). *A Study of the academic performance of tribal college transfer students in four-year institutions*. Paper presented at the Annual Meeting of the American Educational Research Association, Chicago.

Wright, B., & Tierney, W. G. (1991). American Indians in higher education: A history of cultural conflict. *Change*, 23, 11–18.

Wright, D. J. (Ed.). (1987). *Responding to the needs of today's minority students*. New Directions for Student Services, no. 38. San Francisco: Jossey-Bass.

Yang, J. (1991). Career counseling of Chinese American women: Are they in limbo? *Career Development Quarterly*, 39, 350–359.

7

Adviser Development and Training

The day has passed when an administrator or department chair can assign advisees to a faculty member or other professional without providing guidance in academic advising processes and skills as well as the substantive materials that are needed to perform effectively. Advising has become an important function on most college campuses and requires well-planned training and development activities if academic advisers are to possess the skills and knowledge necessary to the task. All too often in the past, if held at all, training was seen as a one time event at the beginning of the school year. Effective advising today requires more extensive, ongoing training activities. Kramer (1986) suggests that programs to improve advising may be viewed as rites of renewal. Adviser development efforts may be seen as one of these rites.

According to the standards set for academic advising by the Council for the Advancement of Standards for Student Services/Developmental Programs (1986), professional academic advisers should have an ''understanding of student development; a comprehensive knowledge of the institution, its programs, academic requirements, majors, minors, and student services; a demonstrated interest in working with and assisting students; a willingness to participate in pre-service and in-service training and other professional activities; and demonstrated interpersonal skills'' (p. 12). These standards emphasize the need for training programs and imply the breadth of topics to be covered.

This chapter focuses on the important aspects of adviser development relating to the issues, types, content, methods, and materials necessary for a well-coordinated, relevant training program. The ''Adviser Training Inventory'' below will help to assess the scope of an existing adviser training program. Item(s) that constitute the different facets of a training and development program may be checked. Scoring instructions are at the end of the inventory.

ADVISER TRAINING INVENTORY

1. How many adviser training sessions or programs do you have in one year? (Select one)

   _____ a. three or more

   _____ b. two

   _____ c. one

   _____ d. none

If you answered a, b, or c, continue to answer the rest of the questions.

2. What is the total number of hours spent a year in adviser training? (Select one)

   _____ a. 10 hours or more

   _____ b. 6–8 hours

   _____ c. at least one-half day

   _____ d. less than one-half day

3. Who sponsors these training activities? (Check all that apply)

   _____ a. academic administrators

   _____ b. academic departments

   _____ c. advising coordinator

   _____ d. student affairs

   _____ e. advisers themselves

4. Have you established in writing specific objectives or goals for your training program(s)?

   _____ a. yes

   _____ b. no

5. How do you determine the content of your training sessions? (Check all that apply)

   _____ a. advising coordinator or administrators

   _____ b. training committee

   _____ c. advisers make suggestions

   _____ d. depends on institutional needs

   _____ e. depends on advisers' needs

   _____ f. depends on students' needs

6. Are advisers *required* to participate?

   _____ a. yes

   _____ b. no

7. Is one person or a training committee responsible and accountable for adviser development on your campus?

   _____ a. yes

   _____ b. no

8. Do you use a permanent training manual or adviser handbook as a test?

   _____ a. yes

   _____ b. no

9. Is it updated regularly?

   _____ a. yes

   _____ b. no

10. Is your training program evaluated for: (Check all that apply)

    _____ a. meeting the overall training program objectives?

    _____ b. meeting individual sessions' objectives?

    _____ c. relevance of content?

    _____ d. type of presentation or method used?

Scoring

Question	Points
1. a.	3
1. b.	2
1. c.	1
1. d.	0
2. a.	3
2. b.	2
2. c.	1
2. d.	0
3. a.	1
3. b.	1
3. c.	1
3. d.	1
3. e.	1
4. a.	3
4. b.	0
5. a.	1
5. b.	1
5. c.	1
5. d.	1

Question	Points
5. e.	1
5. f.	1
6. a.	2
6. b.	0
7. a.	3
7. b.	0
8. a.	3
8. b.	0
9. a.	3
9. b.	0
10. a.	2
10. b.	2
10. c.	2
10. d.	2

Sum the total number of points you scored.

If you scored between 39 and 30 you don't need to read this chapter. Lower scores indicate you need to reexamine your training efforts and use some of the ideas offered below.

39–30	Excellent
29–25	Good
24–20	Fair
19–0	Poor

TRAINING ISSUES

Every advising program has a history and tradition, which often includes a training component. Every advising program needs to examine its traditional ways of providing advisers with support and development and through evaluation activities determine if the training component is meeting the needs of its advisers. Is it constantly monitoring the needs of new and experienced advisers, changing local information and higher education in general? Administrative support for adviser training is critical. When advisers (particularly faculty advisers) are aware that the president, provost, and other high-level administrators view advising as a critical function, training becomes an integral part of that effort. The time, funding, and priority given to this function will usually not be forthcoming without this support.

In addition to administrative support, another issue to be considered is whether to require training. Requiring attendance at training sessions will be accepted by most advisers who sincerely wish to improve their knowledge and skills. Raskin and Looney (1982) found that new faculty reported that their skills and aptitude for advising were not discussed when hired, a report somewhat contradictory with the perception of department chairs who felt this issue was addressed. The majority of new faculty felt they needed training and would attend training activities when offered.

Winston, Ender, and Miller (1982) identify format as an issue to be resolved if systematic adviser training programs are to exist. Instead of conducting workshops for experienced advisers before school begins or in-service sessions scheduled periodically throughout the year as needed, Winston, Ender, and Miller suggest that training should take place before the selection of academic advisers. Training then becomes a prerequisite for selection. The need for rewards for participating in training (e.g., additional salary or reduced teaching loads) is recognized if this method is to work. Insuring these rewards means administrative support as well as that of key faculty leaders since this acknowledges that training is the key to effective adviser performance.

Another issue is to determine who needs training. Obviously new advisers need to be exposed to the important knowledge and skills that are required for effective advising. Experienced advisers also need to be updated and acquire new knowledge in areas dictated by change. Everyone connected to advising, regardless of experience or years of advising, can benefit from a well-designed training activity (Gordon, 1984; Grites, 1986).

Responsibility for the training function is another issue. On campuses where there is an advising center, training activities are usually carried out by the director of the center. On larger campuses where advising is decentralized, adviser training is often the responsibility of individual deans or department chairs. A campuswide advising committee composed of representatives from every area participating in training can help to coordinate these efforts. Those responsible for training can use this committee as a sounding board for training schedules and activities. Regardless of how training is administered, one individual or office needs to be responsible so accountability is assured.

The where and when of training activities will depend on advisers' and institutions' needs (Gordon, 1984; Jones, 1963). Some may argue that it is better to meet off-campus where the pressures and distractions of work are not present. On the other hand, if time is a problem, holding training activities on campus may be the best solution. The timing for training activities will depend on the availability of those involved and the press of updating information. The where and when are important considerations for training issues relating to attendance, the need for informational updates, or problems that need to be resolved quickly.

The issue of rewards for training is a concern on some campuses (Bostaph & Moore, 1980; Grites, 1986). Financial incentives or reduced teaching loads are sometimes provided, especially for faculty advisers. More often, however, the rewards for training are in the opportunities to improve one's advising knowledge and skills and the subsequent rewards of student satisfaction and retention. Providing financial support for advisers who wish to attend national or state meetings or workshops on topics related to advising can be an excellent way to show support and the importance of keeping current in the field.

SETTING OBJECTIVES

Grites (1986) suggests some general objectives of an adviser training program might include the following:

1. to provide advisers with accurate and timely information about policies, procedures and processes which affect the advising relationship;

2. to provide advisers with additional skills often required in their advising responsibilities;

3. to increase student satisfaction with advising;

4. to increase adviser satisfaction with advising; and

5. to develop a comprehensive approach to academic planning as a part of the total advising process. (P. 140)

To establish goals and objectives for a training program, one must recognize the needs of individual advisers and advising environments. Ender and Winston (1982) identify 11 essential skills and competencies that all advisers must posses to be truly effective. They then outline goals and objectives for each component.

Establishing objectives for a training program may involve general ones such as those outlined above or more specific objectives that are measurable, such as, "At the end of this training activity, faculty advisers will be able to interpret their advisees' placement scores in English and mathematics." The acquisition of this knowledge can be measured through the use of case studies or other structured means.

Preservice training objectives—that is, goals for training before advisers begin advising—may be more general than in-service training objectives, which involve training for advisers who are already serving in that capacity. Pre-service training is of longer duration, and its purpose is to train new staff in basic knowledge and skills. In-service objectives often involve a onetime or series of training activities that include specific topics or updating of information.

Objectives for a given training activity may be determined by the trainers or by the trainees themselves. A survey of experienced advisers can help determine the knowledge or skills they feel are important to cover. Some advisers, for example, might express a need to expand their expertise in working with special populations or cross-cultural advising (Margolis & Rungta, 1986; Neimeyer et al., 1986). Asking experienced advisers to suggest goals to be met by a training activity can help ensure relevance.

Students may have an indirect voice in setting objectives, since they may have expressed concern about certain aspects of advising. These concerns may lead to the need for training activities to alleviate certain problems that periodically surface.

An extremely important aspect of setting objectives is their use in evaluation. Action-oriented, measurable objectives can lead to expanded knowledge and changes in attitudes and behaviors. A vehicle for measuring each objective should be included in evaluation activities so that progress and positive changes may be documented.

TRAINING PROGRAM CONTENT

The number and type of topics included in training activities are unlimited. In a preservice training effort, the advising process, student characteristics and development, communication skills and techniques, career advising, campus resources, and understanding the college environment from both student and adviser perspectives are a few of the general areas that need to be covered (Gordon, 1980; Kishler, 1985).

Moore, Murphy, and Gore (1985) describe a series of workshops offered for faculty and professional advisers designed to reduce the frustration and burnout reported by advisers in addressing student concerns for which they felt unprepared. The topics covered were (1) advising, interviewing, and referral and (2) choosing majors and careers. Advisers who took part in the workshops identified many topics for future workshops or support group meetings.

As indicated before, Winston, Ender, and Miller (1982) suggest 11 areas or topics and outline outcome objectives for these areas. These areas include human growth and development, communication skills, decision-making strategies, career exploration, study skills, campus resources, and awareness of special populations. Figure 7.1 outlines various topics that might be covered in faculty or staff development activities according to level of expertise and experience. Beginning advisers, for example, will need more basic information or skill-building content than experienced advisers, who will want to refine their approaches. These topics may be relevant for preservice or in-service activities. What one institution may consider a critical topic, however, may not be considered as important by another.

TRAINING METHODS

The method or techniques used to disseminate the content of the training activity will depend on the topic and the skills of the trainer. The learner must always be the focus of the activity. Some advisers will learn optimally by talking in small group discussions, some by reading or the lecture method, and some by experiencing. If only one adviser is being trained, the method can obviously be tailored to that individual's needs. If a large group is involved, a variety of strategies may be used to accommodate all types of learning styles.

Lecture. The lecture method is probably the least desirable method but may

Figure 7.1
Adviser Training Topics by Experience Levels

Beginning Advisers	Some Experience	Very experienced
Knowledge of general education requirements	Student development theory	How to advise special populations (e.g., adults, honors, disabled)
Academic major/program requirements	Career advising	
	Crises intervention	How to advise culturally different students (e.g., Black, Hispanic)
Institutional policies and procedures (e.g., drop/add, withdrawal)	Decision making strategies	
	Basic counseling techniques	Human growth and development
Use of student data base; transcript analysis; degree audit	How campus culture interacts with advising	Ethical issues in advising
	Job market information about major/program area	Retention strategies
Personal record keeping (if needed)		Decision making theory
	Learning styles	
Campus resources including student affairs, career services, learning resources, etc.	Ethical issues in advising	Learning theory
		Plus any areas in other two levels if not covered before
	Plus areas for beginning advisers if not covered before	
Roles and responsibilities of adviser and advises		
Typical advisee problem areas (i.e., freshmen in particular)		
Basic communication and referral skills		
Basic concepts of developmental advising		
Campus demographics and traditions		
Test interpretation		
How to work with parents		

be necessary if a large group is to be trained. A great deal of information can be disseminated by lecturing, but time for questions and comments must be included.

Discussion. Small group discussions are an excellent way to update advisers about new procedures or policies. These may also follow a lecture format where new information or procedures are discussed within a specific context. Advisers often find it valuable to hear their peers' views on certain issues or to share different approaches to certain advising problems.

Observation. Observing another adviser advise a student is one of the most basic and useful training methods since it can offer a new adviser a perspective on what advising entails. Watching an adviser or several advisers in action provides real-life examples of the advising process and offers an opportunity to view different styles of responding to students' presented questions and needs. Observation should be followed by a discussion, however, either with the observed adviser or with the person offering the training. New advisers often have questions about why certain solutions to students' problems were offered or why a certain procedure was used. A follow-up discussion will help the trainee add depth and a more practical understanding of what transpired.

Quizzes. One way to be sure advisers have learned new information and its application is to provide a short quiz that they may grade themselves. This helps them test their understanding of certain material, particularly procedural or other specific knowledge that they need to know.

Case Studies. Using actual student records or cases to help advisers think through their approaches to certain situations can be very informative. The case study approach is especially effective in small group discussions where many views may be expressed. Hearing other advisers' solutions to specific problems can expand one's understanding of how effective resolutions may be reached.

Interviews. Interviewing experienced advisers or students is a technique that is sometimes used when individuals are being trained. Hearing the views of other advisers can be enlightening. When using this method with new advisers, it is important to help them generate relevant questions before the interview since there may be important information about certain advising areas that a new adviser may not have the background to ask.

Simulations. Creating a scenario for a group of advisers to experience can be an effective training tool. Actually acting out a specific advising problem can provide insights into the advising function in a most dramatic way.

Videotaping. An extremely useful tool is to ask experienced advisers to act out an advising scene with a student. As advisers-in-training watch, common problems can be seen in a real advising contact or in one that is set up for this purpose. This often gives a new adviser a sense of what an effective advising transaction might include. Non-verbal communication skills can be noted and critiqued. An advantage of videotaping is that the vignette may be stopped and replayed for discussion purposes. Another use of videotape is to tape an adviser-in-training in a real advising situation (with permission of the student, of course) and then to critique it with the trainee and with the comments of an experienced adviser. This helps an adviser see areas that need improvement as well as areas that were done well.

Role Playing. Advisers or students can present a trainee who is playing the role of adviser with a typical advising situation. Playing the role of adviser forces a trainee to experience firsthand the need to solve problems and use advising materials. Immediate feedback provides new advisers with a sense of how students feel about the exchange. Role playing may also be videotaped so that new advisers may see how they handled the specific situation. It is also a useful vehicle for checking one's nonverbal communication reactions.

Any or all of the above techniques may be used in the course of an adviser training program. Which are used in specific situations will depend on the number and type of advisers being trained, the content that is being offered, and the experience and expertise of the advisers who are providing the training. In Chapter 1 various learning styles were described that were considered important in understanding the academic development of students. The same learning approaches are relevant for a trainer who is sensitive to the different styles evidenced by a group of advisers-in-training. A particularly useful learning style model is offered by Kolb (1981). Understanding Kolb's cycle of learning will help to determine which of the training strategies described above would be suitable for specific individuals and topics. Some advisers might prefer a more concrete experiential method that would include role playing, simulations, or videotaping. Those who learn best through observation and reflection will prefer to watch experienced advisers as they work directly with students. The learner then builds on this experience to expand conceptual knowledge, which can later be tested in new situations. Advisers who prefer a more abstract or conceptual way of learning might prefer the lecture or interviewing methods or even the opportunity to read material on their own. All of these approaches to learning are part of Kolb's learning cycle, but some advisers may feel more comfortable in a learning opportunity that fits their particular style.

Offering many different types of learning strategies to help advisers assimilate the knowledge and skills necessary for optimal advising will provide all trainees with opportunities to select the ones they prefer. The particular topic might also have some bearing on the method used since learning procedural information, for example, might call for a more straightforward presentation. Learning how to apply this knowledge, however, might call for a more action-oriented method in which the adviser is actually experiencing a situation where the knowledge must be interpreted within a given context (e.g., role playing or case study).

TRAINING MATERIALS

Grites (1984) offers a sampling of publications, assessment instruments, resource documents, and other materials that may be useful in a training activity. Most of these are local documents such as admissions materials and college catalogs. Others, such as ACT or SAT interpretive materials or career information materials, can be useful.

A basic tool is the training manual or notebook. Although many training programs use an advisers' handbook (Ford & Ford, 1990; Schubert & Munski, 1985) as a basic text, a specially designed training manual can provide the continuity that ongoing training programs require. Figure 7.2 outlines the content of a sample training manual. While all of the topics may not be relevant for all

Figure 7.2

Sample Content for an Academic Adviser's Training Manual

I. DEAN'S MESSAGE (or other administrator in charge of advising). (This is to show support for the training effort at the highest levels.)

II. INTRODUCTION TO THE TRAINING PROGRAM

   Training Program Objectives
   (This section provides the training program's objectives so that participants are aware of goals of the program activities.)

   Training Program Schedule

III. THE SETTING FOR ACADEMIC ADVISING

   Introduction to the institution

   History and Mission of Institution
   Adviser's Role and Responsibilities
   General Education Rationale and Requirements
   Descriptions, Functions, and Location of Important Institutional Offices
   　　(with which advisers will relate on a regular basis, e.g., Registrar, Admissions, Financial Aid)
   Description of Orientation and Adviser's duties (if any)
   Listing of Student Affairs services, locations, and functions
   Listing, locations, and description of Learning Skills Resources
   Listing, locations, and descriptions of Career Counseling and Information Resources
   Listing and description of other important campus resources
   Description and availability of receptionist and clerical support

IV. INTERPERSONAL DYNAMICS OF ADVISING PROCESS

   Definitions of Academic Advising
   Adviser and student roles and responsibilities
   College student profile (both nationally and locally)
   The Advising Process
   　　Counseling and Advising (differences)
   　　Decision Making and Advising
   　　The Advising Interview
   　　Communication Skills
   　　Referral Skills
   　　Legal Implications

V. BASIC ADVISING TASKS

   Scheduling new freshmen in orientation
   Scheduling transfer students
   Scheduling returning students
   Special scheduling considerations for particular majors
   Procedural advising (institution's policies for drop/add, withdrawal, etc. and paper work needed for each)
   Adviser as Referral Agent (how and when to refer)
   Summarize advising tasks

Figure 7.2 (continued)

VI.   CAREER ADVISING

       Relationship to advising
       Career development theories
       Matching students' career needs and resources
       Campus career planning resources
       Advising undecided students
       Advising students in need of alternative majors

VII.   ADVISING SPECIAL POPULATIONS
       (Define category in institution's terms, describe special needs these students may have, and list
       office location of specialist helping them.)

       Honors students
       Adult students
       Minority students
       Disabled students
       Student athletes
       International students
       Students in academic difficulty
       Other categories of special students unique to institution.

campuses, the basic outline provides the type of information that most well-coordinated training programs should contain.

Training materials may serve as valuable resources to advisers after the training is completed. Notes taken on the materials may help remind advisers later of an important fact or procedure they learned during the program. Each section of the manual can be augmented with case studies, quizzes, and other practical material and examples so that the content may be practiced in different activities. If a training manual is not written and a regular advising notebook is used, it can also serve as a valuable resource when advisers are encouraged to write their notes directly onto the pages of their copy.

SPECIALIZED PRESERVICE TRAINING

An important consideration when discussing adviser training is the importance of training advisers before they assume their duties, that is, preservice programs. Two special training programs exist on some campuses, one created especially for graduate students who may advise later as faculty or professionals and another for undergraduate students who are trained to become peer advisers.

Graduate-Level Advising Courses

Offering a graduate-level course on academic advising is an opportune way of training future faculty in any discipline and graduate students in student affairs, higher education administration, and counseling programs. The basic concepts, issues, and content of advising are covered in-depth and an appreciation for advising can be gained as graduate students obtain positions in higher education after graduation (Goldman, 1988; Gordon, 1982).

As Gordon (1982) points out, most faculty advisers are not trained in advising prior to assuming those duties. This type of in-depth experience provides an understanding of academic advising purposes and processes that serves as a foundation for later responsibilities. It can also foster positive attitudes and enthusiasm for advising as a professional activity.

Gordon (1982) suggests course objectives may include (1) a general introduction to academic advising from historical, philosophical, and practical perspectives; (2) readings and materials to acquaint students with a variety of advising delivery systems, advising skills and techniques, and resources required to accomplish advising tasks; and (3) an opportunity for graduate students to become familiar with academic advising literature and to apply what they read to practical assignments. The specific content of the course can include many of the important aspects of academic advising that would take numerous in-service programs to cover. An introduction to the historical and philosophical aspects of advising is rarely discussed in adviser training programs. Learning the theoretical underpinnings of advising and its many related topics could also be included.

Basic advising techniques and skills, learning to interpret assessment, and other material can be accomplished through role playing and case studies. Assigning students to interview professional as well as faculty advisers would give them a perspective on various philosophies and approaches to advising and expose them to the various settings within which advising is performed.

Training Peer Advisers

As stated in Chapter 2, peer advising has been shown to be a valuable method for delivering advising services. While peer advisers are considered supplemental to an advising program, their involvement can free faculty for more personalized student contact.

The key to an effective peer advising system is training. Ender and Winston (1982) suggest that the quality of students' experiences with peer advising is directly related to the quality and rigor of the training they receive. Some campuses offer a credit course for teaching the knowledge and skills needed for them to perform effectively. This course is often offered in the spring term before the students begin their advising duties in the fall.

Most courses offer training in procedural tasks, referral skills, communication skills, problem-solving skills, and time management so that they can avoid burnout and stress (Ender & McFadden, 1980; Friedman, 1979; Habley, 1979; Stein & Spille, 1974). A student development approach to instruction offers the students an opportunity to apply what they learn to their own development as well as the students they are advising (Miller & Prince, 1976).

Ender, McCaffrey, and Miller (1979) developed a training manual for peer advisers. The student helper's role is defined, and certain basic skills are taught to help the peer advisers examine and understand themselves as persons. The manual offers basic principles of college student development and helps the trainees to assess their skills and competencies as self-directed learners.

Gordon (1984) points out that teachers of training courses need to be well versed in student development concepts as well as communication and counseling skills. Assignments must be of the same level of difficulty as any other course offering, and testing should be included so that peer advisers' learning may be monitored.

In addition to credit courses, peer advisers may be trained in a workshop format while experiencing supervised, on-the-job training. If a course is not offered, frequent training meetings are necessary so that peer advisers' contacts with advisees can be carefully supervised and monitored.

EVALUATING TRAINING EFFORTS

As in any advising endeavor, training activities must be evaluated to assure they are meeting the objectives set forth for this important function. Both formative and summative evaluation strategies should be used. Feedback from the trainees should be solicited after each training activity as to its value and relevance. Evaluation may also include vehicles for testing the knowledge and skills learned. Formative evaluations can provide immediate feedback so that the positive elements of the program can be retained and areas to be improved can be identified. An annual evaluation, for example, on the year's training program (summative evaluation) may include individual reactions as well as an assessment of the objectives that were established at the beginning of the program. An annual survey can provide information on how advisers feel about their progress in the knowledge or skills taught and can solicit their ideas for future training topics or activities (Gordon, 1984). Questionnaires and interviews can also solicit advisers' opinions about how the training program has served them. This information can then be used to change or improve future training efforts. Overall, training programs should provide pronounced improvement in advising services as evidenced by increased student usage and adviser satisfaction.

SUMMARY

Training is a critical component of any effective advising program. Training efforts should reflect the unique needs of an institution. The first step is to establish objectives or goals for what needs to be accomplished. Objectives need to be stated in measurable terms. Careful consideration should also be given to content, method, timing, and location. The issue of rewards, if training requires additional time, needs to be resolved as well, particularly for faculty advisers. A training committee that is established on a permanent basis with rotating members is a most effective way to make sure this function is responsive to campus needs. One individual or office should coordinate and be accountable for all training activities. Perhaps one of the most valuable outcomes of an advising training program is the interaction of advisers with each other. Listening to other advisers' experiences and concerns helps bring one's own advising perspectives into focus.

REFERENCES

Bostaph, C., & Moore, M. (1980). Training academic advisers: A developmental strategy. *Journal of College Student Personnel*, 21, 45–50.

Council for the Advancement of Standards for Student Services/Development Programs (CAS). (1986). Iowa City, IA: American College Testing Program.

Ender, S. C., McCaffrey, S., & Miller, T. (1979). *Students helping students*. Athens, GA: Student Development Associates.

Ender, S. C., & McFadden, R. B. (1980). Training the student paraprofessional helper. In F. Newton and S. Ender (Eds.), *Student development practices: Strategies for making a difference* (pp. 129–142). Springfield, IL: Charles C. Thomas.

Ender, S. C., & Winston, R. B. (1982). Training allied professional academic advisers. In R. Winston, S. Ender, and T. Miller (Eds.) *Developmental approaches to academic advising* (pp. 85–103). New Directions for Student Services, no. 17. San Francisco: Jossey-Bass.

Ford, J. & Ford, S. S. (1990). Producing a comprehensive academic advising handbook. National Clearinghouse for Academic Advising. Columbus, OH: Ohio State University.

Friedman, R. E. (1979). The advising structure of McMicken College of Arts and Sciences of the University of Cincinnati and the institution of peer advising structure: Some encounters and observations. In D. S. Crockett (Ed.), *Academic advising: A resource document* (pp. 1.198–1.211). Iowa City, IA: American College Testing Program.

Goldman, B. A. (1988). It's time to provide higher education courses in enrollment management, academic advising, and retention. *College Student Journal*, 22, 42–46.

Gordon, V. N. (1980). Training academic advisers: Content and method. *Journal of College Student Personnel*, 21, 334–339.

Gordon, V. N. (1982). Training future academic advisers: One model of the pre-service approach. *NACADA Journal*, 2, 35–40.

Gordon, V. N. (1984). Training professional and paraprofessional advisers. In R. Winston, T. Miller, S. Ender, T. Grites, and Associates (Eds.), *Developmental academic advising* (pp. 440–465). San Francisco: Jossey-Bass.

Grites, T. J. (1984). Techniques and tools for improving advising. In R. Winston, T. Miller, S. Ender, T. Grites, and Associates (Eds.), *Developmental academic advising* (pp. 197–225). San Francisco: Jossey-Bass.

Grites, T. J. (1986). Training the academic adviser. In D. Crockett (Ed.), *Advising skills, techniques and resources* (pp. 139–159). Iowa City, IA: American College Testing Program.

Habley, W. R. (1979). The advantages and disadvantages of using students as academic advisers. *NASPA Journal*, 17, 46–51.

Jones, R. L. (1963). A suggested training program for academic advisers. *Journal of College Student Personnel*, 4, 186–187.

Kishler, T. C. (1985). Developing an all-university adviser's training program: A short history of one model. (ERIC Document Reproduction Service No. 261 578).

Kolb, D. A. (1981). Learning styles and disciplinary differences. In A. W. Chickering and Associates (Eds.), *The modern American college* (pp. 232–255). San Francisco: Jossey-Bass.

Kramer, H. C. (1986). Advising systems: The use of rites and ceremonials. (ERIC Document Reproduction Service No. ED 272 061).

Margolis, R. L., & Rungta, S. A. (1986). Training counselors for work with special populations: A second look. *Journal of Counseling and Development*, 64, 642–644.

Miller, T. K., & Prince, J. S. (1976). *The future of student affairs: A guide to student development for tomorrow's higher education.* San Francisco: Jossey-Bass.

Moore, C. A., Murphy, P. P., & Gore, M. R. (1985). Advising the advisers: A preventative intervention strategy. (ERIC Document Reproduction Service No. ED 260 614).

Neimeyer, G. J., Fukuyama, M. A., Bingham, R. P., Hall, L. E., & Mussender, M. E. (1986). Training cross-cultural counselors: A comparison of the pro-counseling and anti-counseling triad models. *Journal of Counseling and Development*, 64, 437–439.

Raskin, M. S., & Looney, S. (1982). Last but not least: Academic advising. (ERIC Document Reproduction Service No. 232 509).

Schubert, G. W., & Munski, D. C. (1985). An academic advising handbook as a tool to help faculty. *Journal of College Student Personnel*, 26, 360–361.

Stein, G. B., & Spille, H. A. (1974). Academic advising reaches out. *Personnel and Guidance Journal*, 53, 61–64.

Winston, R. B., Ender, S. C., & Miller, T. K. (Eds). (1982). *Developmental approaches to academic advising.* New Directions for Student Services, no. 17. San Francisco: Jossey-Bass.

8

Evaluation

Evaluating or assessing the value of academic advising as a process or of a program or of an individual adviser has become increasingly important over the last decade. Accountability, retention, limited financial resources, and other issues have forced advising administrators to think seriously about ways to prove advising is a critical function that makes a difference. While great strides have been made, many institutions still do not have evaluation programs in place. In a national survey, Habley and Crockett (1988) found that only 42.5 percent of institutions reported that they conducted systematic evaluations of advising on their campuses. This figure, however, had doubled since the survey conducted five years earlier.

Many advising programs that have an adviser evaluation vehicle in place are now recognizing the need for more elaborate programmatic evaluations using more sophisticated evaluation techniques. For the past two years, "evaluation and assessment" have been the topics for which most requests were received by the National Clearinghouse for Academic Advising (Gordon, 1991).

DEFINITIONS

Evaluation may be defined in many forms, but for advising purposes it may be viewed as a purposeful set of activities that help to determine the value of a program and its parts. Evaluation is examining and judging how we have accomplished the goals we have set.

Evaluation and assessment are often used interchangeably, but Hartle (1985) suggests that they are not the same. He maintains that assessment is much broader and that testing is one of its important components. While research and evaluation are related, they are also different in purpose (Wheeler & Loesch, 1981). While some knowledge of empirical investigation is helpful, evaluation skills require a more situational approach, and an evaluator needs to develop other types of skills, such as interviewing techniques and problem solving (Anderson & Ball, 1978; Oetting, 1976).

Astin (1991) has provided a most useful distinction between assessment and evaluation. He considers assessment to include the gathering of information so as to "improve the functioning of an institution and its people" (p. 2). Assessment, according to Astin, refers to two very different activities: gathering information and then using it for institutional and individual improvement. How we *use* the information we gather is the critical aspect of assessment. Evaluation is the rendering of value judgments, according to Astin, and what we might call evaluation (as in giving course grades, for example) is often "measurement."

Stufflebeam et al. (1971) suggest that the purpose of evaluation is "not to prove but to improve." They view evaluation as the process of gathering data as an aid to decision making. Kuh (1979) indicates that evaluation is to make judgments about the elements or worth of a program. He also points out that evaluative judgments can be formal and explicit or informal, depending on the situation.

According to House (1983), conceptions of evaluation depend on what it entails. Sometimes the emphasis is on programs and their parts, sometimes on inputs or outputs, and other times on outcomes. A metaphoric example might be to examine industrial production, as it uses a systematic approach (Rossi, Freeman, & Wright, 1979). According to this approach, evaluation may be thought of in terms of time (student appointments, paperwork, training), costs (overall and per student cost for advising services), procedures (the advising process), and product (student satisfaction, retention, student knowledge, etc.).

EVALUATION MODELS

Brown (1978) describes three models of evaluation that attend to issues sometimes neglected when considering evaluation strategies. "Goal-free evaluation" refers to the approach of the evaluator, not the goals of the program itself. The goal-free evaluator looks for the actual effects of the program and attends to any possible outcomes, rather than just the specific intents of the program. Goal-free evaluation can often be complementary to goal-based efforts.

The second model Brown describes is the "responsive approach." Evaluators in this model document the existence and events of a program in addition to program outcomes. Responsive evaluation is not overly concerned with formalized statements of objectives but responds to the nature of the program and the concerns of those involved. Emphasis is on communication and feedback.

The third model, "transactional evaluation," confronts conflicts and tries to transform the energy given to conflict into productive activity. The emphasis is on the change that is taking place rather than with the outcomes of the activity. Brown contends that these three approaches are useful to program planners and administrators because they attend to philosophical issues generally not employed in experimental models of evaluation.

Astin offers a model for assessment that includes three variables: Inputs, Environment, and Outputs (The I-E-O Model, p. 18). For example, if we are assessing an advising program, the components of the present program must be identified (input). If we want to change our program to become more effective for students, we must take into account the total institutional environment that will have an impact on both students and our program. Outcomes are the concrete changes we wish to make in students' development as a result of advising services.

Wilson (1984) describes the many approaches to evaluation, including goal-free, goal-directed, decision-oriented, responsive, juried, quasi-experimental, and behavioral premises. According to Wilson each has its advantages and disadvantages. Kozloff (1987) argues for a more student-centered model of evaluation and assessment rather than a management approach. She maintains that measuring personal and cognitive development must be an integral part of assessing student outcomes.

Crockett (1988) defines the differences between formative and summative evaluation. Both share the goal of improving advising and involve gathering and interpreting data. Summative evaluation uses the data to make decisions about advisers while formative evaluation is used to help advisers improve their performance.

The standards for advising programs as set forth by the Council for the Advancement of Standards for Student Services/Development Programs (CAS) (1986) indicate that systematic and regular research and evaluation need to be implemented to determine whether the educational goals and needs of students are being met. Although methods of evaluation may vary, these standards direct that both quantitative and qualitative measures must be used. Evaluation data must be collected from students and other "significant constituencies." The standards also mandate that the results of these regular evaluations must be used in revising and improving program goals and implementation of advising services.

Another aspect of evaluation that is often ignored is evaluating the process, which is as important as the product. Kuh (1979) discusses the difference between process and product. The product of advising may be the choice of major or the adherence to an institutional policy. The process involves what leads up to the product. The products of the advising process (materials and formats) can also be assessed as student outcomes. The process includes what transpires or changes. Examples of process questions include: How long did students wait in line to see an adviser? Are the registration materials understandable?

Potter (1989) urges that before evaluation begins, an adequate assessment design should be in place. He emphasizes that developing a plan is essential if time and financial resources are to be well spent. If a quantitative approach is used during the data-gathering phase, population samples must be representative, response rates must be high (generally 75 percent–80 percent), and statistical procedures must be appropriate.

Barak (1982) outlines the following steps in developing an evaluation plan:

- Identify evaluation purposes
- Conceptualize the process
- Develop consensus
- Select reviewers
- Collect data
- Assess the data
- Conduct the evaluation
- Develop recommendations
- Implement and use the results
- Evaluate the review process

These steps can help conceptualize the important elements and flow of the evaluation process. Identifying the purpose of evaluation is especially important since it calls into question what will be accomplished by the evaluation itself. The last step, evaluating the review process, is rarely taken. Were the evaluation methods realistic? Was the information generated useful? How could the process be improved?

FACTORS IN DEVELOPING AN EVALUATION PROGRAM

While some institutions evaluate academic advisers on a regular basis, there are many factors to consider when evaluation needs to extend far beyond this one component.

Administrative Support. Strong support from administrative areas is essential if an evaluation program is to succeed. Administrative commitment will ensure that changes revealed by the evaluation will take place and that the evaluative information will be used for decision making (Brown & Sanstead, 1982). Evaluation can also be used to prove organizational effectiveness (Kramer, 1983).

Who Should Be Responsible? The evaluator(s) of advising programs are often the program administrator or individuals responsible for advising services. This is the pattern when a self-study method is used. If an advising committee exists, it may assume responsibility. Whoever is accountable for the outcomes of advising services needs to be involved in all phases of the evaluation planning and implementation process. The area of evaluation has become so complex that advising specialists are now recognized professionals (Stufflebeam et al., 1971). Even an outside evaluator, however, must report to the administrator who oversees advising services.

Involvement of Advisers. Perhaps the most important aspect of establishing an evaluation program is to involve the advisers who will be most affected by the results and possible changes that may ensue. Crockett (1988) discusses the resistance that some faculty have to evaluation in general. This may be overcome by involving them in the planning process since a feeling of ''ownership'' may eliminate some potential problems. If advisers are involved in establishing objectives or goals for the advising program, evaluation will be a natural part of assessing those objectives. If an advising committee exists, developing evaluative activities can be part of the group's responsibility. Participatory involvement will often provide excellent suggestions for how, where, and what to evaluate and the necessary evaluation activities to carry out these suggestions.

Establishment of Program Goals. Establishing overall goals or objectives for the advising program leads directly to evaluation activities. Many program goals are vague, unclear, and often too general. Participatory involvement can help clarify the purpose and goals of a program. Consulting with those involved and affected by the total advising program will help to obtain consensus about what is important to accomplish. Suchman (1969) offers a continuum of activities across time: immediate, intermediate, and ultimate goals. He suggests a checklist be formulated to address specific problems encountered when developing goals. This approach would be helpful not only in setting goals but in formulating objectives for the overall program as well.

Setting Criteria. Some authors suggest that conducting a criterion-based evaluation is difficult (Pine, 1975; Wheeler & Loesch, 1981). Wilson (1984), on the other hand, suggests that once criteria have been identified, all that is left is to gather data and make decisions. He thinks this simplicity is attractive to evaluators.

Three areas to consider when setting criteria for what needs to be accomplished are improving and expanding knowledge, changing counterproductive behaviors, and improving and changing poor attitudes. What student behavior needs changing? What adviser behavior needs changing? What knowledge must each adviser possess? What attitudes need to be examined or changed? Do students' and faculty's attitudes toward the importance and value of academic advising need changing? How would these goals be accomplished? Knowledge and behavioral goals are easier to measure than attitudinal goals; thus they are used more frequently as criteria.

Data Gathering and Analysis. The selection of evaluation methods is directly related to what is being evaluated. Both quantitative and qualitative methods can be used for measuring outcomes that pertain to knowledge, behaviors, and attitudes. A plan or blueprint should be created specifying the type of information needed, evaluation techniques for gathering this information, and priorities for gathering and analyzing the information (Akpom, 1986). Data gathering is perhaps one of the most important steps in establishing an evaluation program. How and when the data are to be collected are also important considerations.

Impact and Uses of Evaluation Results. Creating an evaluation program is useless unless it is used to confirm what is taking place and to identify problems that need to be resolved. Evaluating a program will implicitly demand that resources be available for improvement. Appropriate action needs to be initiated when evaluation results reveal resources need to be committed. This emphasizes the first factor necessary to an ongoing evaluation process: administrative support is critical (Wergin & Braskamp, 1987).

Formative evaluation can help advisers receive feedback on their performance so they can check their own perceptions against those of others. In this way they can personally decide what steps in self-development they need to take. Summative evaluation activities can determine how effective advisers are in the overall picture (Crockett, 1988).

While the factors above are critical in planning an evaluation program, more practical approaches are outlined below.

EVALUATION METHODS

An important aspect of evaluation is to select the best methods for measuring goals and objectives. These methods may be tailored to program evaluation or adviser evaluation.

Adviser Evaluation

Many studies have examined methods for evaluating individual adviser performance (Guinn & Mitchell, 1986; Kapraum & Coldren, 1980; Lygre, 1985; McAnulty, O'Conner, & Sklare, 1984). In the *Third ACT National Survey of Academic Advising* (Habley & Crockett, 1988), four methods were polled for evaluating advisers: student evaluation, self-evaluation, supervisory performance review, and peer review. Although the authors found none of the methods widely used, the two most common were student evaluation and supervisory performance review.

Student Evaluation

Since students are the prime recipients of direct advising contacts, they are in a position to express their reactions to these contacts. Wheeler and Loesch (1981) speak to the threat (implicit or explicit) that some faculty or professional advisers feel about evaluation since they think their job security rests on a positive reaction. Others may be opposed to change.

Lechtreck (1987) offers the view that students are often biased in evaluating faculty performance, and this could also be true of adviser roles. It is unrealistic, according to Lechtreck, to expect untrained individuals to give evaluations. Neale and Sidorenko (1988) offer the opposite view, indicating the persons receiving the service should be the ones to evaluate it. Crockett (1988) is convinced that students should be asked to evaluate the effectiveness of their advisers in spite of the problems.

The most common form for soliciting student evaluation is through surveys that can be nationally or locally developed. The advantage of using nationally distributed surveys, such as the ACT Survey of Academic Advising or the Academic Advising Inventory (Winston & Sandor, 1984), is the ability to compare local advising with national norms.

Srebnik (1988) offers an excellent review of academic advising assessment instruments. The survey instruments are in four categories: those for students evaluating advisers, those for students evaluating advising centers, those with dual forms for advisers and students, and those given to advisers alone. The number and wide·variety of instruments described underscore that many are available. As Srebnik points out, budgets, time accessibility to students, and other variables specific to the institution all play a role in the choice of instrument.

Trombley (1984) analyzed the complexity of academic advising tasks and found that three factors—academic counseling, personal counseling, and informational—emerged from a pool of 40 tasks that were typically performed by advisers. She concludes that two roles underlie the advising function: the informational role and the counseling role. Questions generated to measure these two categories would be useful in creating evaluation surveys.

Trombley's (1984) categories and items describing the advising function might serve as an impetus for generating ideas at the local level about the important roles and functions of an adviser. Surveys or questionnaires developed locally can provide more specific information and are generally used most frequently (Frisz & Lane, 1987; Peabody, Metz, & Sedlacek, 1980; Vowell & Karst, 1987).

Lygre (1985) evaluated a cadre approach to academic advising by using a questionnaire to measure the number of times students met with their advisers, whom the students consulted when making decisions about courses, whether advising met with the students' expectations, and the students' overall satisfaction with the advising experience.

In addition to written surveys or questionnaires, other methods include telephone surveys (Beasley-Fielstein, 1986) and computer evaluation (Neale & Sidorenko, 1988). Interviewing students or others who have contact with advisers is another vehicle for evaluation. The interviewing method requires careful planning and implementation. Questions need to be formulated in a systematic manner so that qualitative methods for compiling the results may be used.

Kapraum and Coldren (1980) suggest that a self-help guide could be developed as a result of adviser evaluation surveys so that advisers could follow up on improving their knowledge and skills based on students' and other evaluations of their performance. Workshops and other training activities would be a direct follow-up to help improve those areas that the evaluations reveal to be weak.

Supervisory Evaluation

A distinction must be made in some areas when discussing faculty and professional advisers. Advising is often considered part of the faculty adviser's teaching role. Professional advisers, however, require a more extensive type of evaluation if their titles, promotion, and salary are based on their competencies in the advising function. Some institutions have developed elaborate performance appraisal systems that spell out in detail the expectations of professional advisers. These are discussed in more detail in Chapter 9.

Program Evaluation

Crockett (1988) suggests that overall advising program evaluation should take place every two or three years. The CAS Standards outlined earlier are an excellent vehicle for delineating program components to evaluate. The Academic Advising Audit (Crockett, 1987) is a four-step process for evaluating an advising program. The audit may be used as an initial self-study. While it is not a scientific instrument, it can serve as an effective self-scoring evaluation tool. The steps in the audit include (1) information gathering, (2) evaluation of the information, (3) analyzing the information, and (4) action planning as the final step.

A task force or advising committee may be charged with the responsibility for program evaluation. Appleton (1983) describes a year-long study by a presidentially appointed commission. Questionnaires and interviews initiated by the commission revealed that advising services were not responsive to the institution's types of students and that many faculty ignored or gave advising a low priority among their professional activities. As a result of the evaluation, organizational and other changes were implemented. Student and faculty use of services increased dramatically, and retention increased.

Perhaps the most common method for program evaluation is the self-study. Kauffman (1984) indicates there are four essential elements in a self-study. These include describing the resources that are available for specific program purposes, clarifying the organizational structure and the persons responsible, delineating those who carry out the program and provide the services, and summarizing the various kinds of survey data documenting user perceptions of the worth of the program.

Balenger, Sedlacek, and Osteen (1989) describe a self-study process that, although used to evaluate student services, is adaptable to advising programs. A staff member conducted a unit self-study with the consultative help of an experienced evaluator coordinator. For each unit, the evaluation coordinator developed a Prescriptive Evaluation Plan (PEP) to guide the self-study. Lecher (1984) also describes a self-study that developed an instrument to measure the program's effectiveness and included external evaluations and student evaluations.

Bringing outside consultants to conduct a program evaluation is common practice. As Boyer (1987) points out, 6 regional accrediting bodies and 154 professional accrediting bodies look at specialized programs in higher education institutions today. The advising component may be part of a regional accreditation of the institution. The National Academic Advising Association maintains a Consultants' Bureau from which outside evaluators may be obtained.

Parsons and Meyers (1984) suggest that the consultation process moves through a series of clearly defined stages. The stages are (1) entry into the system, (2) goal identification, (3) goal definition, (4) intervention planning and implementation, (5) assessment of the impact of consultation, and (6) conclusion of the relationship. The first three steps are primarily concerned with data gathering and problem identification. Although intervention strategies need to be developed and implemented, interventions may occur at all phases of the consultation. Parsons and Meyers emphasize that many forms of assessment are possible beyond traditional psychometric areas. Concluding the relationship can be accomplished in many ways, but when the expectations set forth at the outset are accomplished, termination may be expected.

Young (1985) defines the various roles of an advising consultant. He emphasizes the need to agree on the consultant's role before the consultation takes place. An evaluator can help clarify the program's purposes and commitments as well as evaluate it. Since academic advising is often a "boundary-spanning" function, a consultant will usually be working with individuals at many levels performing many functions. Providing the consultant with pertinent information prior to the visit or visits is imperative. A consultant may request that some data be gathered through questionnaires or surveys prior to the visit. A consultant's help with this step may be needed. At the end of the consultation an oral summation, followed by a written report outlining the findings and recommendations, is usually given. Follow-up contacts may be needed, depending on the needs of the institution and the consultant's findings.

SUMMARY

Evaluation is an important part of administering an effective advising program. There are many models to follow, including systematic, goal-directed, or student-centered approaches. The CAS Standards describe the components of an advising program and can be used as a guide when creating an evaluation plan. Many factors need to be considered when developing an evaluation program. Administrative support, involvement of advisers, establishing program goals, setting criteria, gathering and analyzing data, and using the information are all important considerations. Evaluating individual advisers is an important part of the overall evaluation plan as well. Most advisers appreciate knowing how effective they are, although some may resist being evaluated.

Many methods are available to evaluate both advising programs and individual advisers. Surveys and questionnaires are commonly used, but computer and interview techniques are also useful. In addition to using the CAS Standards or an Advising Audit, programs can be evaluated through self-studies and task forces or commissions and by using outside consultants.

Crockett (1986) summarizes the objectives of a well-developed evaluation program: (1) to determine how well the advising system is working, (2) to obtain information on individual adviser performance for the purpose of self-improvement, (3) to gain information on areas of weakness to develop better in-service training strategies, (4) to provide data for use in administering a recognition or reward system for individual advisers, and (5) to gather data to support requests for funding or gain improved administrative support of the advising program.

REFERENCES

Akpom, K. (1986). Planning program evaluation to meet management information needs. *Evaluation Practice*, 7, 35–36.

Anderson, S. B., & Ball, S. (1978). *The profession and practice of program evaluation.* San Francisco: Jossey-Bass.

Appleton, S. (1983). The impact of an academic advising program: A case study. *NACADA Journal*, 3, 57–63.

Astin, A. W. (1991). *Assessment for excellence.* New York: ACE/Macmillan.

Balenger, V. J., Sedlacek, W. E., & Osteen, J. M. (1989). *Prescriptive evaluation plans: A method of large-scale evaluation in student affairs.* (Research Report 16–19.) (ERIC Document Reproduction Service No. ED 312 310).

Barak, R. J. (1982). *Program review in higher education: Within and without.* Boulder, CO: National Center for Higher Education Management Systems.

Beasley-Fielstein, L. (1986). Student perceptions of the developmental advisor-advisee relationship. *NACADA Journal*, 6, 107–117.

Boyer, E. L. (1987). *College: The undergraduate experience in America.* New York: Harper & Row.

Brown, R. D. (1978). Implications of new evaluation strategies for accountability in student affairs. *Journal of College Student Personnel*, 19, 123–126.

Brown, R. D., & Sanstead, M. J. (1982). Using evaluation to make decisions about academic advising programs. In R. Winston, S. Ender, & T. Miller (Eds.), *Developmental approaches to academic advising* (pp. 55–66). New Directions for Student Services, no. 17. San Francisco: Jossey-Bass.

Council for the Advancement of Standards for Student Services/Development Programs. (1986). Iowa City, IA: American College Testing Program.

Crockett, D. S. (1986). Assessing your advising program. In D. S. Crockett (Ed.), *Advising skills, techniques, and resources* (pp. 315–320). Iowa City, IA: American College Testing Program.

Crockett, D. S. (1987). *Academic advising audit.* Iowa City, IA: American College Testing Program.

Crockett, D. S. (1988). Evaluating and rewarding advisers. In W. R. Habley (Ed.), *The status and future of academic advising* (pp. 169–199). Iowa City, IA: American College Testing Program.

Frisz, R. H., & Lane, J. R. (1987). Student user evaluation of peer advising services. *Journal of College Student Personnel*, 28, 241–245.

Gordon, V. N. (1991). *Annual report of the National Clearinghouse for Academic Advising.* Columbus, OH: Ohio State University.

Guinn, D., & Mitchell, R. (1986). Academic advising: And different expectations. *NACADA Journal*, 6, 99–105.

Habley, W. R., & Crockett, D. S. (1988). The Third ACT National Survey of Academic Advising. In W. R. Habley (Ed.), *The status and future of academic advising* (pp. 11–76). Iowa City, IA: American College Testing Program.

Hartle, T. W. (1985). *The growing interest in measuring the educational achievement of students*. Paper presented at the National Conference on Assessment in Higher Education, University of South Carolina, Columbia.

House, E. R. (1983). How we think about evaluation. In E. R. House (Ed.), *Philosophy of evaluation* (pp. 5–25). New Directions for Program Evaluation, no. 19. San Francisco: Jossey-Bass.

Kapraum, E. D., & Coldren, D. W. (1980). An approach to the evaluation of academic advising. *Journal of College Student Personnel*, 21, 85–86.

Kauffmann, J. F. (1984). Assessing the quality of student services. In R. A. Scott (Ed.), *Determining the effectiveness of campus services* (pp. 23–36). New Directions for Institutional Research, no. 41. San Francisco: Jossey-Bass.

Kozloff, J. (1987). A student-centered approach to accountability and assessment. *Journal of College Student Personnel*, 28, 419–423.

Kramer, H. C. (1983). Advising implications for faculty development. *NACADA Journal*, 3, 25–31.

Kuh, G. D. (1979). Evaluation: The state of the art in student affairs. In G. D. Kuh (Ed.), *Evaluation in student affairs*. Cincinnati, OH: University of Cincinnati.

Lecher, A. (1984). Academic advisement center self-study report. (ERIC Document Reproduction Service No. ED 256 418).

Lechtreck, R. (1987). College faculty evaluation by students: An opportunity for bias. *College Student Journal*, 21, 297–299.

Lygre, J. G. (1985). A cadre approach to freshman academic advising. (ERIC Document Reproduction Service No. ED 257 355).

McAnulty, B. H., O'Conner, C. A., & Sklare, L. (1984). Analysis of student and faculty opinion of academic advisement service. (ERIC Document Reproduction Service No. ED 253 189).

Neale, A., & Sidorenko, C. (1988). Student evaluation: A model for improving advising services. *NACADA Journal*, 8, 72–82.

Oetting, E. R. (1976). Planning and reporting evaluative research: Part II. *Personnel and Guidance Journal*, 52, 434–438.

Parsons, R. D., & Meyers, J. (1984). *Developing consultation skills*. San Francisco: Jossey-Bass.

Peabody, S. A., Metz, J. F., & Sedlacek, W. E. (1980). A survey of academic advising models used by Maryland state public institutions of higher education. (ERIC Document Reproduction Service No. ED 207 460).

Pine, G. (1975). Evaluating school counseling programs: Retrospect and prospect. *Measurement and Evaluation in Guidance*, 8, 136–144.

Potter, E. B. (1989). *Cooperative advising and assessment: Prospectus III*. Paper presented at the meeting of the National Academic Advising Association, Houston, TX.

Rossi, P. H., Freeman, H. E., & Wright, S. R. (1979). *Evaluation: A systematic approach*. Beverly Hills, CA: Sage.

Srebnik, D. S. (1988). Academic advising evaluation: A review of assessment instruments. *NACADA Journal*, 8, 52–62.

Stufflebeam, D. L., et al. (1971). *Educational evaluation and decision-making*. Itasca, IL: F. E. Peacock.

Suchman, E. A. (1969). Evaluating educational programs: A symposium. *Urban Review*, 3, 15–17.

Trombley, T. B. (1984). An analysis of the complexity of academic advising tasks. *Journal of College Student Personnel*, 25, 234–239.

Vowell, F., & Karst, R. (1987). Students satisfied with faculty advising in an intrusive advising program. *NACADA Journal*, 7, 31–33.

Wergin, J. F., & Braskamp, L. A. (Eds.). (1987). *Evaluating administrative services and programs*. New Directions for Institutional Research, no. 56. San Francisco: Jossey-Bass.

Wheeler, P. T., & Loesch, L. (1981). Program evaluation and counseling: Yesterday, today, and tomorrow. *Personnel and Guidance Journal*, 59, 573–578.

Wilson, R. F. (1984). Critical issues in program evaluation. *Review of Higher Education*, 7, 143–157.

Winston, R. B., & Sandor, J. A. (1984). Developmental academic advising: What do students want? *NACADA Journal*, 4, 5–13.

Young, W. H. (1985). Some principles of effective adviser consulting. *NACADA Journal*, 5, 77–82.

9

Advising as a Profession

Advising by full-time professionals has existed in many forms for many years but has recently taken on new significance. Within the past several decades advising by full-time professionals has increased as the numbers and diversity of students have grown and as pressures on faculty to research and publish have continued. Historically, as traced in Chapter 1, academic advising has been performed by faculty. From the earliest colonial colleges, advising has been the purview of faculty, who have acted as role models and experts in the academic disciplines that students pursue. The first "professional" advisers were faculty who took responsibility for student service activities. Eventually these professionals came from many backgrounds and academic disciplines (Dameron & Wolf, 1974). Today 66 percent of advising is performed by full-time advisers in advising offices (Habley & Crockett, 1988), and this trend is expected to continue. As detailed in Chapter 3, many delivery systems use full-time professional advisers along with faculty advisers in a coordinated effort. This chapter discusses the role and responsibilities of professional advisers and the issues related to this phenomenon.

WHAT IS A PROFESSION?

Are full-time advisers part of a profession? A prior question that bears consideration is, What constitutes a profession? Many perspectives are needed fully to understand the issues involved. Within the professional category of its occupational classification system, the U.S. Census Bureau includes such occupations as accountant, librarian, natural scientist, teacher, optometrist, and college professor. Greenwood (1962) finds that these groups have the following attributes in common: (1) systematic theory, (2) authority, (3) community sanction, (4) ethical codes, and (5) a culture. Similar attributes have been offered by writers in fields in which a professional identity has been sought. Gordon et al. (1988), for example, examined definitions from the student affairs area. Wrenn and Darley (1949) set out eight traditional criteria to determine if student affairs was a profession:

1. the application of standards of selection and training;
2. the definition of job titles and functions;
3. the self-imposition of standards of admission and performance;
4. the legal recognition of the vocation;
5. the development of a professional consciousness and of professional groups;
6. the performance of a socially necessary function;
7. the possession of a body of specialized knowledge and skills; and
8. high moral and personal integrity in lieu of the development of a code of ethics.

Wrenn and Darley found that student affairs did not measure up to some of these criteria, such as application of standards of selection and training; definition of job titles; self-imposition of standards of admission and performance; and the legal recognition of the vocation.

Lieberman (1956) sets forth criteria for a profession within an educational setting:

1. a unique, definite, and essential social service;
2. an emphasis upon intellectual techniques in performing its service;
3. a long period of specialized training;
4. a broad range of autonomy for both the individual practitioners and the occupational group as a whole;
5. an acceptance by the practitioners of broad personal responsibility for judgments made and acts performed within the scope of professional autonomy;
6. an emphasis upon the service to be rendered, rather than the economic gain to the practitioners, as the basis for the organization and performance of the social service delegated to the occupational group;
7. a comprehensive, self-governing organization of practitioners; and
8. a code of ethics that has been clarified and interpreted at ambiguous and doubtful points by concrete cases.

Christensen (1980) outlines five major, interrelated components of a profession that could apply to advising. These include (1) history and philosophy, (2) relevant theories, (3) models of practice, (4) professional competencies, and (5) management and organizational competencies. While the professional identity of advisers is fairly new, the five components above can be identified as part of the current professional awareness of this group. All of these components have been discussed in previous chapters. The history of advising can be traced to the early years of higher education, and many individual institutions are developing a philosophy of advising relevant to their situation. Advising draws from many theoretical frameworks, including developmental, learning, career development, philosophical, sociological, psychological, and economics. Organizational models for delivering academic advising services, as well as professional and management competencies, have been identified by many writers in the field. Christensen stresses the interrelationship of these components and states that all must be included when defining the structure as a whole.

Penney (1969) offers a different perspective on professional recognition. He suggests that a profession must have a basic literature in both quantity and quality. He makes a case for a need to produce a large body of permanent, fundamental literature both generally and for specializations within the profession.

A most useful approach to examining a profession is offered by Rickard (1988), who outlines a multiple perspective that encompasses all dimensions of an evolving professional field. This multidimensional framework "acknowledges the need for generalists as well as specialists and affirms the value of institutional diversity and autonomy" (p. 390). His professional paradigm consists of six dimensions: the foci or sphere of professional work, professional roles, professional skills, supporting disciplines and professions, theories and models, and functional areas. If one adapts this model to professional advising, the heart or core of a concentric circle contains the foci of professional activity, which include advising, student development, and administration. These dimensions, according to Rickard, circumscribe the total scope, extent, and magnitude of professional work. How these activities are performed will vary with institutionally defined roles and other unique institutional factors.

The second concentric circle in Rickard's model includes the professional roles that might be assumed by the adviser, for example, counselor, educator, manager, administrator, researcher, or evaluator. The third component is a series of skills such as administering, organizing, planning, assessing, researching, and evaluating. The fourth component consists of the disciplines and professions most closely related to the three foci, such as organizational development, psychology, sociology, counseling, business, law, philosophy, and education. The fifth component includes the models and theories used by advising, such as developmental, structural, human resource, typological, psychosocial, existential, and behavioral.

The last dimension in this professional paradigm consists of functional areas such as academic advising, career advising, counseling, learning, orientation, registration, and working with special populations of students (e.g., minorities, commuters, adults, honors). When viewed from this perspective, advising can be depicted as a profession with a multiprofessional nature that encompasses many types of knowledge and skills taken from many theoretical frameworks and disciplines.

Although some may view this discussion of defining a profession as not relevant, there does exist at this time a growing group of full-time professionals who consider themselves part of a profession. In a survey by Gordon et al. (1987), 95 percent of the adviser respondents reported they were satisfied with their work, and 87 percent intended to continue in the field in the future.

Perhaps the best view is presented by Young (1988), who suggests that student affairs (and advising as well) should be thought of as dynamic and "professionalizing," rather than as static and fully professionalized. While at the present time advising does not qualify as a full "profession" under many of the criteria set forth earlier, it can be viewed as an "emerging" profession with many of the earmarks of a profession in place. A professional identity has been established, national standards have been set, a broad range of autonomy for individual practitioners does exist, national organizations have been formed, and a code of ethics is being developed. At this writing, the National Academic Advising Association is studying the titles, salaries, and levels of work for professional advisers. Minimum professional development requirements are also being discussed. As with any professional group certain issues have emerged as the importance of examining advising as a profession is recognized.

ROLES OF PROFESSIONAL ADVISERS

Kramer and Gardner's (1983) discussion of faculty advising roles, as outlined in Chapter 2, applies to professional advisers as well. They point out that advisers assume certain roles in the advising relationship with students and in their interaction with the institution. While these roles are implicit in most advising positions, some may assume more significance in certain settings than others. Examples of the roles professional advisers play are as follows:

- *Curriculum expert*—assists students with selection of major, general education requirements, course selection, graduation requirements, and other curricular matters.
- *Registrar*—assists students with scheduling and related procedures.
- *Counselor*—listens to students' concerns and helps them set goals commensurate with their values and abilities.
- *Career counselor and planner*—helps students understand the relationships between academic and career alternatives and supports students as they make career decisions.
- *Student development specialist*—understands how students change and grow during the college years and challenges them to grow in positive ways.
- *Student advocate*—acts as intermediary for students in disputes between institution and student.
- *Educator*—teaches students how to think and learn about the various aspects of curricular and extracurricular activities.
- *Manager*—manages people, paperwork, and procedures associated with advising tasks.
- *Administrator*—oversees various aspects of the advising enterprise and ensures that it functions properly.

- *Broker*—negotiates various aspects of advising between the student and the institution.
- *Evaluator*—assesses the effectiveness of personal advising and advising programs.
- *Researcher*—studies different aspects of advising-related problems or questions.
- *Specialist*—is an expert on a specific aspect of advising or advising a specific student population.
- *Friend*—has special relationship with advisee in which both esteem and respect each other.
- *Mentor*—is a trusted counselor or guide.

While carrying out institutional policies and procedures, advisers are also concerned with individual students' best interest. When an institutional policy does not make sense in a specific situation, it is sometimes necessary for the adviser to search for a compromise or exception on the students' behalf. Kramer and Gardner suggest that in certain situations, students perceive advisers in a different role than advisers perceive themselves. For example, a student may see an adviser as an authority when scheduling takes place, while advisers may perceive themselves as teachers in that situation. Occasionally, one role may clash with another. For example, the expectation of adviser as agent of the institution may clash with the expectation of adviser as friend or advocate. Kramer and Gardner suggest that when a student does not understand the adviser's role, confusion results. This confusion may be overcome by recognizing that students' perceptions need to be checked frequently so that accurate communication may result.

ISSUES IN PROFESSIONAL ADVISING

Many of the issues involved in advising as a profession center around adviser job descriptions and levels of responsibility and titles; preparation, including training and professional development; career advancement and mobility; unionization on some campuses; performance appraisal; research opportunities and expectations; recognition and rewards; and overall standards. Other concerns focus on ethical behavior and legal issues.

Job Descriptions

The overall responsibilities and specific duties of professional advisers are as varied as the settings in which they work. One example can demonstrate the wide variety of tasks involved. The Academic Professional Model in University College at the University of Minnesota divides adviser responsibilities into three categories: advising activities, program operation activities, and professional activities. Under advising activities are teaching, evaluating, counseling, brokering, and student program management. Activities within program operation include program development, action research, administration, and governance.

Professional activities include professional development and professional service. Each of these is described in detail so that each responsibility within the position is clearly defined. For example, evaluating is defined as "evaluating students' curricular plans with respect to the educational expectations and graduation criteria of the program and assessing whether the aggregate of learning experiences meets the students' identified objectives and goals."

Program development is defined as efforts to improve or expand the program, which may involve "designing new or altered structures and systems; reviewing and revising program policies and processes; participating in program planning; and developing programmatic materials." When professional responsibilities are clearly defined as in the Minnesota program, criteria for evaluating advisers are easily established. In a less elaborate system, professional advisers may be responsible for many activities typically associated with the advising process. Some examples follow:

• assist students in the choice of academic and career goals commensurate with their aptitudes and interests;

• assist students in the selection of courses consistent with their developing goals and interests;

• provide advice and assistance on matters affecting academic progress;

• interpret test results and general education requirements;

• monitor advisees' academic progress and offer special counseling when appropriate;

• act as referral agent to other campus resources when a need is indicated;

• keep records of significant advisement contacts with students for inclusion in the student's permanent record.

This is just a partial list of possible activities in which professional advisers may become involved.

In a national survey, Gordon et al. (1987) found that some professional advisers assumed other responsibilities in addition to the advising function. These included responsibilities for teaching and administration. In smaller institutions in particular, advisers could be involved in orientation, counseling, career planning, and other student services activities. Forty-nine percent of the advisers in the survey taught courses in academic disciplines, freshmen orientation, study skills, or career planning. Advising administrators, particularly in advising centers, were often professional advisers who assumed that responsibility after serving as full-time professional staff. As indicated earlier, some faculty moved into full-time administrative positions to coordinate or direct campus advising services.

In the same national survey (Gordon et al., 1987), it was found that advisers held many titles, although "academic adviser" and "academic counselor" were the most common. Some institutions have established levels or "career ladders" for advisers within which professionals can move. While the most common entry-level position is entitled "academic adviser," the next levels have a variety of titles, such as associate advisers, professional counselors, staff associates, educational advisers, academic advising specialists, or senior advisers. As the level of competence increases, an adviser might move to higher levels of responsibility and the accompanying salary increases. Since each institution has its own personnel classification system, most advisers have titles unique to that system. Fifty-eight percent of titles were listed in an administrative or professional system, 17 percent were under a faculty system, 23 percent were under a civil service system, and 2 percent were under a clerical system.

Preparation

Like titles, the level of preparation required by institutions for an advising position varies dramatically. In some institutions no academic degree requirement is stated while others require a graduate degree. The academic discipline required for a degree is rarely stated unless there is a need for additional specific expertise, such as counseling or advising within an academic department. The graduate degree is almost always required for administrative positions.

Preservice training can range from a formal training program to ad hoc "learning on the job." In the Gordon et al. (1987) survey, 53 percent of the respondents were in favor of a national certification program for full-time professional advisers. Over a quarter of the respondents recommended the following criteria for determining certification of professional advisers: an advanced degree, specified number of years of experience, and a specified number of in-service certifiable training hours. Sixteen percent recommended a nationally recognized training program providing a certificate. Other less popular suggestions included a national test that assesses general advising knowledge and skills, letters of endorsement, or sponsorship.

Other issues concerned with a national certification of professional advisers involve who the certification body would be (83 percent indicated the National Association of Academic Advisers [NACADA]) and the topics for inclusion in certified training. Recommendations for topics included interview skills, use of information, counseling skills, decision making skills, career counseling skills, referral skills, knowledge of human development and communication theories, legal aspects of advising, knowledge of special populations, and research skills and knowledge.

Goetz and White (1986) surveyed graduate programs that addressed the preparation of academic advisers. Although 25 percent of the departments responding indicated they offered graduate courses on advising on a regular basis, a closer examination indicated only five official courses listed by title as academic advising courses. Advising was more frequently incorporated into offerings in higher education, student personnel, and special seminar courses covering issues in higher education. In the Gordon et al. (1987) survey, only 21 percent of the respondents reported they would ever pursue a graduate degree in advising.

Gordon (1982) provides an example of a preservice approach to training academic advisers through a graduate-level course that is part of the higher education curriculum. Course topics include the history of academic advising; definitions of advising, including philosophical and theoretical underpinnings; administrative or delivery systems; advising techniques and skills; student development; career advising; and advising special groups of students such as minorities, honors, and adult students. Future faculty can be trained through such courses in addition to students in graduate programs in student personnel, counseling, and related fields.

Since no stated preparation exists at the national level, each institution determines the type of preparation and training professional advisers are required to have to function within that setting. The quantity and quality of preservice and in-service training varies tremendously from institution to institution.

Mobility

Like other aspects of professional advising, mobility rests with the type of institution and the evolving expertise and competence of the individual adviser. Becoming specialized in a particular area of advising might increase the chances for mobility if that particular expertise were needed in a particular setting. Mobility implies career advancement, but Sherburne (1970) points out that there is a need to develop a quantitative method for measuring mobility so that more specific elements may be identified.

Salaries

Of concern to many professional advisers is the unevenness of salary ranges not only among institutions but sometimes within an institution itself. The *Chronicle of Higher Education Almanac* (1991) listed the national median salary for an academic adviser as $27,040. The survey does not indicate what levels or titles are represented (e.g., entry-level, advising administrators). In this survey the title of academic adviser is listed under the student services section. Advisers' salary ranked 36th out of the 39 positions listed.

Since there are no national standards for preparation, titles, or levels of responsibility, it is difficult to ascertain a realistic appraisal of an adviser's worth within a range of position titles. As in many positions in higher education, salaries in an institution's professional and administrative classification system depend on the type, size, and geographical location of the college or university.

Unionization

Bee, Beronja, and Mann (1990) suggest that the "middle-management" group, of which professional advisers are a part, has been hindered by its relatively small numbers in obtaining economic, career, and professional goals. Unionization of advisers on the authors' campus addressed the job security needs of advisers by establishing grievance procedures and retrenchment policies. As a result of unionization, the work load requests for advisers are defined and nonadvising responsibilities are monitored.

Performance Appraisal

The evaluation of professional advisers' performance varies considerably among institutions as well as within institutions. Some have established elaborate evaluation procedures specifically for professional advisers, some use an institutional format, while others use an informal or ad hoc approach. The criteria discussed below have been excerpted from those used by the University of Minnesota, the Ohio State University, the University of Washington, and Iowa State University. The plans developed by these institutions incorporate many of the same evaluation categories. Professional advisers may be evaluated within the following categories:

Individual Advising

Knowledge

- knowledge of academic programs, requirements, and specific majors
- knowledge of the institution's general requirements and the curricular requirements of individual programs
- knowledge of the institution's policies, procedures, and regulations
- knowledge of career opportunities related to academic program areas
- knowledge of campus resources, both academic and non-academic
- knowledge of developmental needs of college students as individuals
- specialized knowledge when applicable (e.g., advising athletes, honors students)

Skills

- communication skills (articulating information, listening skills, writing skills)
- interpersonal skills (sensitivity to individual students' needs, flexibility in dealing with various types of people, ability to be assertive when needed, positive reaction to difficult situations)
- referral skills (ability to know when, how, and where to refer students to campus and community resources)

Group Advising

- develop, implement, and evaluate group advising workshops or sessions (e.g., for probation students, "exploring major" group sessions)
- teach an orientation course (when applicable)
- effectively conduct group or class discussion

Administrative Responsibilities

- quality of petitions and other institutional forms as assigned, for example, evaluates readiness for graduation
- facilitates development of degree plans
- processes paperwork in prompt and orderly manner
- maintains records of advisees
- participates in decision making through staff meetings and other situations
- acts as information resource for other staff members within and outside advising office
- participates in program or college governance activities
- can set goals and objectives and establish priorities
- organizes time effectively and appropriately
- develops systems, resources, and contacts to improve academic advising overall

Professional Development Activities

- participates in institutionwide committees and other functions
- participates in professional organizations, locally, regionally, and nationally
- attends conferences, workshops, and courses to improve professional skills and expertise
- gives presentations at regional or national conferences
- initiates and authors or coauthors publications and/or reports
- seeks new opportunities for professional growth

Professional Conduct

- is dependable (attendance, punctuality, doesn't need constant supervision)
- takes initiative (takes responsibility, independent action, attends to problems as they emerge)
- is creative (suggests new and improved ways to approach situations, problems, advising tasks)
- cooperates with other advisers and staff members
- attends and contributes to staff and committee meetings

The above categories and duties are only examples of the type of performance appraisal criteria that can be used to evaluate professional advisers. An evaluation instrument is best developed locally since the duties of advisers vary so greatly. Some questions to ask when developing or improving an evaluation plan follow:

- Are the present evaluation system's objectives realistic and measurable? What else needs to be included?
- What are the present criteria? Do they encompass all areas needing to be evaluated? Are current job descriptions, levels, and performance standards accurate and adequate?
- What parts of the evaluation plan need to be expanded? Changed? What specific steps are needed to implement change?

- Who (advising committee, individual advisers, administrators) should be involved in examining evaluation procedures?
- How should the results of the evaluation be used? (E.g., for salary considerations, promotion, awards, support of professional activities?)
- What time line is realistic for improving/changing the evaluation practices and documents?

The Council for the Advancement of Standards for Student Services/Development Programs (CAS) (1986) indicates that professional academic advisers should have, in addition to a graduate degree, "an understanding of student development; a comprehensive knowledge of the institution, its programs, academic requirements, majors, minors, and student services; a demonstrated interest in working with and assisting students; a willingness to participate in preservice and in-service training and other professional activities; and demonstrated interpersonal skills." These provide the minimum standards to be used in evaluating professional advisers.

Research Opportunities

One earmark of a profession is its contributions to the literature of the area. A surprising finding in the Gordon et al. (1987) survey was the low number (6 percent) who recommended "research skills and knowledge" as a topic for inclusion in professional certification. If advising is to be recognized as a legitimate profession, its practitioners need to establish a sound research reputation. Acquiring basic knowledge and skills in conducting and/or interpreting research is a fundamental grounding of a profession.

Since advisers come from such diverse backgrounds and academic disciplines, the interest in, experience with, and ability to perform research may vary considerably. Research may be viewed by some as in-depth studies accompanied by complicated statistical analyses. Research may encompass simple studies, however, that can contribute significantly to the knowledge of the field. Evaluation studies may yield important information to a local advising effort that is attempting to improve or change delivery systems, identify potentially high-risk students, or check students' perceptions of the advising they receive. Professional advisers are confronted daily with situations or student behavior about which they have questions. Advisers always need to be sensitive to the opportunities to research a specific question that might shed light, not only on local advising practices, but for the benefit of a national audience as well.

ETHICAL BEHAVIOR

Academic advisers are confronted almost daily with ethical problems that arise in many areas: student conduct, interaction with colleagues, supervisory relationships, and institutional policies and procedures. According to Bok (1988), higher education has not demonstrated deep concern with moral development of the individual student, despite its importance. Higher education should be the first to "reaffirm the importance of basic values, such as honesty, promise keeping, free expression, and nonviolence" (p. 50).

Chambers (1981) warns us that the difficulty with ethics is that it is not "a well indexed code of behavior . . . but how individuals translate their inner motivations into external actions having social consequences" (p. 5). Ethics is based upon cultural tradition and heritage. The foundations of ethical responsibility in higher education need to be reexamined periodically.

The Ethics Committee of the American Association of Counseling and Development's report for 1989 to 1990 indicates a substantial increase in the number of complaints, formal inquiries, and other questions about ethical behavior directed to the committee. They speculate that "clients and students may be more informed about their rights and are more willing to file complaints" (p. 279). They hope to establish historical data to monitor the number and type of unethical behaviors reported.

Kitchner (1985) proposes a model of ethical decision making in which the particular situation and the facts of that situation dictate the ethical reasoning that takes place. She describes three levels of ethical reasoning: ethical rules and codes of ethics; ethical principles, which provide a framework for identifying central issues; and ethical theories, which provide a rationale for deciding when ethical principles are in conflict.

Ethical rules, according to Kitchner, provide the first level of ethical justification. Some ethical dilemmas may be resolved by pointing to established rules or codes of conduct. There is an inherent danger here that codes, while acknowledging certain conflicts, cannot totally resolve them. "An act considered ethical by one organization can be considered unethical by another" (p. 19).

Ethical principles are more general than rules and can offer a more consistent framework within which a particular issue or case may be considered. Kitchner outlines four ethical principles that may be considered the underpinnings of the rules or codes themselves. These include nonmaleficence or "do no harm"; both psychological and physical harm and both intentional and unintentional harm to others must be avoided. The ethical obligation to intervene increases with the magnitude and risk of harm. The second principle is beneficence or "act to benefit others," which incorporates the obligation to make a positive contribution to another's welfare or promote the personal growth of another. Beneficence often needs to be balanced against doing no harm to one party while helping another.

The third principle is promoting justice. This means fair treatment of all persons and fair distribution of goods, services, and rewards. Three standards should be observed when promoting justice: reciprocity, impartiality, and equity. The fourth principle, fidelity, includes the obligation to keep promises, to be loyal, and to be truthful. Special obligations come with contracts between individuals of unequal knowledge or power. The last principle is respecting one's autonomy.

This includes the right to act as a free agent and to have freedom of thought or choice, freedom of action, the right of self-determination, respect for the autonomy rights of others, and the right to privacy, confidentiality, and informed consent (Beauchamp & Childress, 1979).

Kitchner (1985) warns that there is no absolutism-subjectivism when thinking of ethical principles. Following moral principles absolutely would in some cases "lead to immoral acts." On the other hand, subjectivism, or the claim that values are strictly a personal affair, has no greater validity since it purports that each person's moral behavior and judgments are as valid as any group's set of ethical rules.

A critical aspect of establishing a code of ethics for academic advising is that the existence of a code of ethics is at the very heart of what it means to be a profession. Winston and Saunders (1991) view ethics within the context of professional standards. Ethics in this context is concerned with the content of the rules, who has the right to make the rules, and how the rules are to be interpreted and enforced.

Winston and Saunders (1991) describe how ethical and professional standards can be viewed in practical situations. First, these standards are a code of ethics for those preparing to become professionals and to promote awareness of ethical principles in professional practice. Students need to be informed of the standards of the profession for which they are preparing and given time to reflect on how they would react in certain situations before being confronted in the actual work setting. Individual practitioners need to have guidelines for the practical decisions they are making on a daily basis.

When advisers are confronted with a moral dilemma, they might think in terms of Rest's (1986) components for making moral decisions:

1. interpreting the situation as moral, or being aware of the moral dimension within the situation, that is, that the welfare of the individual is at stake; recognizing how possible courses of action affect all parties involved;
2. defining the morally ideal course of action; determining what one ought to do; formulating a plan of action that applies a moral standard or ideal (e.g., fairness, justice);
3. deciding what one intends to do; evaluating the various courses of action for how they would serve moral or nonmoral values (e.g., political sensitivity, professional aspirations); and
4. executing and implementing a moral plan of action; acting as one intended to act; assisted by perseverance, resoluteness, strong character, and the strength of one's convictions.

Winston and Dagley (1985) also suggest that an ethical set of standards is helpful when clarifying responsibilities of a professional. Standards ensure that each member of the profession must possess the qualifications, experiences, and expertise for the functions performed by that profession. Winston and Dagley suggest that these include "specifying the need for specialized preparation, representing qualifications and experiences accurately, supporting the legitimate professional endeavors of colleagues, and supporting the missions of the institution at which they are employed'' (p. 51).

Other uses of a code of professional ethics, according to Winston and Dagley, are protection of the profession and the individual practitioner, in public affirmation of the profession's role and functions and in performance appraisal. Standards can be used to define what activities should be evaluated and how they should be evaluated.

Advisers can play an important role in helping students realize their responsibility for moral behavior. In a survey to chief student personnel officers, Dalton, Barnett, and Healy (1982) found the respondents' greatest concern was with the potentially negative ethical implications of alcohol and drug abuse by students. They agreed upon the importance of honesty and respect for others as critical values necessary to student development. The authors recommended a values education program for students but strongly emphasized students' responsibility for their own actions in this area.

Bok (1988) presents several elements of a comprehensive program of moral education that colleges and universities could follow. When dealing with student conduct, Bok points out that although institutions have rules of conduct, the official literature rarely explains why certain conduct, such as substance abuse, is wrong. Bok suggests that efforts should be made to explain why such rules exist rather than arbitrarily enforcing them.

Moral responsibility cannot develop through rules and regulations alone. Students must grow by experiencing situations where one's actions have an effect on others. Bok suggests extracurricular activities and community service programs as vehicles for bringing students into collaborative or communal relationships.

Bok also stresses that institutions have ethical standards, as do the students, faculty, and staff working within that environment. Examples of moral problems that institutions periodically encounter are investing their stock, interacting with the surrounding community, athletic situations, and implementing affirmative action.

In addition to discussing rules of conduct with students and building programs of community service, other areas where moral education could be conducted are offering classes in applied ethics, striving for high ethical standards in dealing with moral issues that face the institution, and being more alert to the countless signals that institutions send to students so that these messages ''will support rather than undermine basic norms.''

Toward a Code of Ethics

The academic advising profession must have a code of ethics that reflects the highest standards of integrity and conduct. A document that describes the principles and standards for career services at The Ohio State University (1991) states that as a consequence of a code of conduct, professionals "act or refrain from acting, not only because one is legally compelled to act or is restrained from action, but because professional spirit and the ideals of service to the profession dictate conduct." Even with an established code of ethics, advisers will be guided by the ethical principles of respecting autonomy, doing no harm, benefiting others, being just, and being faithful (Krager, 1985).

Rich (1984) discusses the structure or basic framework of ethical codes. Ethical codes serve to "convey the collective wisdom of the profession and develop esprit de corps among members" (p. 31). Codes have a preamble or set of objectives, a body describing the basic principles, and other sections on implementation and enforcement. Codes also consist of ideals, principles, standards, rules, and procedures.

Advisers must confront unethical situations, not ignore or hide from them. They should not only teach students ethical behavior and encourage them to take courses in ethics but be well informed on the subject and act ethically themselves. If ethical behavior has not been discussed in in-service training efforts on their campus, they should take the initiative to organize one. They should be aware of the critical issues involved in the adviser-advisee relationship so that possible ethical dilemmas may be discussed and resolved before they actually happen. By being aware of the importance of ethical behavior, advisers may be involved in one of the most distinguishing criteria for being part of a profession.

LEGAL ISSUES

The changing relationship between institutions of higher education and the courts has been well documented (Barr, 1983; Gehring, 1984; Kaplan, 1978; Laudicina & Tramutola, 1974; Likins, 1979; Owens, 1980). In the past the courts have been reluctant to become involved in the affairs of higher education. According to Elliott (1983), increasing litigation in academic affairs indicates that the courts are more willing to enter the classroom. Likins (1979) offers several reasons for this increased litigation. First is a growing use of litigation by society in general. This growing orientation toward legal resolutions has carried over into higher education.

A second reason offered by Likins is that higher education has lost some of its autonomy. As the judicial branch of government has become more involved in the affairs of higher education (e.g., in admissions, financial aid, educational policy), autonomy has diminished.

A third reason for the changing relationship offered by Likins is changing interpretations of student-university relationships. With the demise of in loco parentis, a new student-institution relationship is one of contract. Instead of being viewed as paternalistic, colleges or universities are now considered a provider of services.

The campus unrest of the late 1960s made students more aware of the legal issues within higher education. The change of legal age from 21 to 18 years of age also had an effect. The courts also began to delineate the parameters of individual freedom and institutional responsibilities to the student. Challenges to many previously held notions of the student-institution relationship changed that relationship considerably.

Courts in the past were most often involved in determining whether institutions had proper jurisdictional authority, but more recently they are involved in examining the relationships between individuals and institutions. The discretionary role of administrators in the past is now limited, and the increased legal awareness of students has created a different atmosphere, within which advisers could be vulnerable (Laudicina & Tramutola, 1974).

Another reason for increased court involvement is consumerism (Buchanan & Lamb, 1980). Faulty and misleading information provided by institutions for students has included lack of disclosure regarding institutional policies, practices, faculty, facilities and programs. Legislative action has tried to ensure that institutions are dealing with students in a "fair and ethical manner." This fair treatment includes pre-enrollment rights, the right to be treated fairly while enrolled, and postgraduation rights.

According to Young (1982), legal issues involving advisers fall into four major areas. A contractual relationship exists between students and institutions. Catalogs, admissions materials, student handbooks, and other printed documents are part of that contract. Both parties have responsibilities: the student to meet the required standards for completing academic programs, and the institution to respect its own regulations. Advisers are generally not personally liable for erroneous advising, according to Young, "in the absence of gross negligence, irresponsible behavior, or arbitrary or capricious treatment of students" (p. 43).

Privacy of students' records is another area where advisers need to be legally responsible. The Family Educational Rights and Privacy Act of 1974 provides students the right to access their advising files and ensures them that only college personnel with a legitimate educational reason may look at students' files. The institution, however, decides who these college personnel are and defines what "legitimate educational reasons" are. Information may not be sent to students' parents without students' written consent. If parents or guardians can prove dependency, however, they can view the students' records. Advisers' personal notes in students' files are excluded but should be removed when the adviser ceases to be involved.

A third area involves privileged communications. Advisers can discuss confidential information about a student with others who are involved professionally with that student. In all cases advisers need to determine if sharing that information is in the student's best interest. Gehring (1982) discusses the adviser's role in transmitting information concerning advisees. Advisers enjoy qualified privilege as long as they act in good faith.

When making statements, advisers need to be aware of not disclosing personal information that would constitute a clear invasion of privacy. Disclosing information without the advisee's consent could be a violation of privacy laws. Knapp and Vandecreek (1983) warn that confidentiality and privileged communication should not be used interchangeably. Privileged communication is a narrower concept dealing with the admissibility of evidence into court.

Information that is shared by students with an adviser that could involve possible harm to themselves or others is exempted, and advisers should share this information with the appropriate party, such as police, parents, or an intended victim. In this situation an adviser would be held to a reasonableness standard in predicting dangerousness. When a special relationship exists, as between adviser and advisee, and there is reasonable knowledge of conduct that may harm, then a legal duty to warn is in effect (Gehring, 1982).

The last area, according to Young, is academic due process. Most institutions have clearly defined grievance processes, and the courts will generally respect the institution's procedures for handling grievances, such as erroneous advising or disputed grades. Due process also is afforded in alleged cheating and plagiarism since these offenses reflect upon a student's good name, reputation, and integrity (Young, 1984).

Young (1982) recommends that institutions clearly define and publish the responsibilities of both adviser and advisee in that relationship. Information relevant to academic programs and graduation requirements should be clearly defined and published in easily accessible materials. Young also indicates that a well-documented and orderly procedure of appeal should be "established and promulgated" and a committee should be appointed to "hear complaints by students against advisers for alleged advising errors or negligent and irresponsible advising" (p. 45). According to Young, channeling complaints through a committee would provide a fair procedure for bringing forth alleged advising errors or negligent and irresponsible advising.

Schubert and Schubert (1983) discuss two areas where legal action could occur in academic advising: tort claims or contract claims. Tort action is a civil action for which the court may allow money damages. Schubert and Schubert outline three areas under tort law where advisers could be involved: negligence, nondisclosure and misrepresentation, and defamation.

Under the law of torts, once a professional undertakes to perform a duty, the law of negligence requires that it be done with care (Patterson, 1980). A special relationship between adviser and advisee exists; therefore, when a duty is breached, a person who has trusted that professional may claim negligence. An adviser is held publicly to have special knowledge, and because of access to certain information, the adviser may have a duty to an advisee. Advisers need to be careful in gathering information, and "if the information is made available with disregard for the truth, then the adviser may be negligent" (p. 2).

Advisers must also be careful about misleading or not offering information that is important for a student to know. The law today, according to Schubert and Schubert (1983), is that "full disclosure of all materials facts must be made whenever conduct demands it." If a statement or information is misrepresented, then negligence might possibly have occurred. Misrepresentation is negligent behavior and can be deliberate concealment of facts or false denial of knowledge. When reliance by the advisee on information is reasonable and that information is misrepresented, then the adviser may be liable for damages based upon negligence.

Defamation is made up of separate torts of libel and slander. Libel is "written communication which can harm one's reputation, and slander is an oral statement made to injure a party's reputation or standing in society" (p. 4). Advisers often have a confidential relationship with their advisees. They must process and communicate information concerning an advisee's scholastic performance and social behavior, and they should not volunteer information. Academic advisers who are responsible for interpreting highly sensitive information are particularly vulnerable to the defamation action. When malice or bad faith by the adviser can be shown, charges of libel or slander may ensue.

In addition to tort law, contract law involves an agreement made between two or more parties that creates an obligation. This includes both written and oral contracts. Most of the court action in the 1960s involved disciplinary dismissal or academic grade deficiencies. The courts, however, would not enter the case unless the action by the institution was arbitrary, capricious, or unfair to the student (*University of Miami v. Militana*, 184 So.2d 701 [FL 1966], 236 So.2d 162 [FL 1967]). The standard set by the court for intervention into academic affairs (*Connelly v. University of Vermont and State Agricultural College*, 244 F.Supp. 156 [VT 1965]) was that colleges and universities have broad discretion where academic requirements are concerned, and the administrators have the necessary information to determine the requirements necessary to attain academic success. The courts will intercede only if the administrator's decision is clearly arbitrary and capricious.

In *Giles v. Howard University*, 428 F. Supp. 603 (DC 1977), the court found that advising was an implied contract between student and an institution, that terms prescribed by the institution for graduation are binding, and that additional requirements may not be placed upon a student after the student completes the requirements that were outlined for the student by the proper officials. However, additional requirements could be required after a student was admitted to the institution as long as the requirements were reasonable and the student had proper notification before the program was completed (Schubert & Schubert, 1983).

Shur (1983) suggests that catalogs, brochures, and other printed material be reviewed periodically and carefully so that claims are always deliverable. Appropriate disclaimers should be made in this material. All employees should understand that anything they say or write can be potentially binding. Advisers are sometimes asked to write letters of recommendation for students, but some advisers fear writing negative letters because of being sued. As long as there is evidence to support those judgments, advisers should feel free to write the truth when it is requested.

In cases involving academic dismissal, courts have indicated that arbitrary and capricious action must be proven before a student prevails (*Watson v. Univ.*

of So. Alabama College of Medicine; Ayton v. Bean, 436 Y.Y.S.2d 781 [NY 1981]). When students fail to achieve satisfactory progress, the student breaches the contract.

Advisers must be careful not to offer information or make agreements in conflict with the institution's written policies. Oral statements can be just as binding as written ones. Since advisers are the institution's representatives or agents, they must be viewed as reasonable and prudent persons. Advisers should provide only that level of knowledge that they are trained to do. Schubert and Schubert (1983) suggest that advisers should stress to the student that their responsibility is to advise and that the final decision is the student's.

Some advisers are concerned about acquiring liability insurance. Hendrickson (1982) reviews areas of "tortuous harm" that counselors may encounter, such as negligence, institutional interference, defamation, and misrepresentation. Risk to advisers can be minimized by acting reasonably and within ethical and professional standards. Insurance coverage, according to Hendrickson, is advisable for any professional who feels at risk of litigation.

Patterson (1980) lists some preventive measures, such as identifying actions that tend to invite suits based on negligent actions, analyzing how these actions can be changed, and taking the steps necessary to alleviate them.

In summary, academic advisers should be aware of the legal ramifications of their actions as an agent of the institution and as an individual. As long as advisers do not act arbitrarily or capriciously, do not misrepresent information or policies orally or in writing, do not abuse the confidentiality of the adviser-advisee relationship, do not impinge on the privacy of the individual student, and always act in good faith, the chances of facing legal action are minimized. Nowicki (1987) suggests that advisers should be familiar with major federal statutes that affect student rights. These include Title VI of the Civil Rights Act of 1964, Title IV of the Education Amendments of 1972, Section 504 of the Rehabilitation Act of 1973, and the Family Education Rights and Privacy Act of 1975. A description of these statutes and regulations affecting academic advising is provided by Gehring (1984).

SUMMARY

This chapter has outlined the issues associated with the professionalism of academic advisers and their roles and responsibilities. Professional advising is an emerging profession, with many policies and tasks associated with a profession thus far unfulfilled. Professional advisers need to examine the standards that identify the profession; define the tasks specifically involved in the advising process; set standards for preparation and training; and recommend titles, levels of responsibility, and minimum salary ranges for those responsibilities. A code of ethics by which the profession can abide needs to be established. Advisers need to be aware of their legal obligations to students, the institution, and themselves.

REFERENCES

Barr, M. J. (Ed.). (1983). *Student affairs and the law*. New Directions for Student Services, no. 22. San Francisco: Jossey-Bass.

Beauchamp, T. L., & Childress, J. F. (1979). *Principles of biomedical ethics*. Oxford: Oxford University Press.

Bee. R. H., Beronja, T. A., & Mann, G. (1990). Analysis of the unionization of academic advisers. *NACADA Journal*, 10, 35–40.

Bok, D. (1988). Ethics, the university, and society. *Harvard Magazine*, 90, 39–50.

Buchanan, E. T., & Lamb, S. H. (1980). Legal rights related to student progress through postsecondary education. *Community College Review*, 8, 41–44.

CAS Standards and Guidelines for Student Services/Development Programs. (1986). Iowa City, IA: American College Testing Program.

Chambers, C. M. (1981). Foundations of ethical responsibility in higher education. In R. Stein & M. C. Baca (Eds.), *Professional ethics in university administration* (pp. 1–13). New Directions in Higher Education, no. 33. San Francisco: Jossey-Bass.

Christensen, V. R. (1980). Bringing about change. In U. Delworth & G. R. Hanson (Eds.), *Student services* (pp. 456–472). San Francisco: Jossey Bass.

Chronicle of Higher Education Almanac. (1991). Median salaries of college and university administrators, 1990–1991. August 28, p. 29.

Dalton, J. C., Barnett, D. C., & Healy, M. A. (1982). Ethical issues and values in student development: A survey of NASPA chief student personnel officers. *NASPA Journal*, 20, 14–21.

Dameron, J. D., & Wolf, J. C. (1974). Academic advisement in higher education: A new model. *Journal of College Student Personnel*, 15, 470–473.

Elliott, L. C. (1983). The legal ramifications of proper instruction: Some considerations for division heads in community colleges. *Community College Review*, 11, 3–12.

Gehring, D. D. (1982). The counselor's "duty to warn." *Personnel and Guidance Journal*, 61, 208–210.

Gehring, D. D. (1984). Legal issues in academic advising. In R. B. Winston et al. (Eds.), *Developmental academic advising* (pp. 381–411). San Francisco: Jossey-Bass.

Gehring, D. D. (1987). The legal limitations on statements made by advisers. *NACADA Journal*, 7, 64–68.

Goetz, J. J., & White, E. R. (1986). A survey of graduate programs addressing the preparation of professional academic advisers. *NACADA Journal*, 6, 43–47.

Gordon, V. N. (1982). Training future academic advisers: One model of a pre-service approach. *NACADA Journal*, 2, 35–40.

Gordon, V. N., et al. (1987). *Advising as a profession*. NACADA Task Force Report. Columbus, OH: Ohio State University.

Gordon, V. N., et al. (1988). Advising as a profession. *NACADA Journal*, 8, 59–64.

Greenwood, E. (1962). Attributes of a profession. In S. Nosow & W. H. Form (Eds.), *Man, work and society* (pp. 207–218). New York: Basic Books.

Habley, W. R., & Crockett, D. S. (1988). The third ACT national survey of academic advising. In W. R. Habley (Ed.), *The status and future of academic advising* (pp. 11–76). Iowa City, IA: American College Testing Program.

Hendrickson, R. M. (1982). Counselor liability: does the risk require insurance coverage? *Personnel and Guidance Journal*, 61, 205–207.

Kaplan, W. A. (1978). *The law of higher education: Legal implications of administrative decision making*. San Francisco: Jossey-Bass.

Kitchner, K. S. (1985). Ethical principles and ethical decisions in college student affairs. In H. J. Canon & R. D. Brown (Eds.), *Applied ethics in student services* (pp. 17–29). New Directions for Student Services, no. 30. San Francisco: Jossey-Bass.

Knapp, S., & Vandecreek, L. (1983). Privileged communication and the counselor. *Personnel and Guidance Journal*, 62, 83–85.

Krager, L. (1985). A new model for defining ethical behavior. In H. J. Canon & R. D. Brown (Eds.), *Applied ethics in student services* (pp. 31–48). New Directions in Student Services, no. 30. San Francisco: Jossey-Bass.

Kramer, H. C., & Gardner, R. E. (1983). *Advising by faculty*. Washington, DC: National Education Association.

Laudicina, R., & Tramutola, J. L. (1974). *A legal perspective for student personnel administrators*. Springfield, IL: Charles C. Thomas.

Lieberman, M. (1956). *Education as a profession*. Englewood Cliffs, NJ: Prentice-Hall.

Likins, J. M. (1979). Six factors in the changing relationship between institutions of higher education and the courts. *Journal of NAWDAC*, 42, 17–23.

Nowicki, M. (1987). Legal implications of academic advising. *NACADA Journal*, 7, 83–86.

Owens, H. F. (1980). They'll take you to court if you don't watch out. *Community and Junior College Journal*, 51, 12–16.

Patterson, A. H. (1980). Professional malpractice: Small cloud, but growing bigger. *Phi Delta Kappa*, 62, 193–196.

Penney, J. F. (1969). Student personnel work: A profession stillborn. *Personnel and Guidance Journal*, 47, 958–962.

Principles and Standards for Career Services at Ohio State University (1991). Columbus, OH: Ohio State University.

Report of the AACD Ethics Committee: 1989–1991. (1991). *Journal of Counseling and Development*, 70, 278–280.

Rest, J. R. (1986). *Moral development: Advances in research and theory*. New York: Praeger.

Rich, J. M. (1984). *Professional ethics in education*. Springfield, IL: Charles C. Thomas.

Rickard, S. T. (1988). Toward a professional paradigm. *Journal of College Student Development*, 29, 388–394.

Schubert, A. F., & Schubert, G. W. (1983). Academic advising and potential litigation. *NACADA Journal*, 3, 1–11.

Sherburne, P. R. (1970). Rates and patterns of professional mobility in student personnel work. *NASPA Journal*, 8, 119–123.

Shur, G. M. (1983). Contractual relationships. In M. J. Barr (Ed.), *Student affairs and the law* (pp. 27–38). New Directions for Student Services, no. 22. San Francisco: Jossey-Bass.

Winston, R. B., & Dagley, J. C. (1985). Ethical standards statements: Uses and limitations. In H. J. Canon & R. D. Brown (Eds.), *Applied ethics in student services* (pp. 49–65). New Directions for Student Services, no. 30. San Francisco: Jossey-Bass.

Winston, R. B., & Saunders, S. A. (1991). Ethical professional practice in student affairs. In T. K. Miller & R. B. Winston, Jr. (Eds.), *Administration and leadership in student affairs: Actualizing student development in higher education* (pp. 309–345). 2d ed. Muncie, IN: Accelerated Development.

Wrenn, C. G., & Darley, J. G. (1949). An appraisal of the professional status of personnel work. In E. G. Williamson (Ed.), *Trends in student personnel work* (pp. 264–287). Minneapolis, MN: University of Minnesota Press.

Young, D. P. (1982). Legal issues regarding academic advising. *NACADA Journal*, 2, 41–45.

Young, D. P. (1984). Legal issues regarding academic advising: An update. *NACADA Journal*, 4, 89–95.

Young, R. B. (1988). The profession(alization) of student affairs. *NASPA Journal*, 25, 262–266.

10

Advising for the Future

To speculate on the future of academic advising is to speculate on the future of higher education and our society in general. In *The Third Wave*, Toffler (1980) writes in an optimistic tone of a new, emerging civilization. Although he describes the transition from the second wave to the third as traumatic and unsettling, the new era could be the first truly humane civilization in recorded history. Higher education is currently facing the challenges of financial retrenchment, educating diverse student populations, a global economy, and other issues that reflect society's changing economic, political, and social agendas.

When the class of 2000 graduates,

- the body of knowledge will have doubled four times since 1988;
- graduates will have been exposed that year to more information than their grandparents were in a lifetime;
- only about 15 percent of jobs will require a college education, but nearly all will require job-specific training after high school;
- women's salaries will have grown to within 10 percent of men's;
- ninety percent of the labor force will work for companies employing fewer than 200 people; and
- minorities will be the majorities in 53 of the 100 largest U.S. cities (Cetron, 1988).

RESHAPING AMERICA

The United Way Strategic Planning Institute (1990) has outlined nine forces that are reshaping America. These forces will have a great impact on all facets of society and great implications for higher education and the preparation of college graduates who will shape our social, economic, and political future.

The Maturation of America

The total population of the United States is growing by just 1 percent per year, but the largest growing sector is the elderly. The proportion of middle-aged Americans (35 to 54 years of age) will increase sharply in the 1990s. The proportion of persons aged 65 to 74 will remain stable through 2005, but the proportion of Americans over age 75 will increase dramatically.

This "maturation" of Americans will place great emphasis on consumption, financial planning, health services, nutrition, and other services for this growing population. Colleges and universities will increasingly recruit older Americans (aged 65 and older) as students. The labor force will continue to grow older and more experienced.

The Mosaic Society

According to the United Way report, American society will move away from a "mass society" to a "mosaic society." The population will become increasingly diverse regarding family structure, ethnic makeup, educational levels, and age. By the year 2000, nearly one in three Americans will be a minority. In the twenty-first century, nonwhite and ethnic groups in the United States are expected to have higher growth rates than the Caucasian population. Advances in technology will allow products, service, publications, and information to be targeted toward special groups.

Redefinition of Individual and Societal Roles

According to the United Way study, boundaries and role definitions are blurring between the public and private sectors and between individuals and institutions. As the federal government's role declines, state government's involvement increases. Over half of all large companies will offer remedial education for employees by the year 2000.

There will be greater cooperation between the private and public sectors. Workers will need to be better educated, and concern about the lack of scientific literacy will increase. Individuals will take more responsibility for their own careers rather than wait for large institutions to provide opportunities. Special groups will grow in numbers and influence.

The Information-Based Economy

The way people communicate, work, and play is being changed by developing information technologies. The advances in computers and microelectronics are beginning to create new patterns of economic and societal organizations. There is alarm about the numbers of adults and youth who lack the basic literacy skills necessary to function in an information-based society. People of all ages will need to be educated about technology. Computers will perform functions in the financial and other consumer industries that are unheard of today. The pace of life will quicken with increased technology, so stress will be a factor in the adjustment process. Concerns about individual privacy will increase as more data are collected electronically.

Globalization

The movement of products, capital, technology, information, and ideas around the world is continuing to increase, according to the United Way study. The price, availability, and array of goods will become more dependent on factors in other economies and their political interaction with the United States. Trade agreements will influence the world's food supply. The need for understanding and tolerance of different cultures will continue to increase.

Personal and Environmental Health

Health, environmental, and qualify of life issues are key areas of concern to many Americans. It is projected that national health costs will triple by the year 2000. Twelve percent of the gross national product is spent on health care, and this is expected to increase. Consumers are expected to bear a greater share of their own health care costs.

Economic Restructuring

The United Way study points out that American businesses are being forced to restructure because of international competition, deregulation, new information technologies, and diverse and changing consumer tastes. Small firms are being created in record numbers. Firms of all sizes are affected by volatile market conditions. Economic development programs are needed to create and retain jobs and train and relocate displaced workers. Women, minorities, and immigrants are expected to account for over 80 percent of the net addition to the work force.

Family and Home Redefined

Many functions once performed by the family, such as food preparation and child care, are increasingly offered by commercial concerns. Activities once available outside the home, such as shopping and movie viewing, are now offered in the home. Information technologies enable more Americans to work from their homes, and computer-based services such as banking and shopping will change the role of the home in society. The family makeup is changing as well. There are more single-person households, single-parent families, and two-income families. The growing stresses on family life will make it difficult to continue its support-giving role without help from outside sources. Needs and concerns of families are more diverse and complex than ever before, resulting in a growing number of "high-risk" families.

Rebirth of Social Activisim

More and more people are becoming concerned about the environment, the deterioration of the public infrastructure, pervasive homelessness, lack of affordable housing, racial tensions, and other social problems. They are also concerned with issues that have a direct effect on their communities such as substance abuse, crime, and AIDS. Coalitions of business, government, education, and the non-profit sector will address social problems seen as beyond the government's ability to address alone.

These nine forces reshaping America, as outlined by the United Way Strategic Planning Institute, provide a picture of the type of society that will challenge higher education in the future. These forces describe the political, economic, and cultural forces that will have an impact on funding, on curriculum, on students, and on every facet of campus life. Advisers need to become knowledgeable about future trends and scenarios that will affect their future tasks and the environment in which they will work.

ACQUIRING A FUTURIST'S PERSPECTIVE

As advisers we must be cognizant of our duty to acquire a worldview perspective and the need to help students acquire the knowledge to succeed in a global economy. Understanding and appreciating different cultures and respecting persons from diverse backgrounds are critical for living responsibly and successfully in our future society.

Students will increasingly expect advisers to be conversant with the job market opportunities of the future and the types of knowledge and skills needed to succeed as a college graduate. As mentioned earlier, the work world our graduates will enter will be different from that of their parents. They will encounter an economy that will be more service- than manufacturing-oriented. They will be faced with drug screening, more short-term jobs, and foreign competition. There will be more home-based businesses, more flextime jobs, and a greater emphasis on corporate ethics. High technology will require a familiarity with computers, data processing, and telecommunications. Although the acquisition of more technical knowledge is critical, the liberal learning that a college experience provides will continue to provide students with the communication and problem-solving skills needed in any endeavor.

CHALLENGES TO ADVISERS

Habley (1986) discusses eight challenges for the future of academic advising. One challenge is to develop a significant body of research that can support future decision making. Advisers are confronted with many unanswered questions about advising processes and services. For example, does advising have a direct and positive impact on students' academic and career decisions and on the quality of their lives?

Habley also challenges advisers not only to defend advising as a critical function in time of retrenchment but to elevate its status as a profession. This includes faculty advising as well. As a profession, advising needs to establish a set of standards, develop a conceptual base, and establish a potential for upward mobility in the profession itself. Habley urges that we attract and retain talented professionals in the advising field. If advising is to have a future, these challenges must be taken seriously and strong leadership given to the fulfillment of this agenda.

As individual advisers we need to work within certain areas to ensure that we will be ready for the future. Test your preparedness for the following areas by indicating if you are very prepared (VP), somewhat prepared (SP), or not prepared (NP):

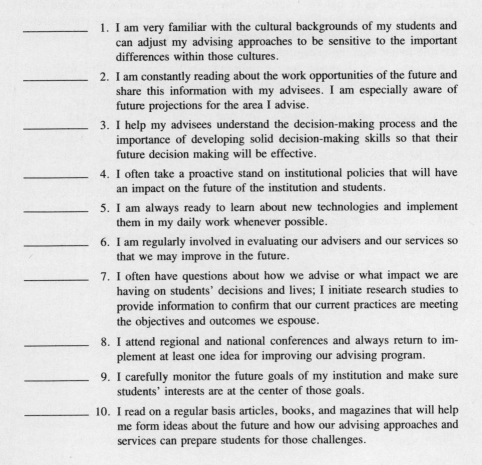

_____ 1. I am very familiar with the cultural backgrounds of my students and can adjust my advising approaches to be sensitive to the important differences within those cultures.

_____ 2. I am constantly reading about the work opportunities of the future and share this information with my advisees. I am especially aware of future projections for the area I advise.

_____ 3. I help my advisees understand the decision-making process and the importance of developing solid decision-making skills so that their future decision making will be effective.

_____ 4. I often take a proactive stand on institutional policies that will have an impact on the future of the institution and students.

_____ 5. I am always ready to learn about new technologies and implement them in my daily work whenever possible.

_____ 6. I am regularly involved in evaluating our advisers and our services so that we may improve in the future.

_____ 7. I often have questions about how we advise or what impact we are having on students' decisions and lives; I initiate research studies to provide information to confirm that our current practices are meeting the objectives and outcomes we espouse.

_____ 8. I attend regional and national conferences and always return to implement at least one idea for improving our advising program.

_____ 9. I carefully monitor the future goals of my institution and make sure students' interests are at the center of those goals.

_____ 10. I read on a regular basis articles, books, and magazines that will help me form ideas about the future and how our advising approaches and services can prepare students for those challenges.

_____ 11. Our advising services have established goals for the future and have
an action plan and time line for meeting those goals.

Advising for the future requires that each individual adviser plan in three areas:
personal, professional, and institutional. A personal commitment to improve
one's knowledge and skills is paramount if daily performance is to be enhanced
and future goals identified. Professionally, advisers need to take an active role
in helping to build a professional identity and image. Faculty advisers need to
join professional advisers to upgrade the image of advising and to expound on
its importance in the lives of the students we serve.

Professional advisers need to be active in furthering the cause of becoming a
profession and thus actively involved in the professional organizations that are
committed to this goal. Advisers need to volunteer to become active in setting
standards, establishing a code of ethics, and being involved in other activities
dedicated to improving advisers and advising in many settings.

Advisers will become increasingly specialized as the diversity of our students
and the complexity of our institutions increase. The need for expanded and
regular training opportunities is at the heart of improving the quality and effectiveness of the advising endeavor. Developmental advising will need to become
the rule rather than the exception.

Advisers' greatest impact for the future may be in working within their own
institutions to establish goals that will make our interactions with students more
personal and professional. We need to take charge of our future now, so that
other forces do not control how we live and operate in the years ahead.

REFERENCES

Cetron, M. J. (1988). Class of 2000: The good news and bad news. *Futurist*, 22, 9–15.
Habley, W. R. (1986). Show us the future: The challenges facing academic advising.
    NACADA Journal, 6, 5–11.
Toffler, A. (1980). *The third wave*. New York: William Morrow.
United Way Strategic Planning Institute. (1990). Nine forces reshaping America. *Futurist*,
    24, 9–16.

Selected Bibliography

Barr, M. J. (Ed.). (1983). *Student affairs and the law*. New Directions for Student Services, no. 22. San Francisco: Jossey-Bass.

Beasley-Fielstein, L. (1986). Student perceptions of the developmental adviser-advisee relationship. *NACADA Journal*, 6, 107–117.

Bok, D. (1988). Ethics, the university, and society. *Harvard Magazine*, 90, 39–50.

Bostaph, C., & Moore, M. (1980). Training academic advisers: A developmental strategy. *Journal of College Student Personnel*, 21, 45–50.

Boyer, E. L. (1987). *College: The undergraduate experience in America*. The Carnegie Foundation for the Advancement of Teaching. New York: Harper & Row.

Brown, D., & Minor, C. W. (1989). *Working in America: A status report on planning and problems*. Alexandria, VA: National Career Development Association.

Bynum, A. S. (1991). *Black student/white counselor* (2nd ed.). Indianapolis, IN: Alexandria Books.

Canon, H. J., & Brown, R. D. (Eds.). (1985). *Applied ethics in student services*. New Directions for Student Services, no. 30. San Francisco: Jossey-Bass.

Change Magazine. (1989). *Asian and Pacific Americans: Behind the myths*, 22, 12–36.

Chartrand, J. M., & Lent, R. W. (1987). Sports counseling: Enhancing the development of the student-athlete. *Journal of Counseling and Development*, 66, 164–167.

Chickering, A. W. (1969). *Education and identity*. San Francisco: Jossey-Bass.

Chickering, A. W. (1974). *Commuting versus resident students: Overcoming educational inequities of living off campus*. San Francisco: Jossey-Bass.

Chickering, A. W., & Associates (Eds.). (1981). *The modern American college*. San Francisco: Jossey-Bass.

Cohen, R. D. (Ed.). (1985). *Working with parents of college students*. New Directions for Student Services, no. 32. San Francisco: Jossey-Bass.

Council for the Advancement of Standards for Student Services/Development Programs. (1986). Iowa City, IA: American College Testing Program.

Courtland, C. L., & Richardson, B. L. (Eds.). (1991). *Multicultural issues in counseling*. Alexandria, VA: American Association for Counseling and Development.

Crites, J. O. (1981). *Career counseling: Models, methods, and materials*. New York: McGraw-Hill.

Crockett, D. S. (1986). *Advising skills, techniques, and resources*. Iowa City, IA: American College Testing Program.

Crookston, B. B. (1972). A developmental view of academic advising as teaching. *Journal of College Student Personnel*, 13, 12–17.

Cross, K. P. (1971). *Beyond the open door: New students to higher education*. San Francisco: Jossey-Bass.

Cross, K. P. (1981). *Adults as learners*. San Francisco: Jossey-Bass.

Dameron, J. D., & Wolf, J. C. (1974). Academic advisement in higher education: A new model. *Journal of College Student Personnel*, 15, 470–473.

Dressel, P. L. (1980). *Improving degree programs*. San Francisco: Jossey-Bass.

Ender, S. C., McCaffrey, S. S., & Miller, T. K. (1979). *Students helping students: A training manual for peer helpers on the college campus*. Athens, GA: Student Development Associates.

Feldman, K. A., & Newcomb, T. M. (1969). *The impact of college on students*. San Francisco: Jossey-Bass.

Fleming, J. (1984). *Blacks in college*. San Francisco: Jossey-Bass.

Frank, C. P. (1988). The development of academic advising programs. *NACADA Journal*, 8, 11–28.

Friedman, P. G., & Jenkins-Friedman, R. C. (1986). *Fostering academic excellence through honors programs*. New Directions for Teaching and Learning, no. 25. San Francisco: Jossey-Bass.

Frost, S. H. (1991). *Academic advising for Student success*. Washington, D.C.: ASHE-ERIC Higher Education Report No. 3.

Fuqua, D. R., Newman, J. L., & Seaworth, T. B. (1988). Relation of state and trait anxiety to different components of career indecision. *Journal of Counseling Psychology*, 35, 154–158.

Gordon, V. N. (1981). The undecided student: A developmental perspective. *Personnel and Guidance Journal*, 59, 433–439.

Gordon, V. N. (1984). *The undecided college student*. Springfield, IL: Charles C. Thomas.

Gordon, V. N., & Grites, T. J. (1984). The freshman seminar course: Helping students succeed. *Journal of College Student Personnel*, 25, 315–320.

Grites, T. J. (1977). Student development through academic advising: A 4X4 model. *NASPA Journal*, 14, 33–37.

Grites, T. J. (1979). *Academic advising: Getting us through the eighties*. Washington, DC: AAHE-ERIC Higher Education Research Report, no. 7.

Habley, W. R. (1979). Organizational structures for academic advising: Models and implications. *Journal of College Student Personnel*, 24, 535–540.

Habley, W. R. (1986). Show us the future: The challenges facing academic advising. *NACADA Journal*, 6, 5–11.

Habley, W. R. (Ed.). (1988). *The status and future of academic advising*. Iowa City, IA: American College Testing Program.

Hameister, B. G. (1984). Orienting disabled students. In M. L. Upcraft (Ed.), *Orienting students to college* (pp. 67–77). New Directions for Student Services, no. 25. San Francisco: Jossey-Bass.

Hardee, M. D. (1970). *Faculty advising in colleges and universities*. Washington, DC: American Personnel and Guidance Association.

Hodgkinson, H. L. (1985). *All one system: Demographics of education, kindergarten through graduate school*. Washington, DC: Institute for Educational Leadership.

Hornbuckle, P., Mahoney, J., & Borgard, J. (1979). A structured analysis of student perceptions of faculty advising. *Journal of College Student Personnel*, 20, 296–300.

Hsai, J. (1988). *Asian Americans in higher education and at work*. Hillsdale, NJ: Lawrence Erlbaum.

Johnston, W., & Packer, A. (1987). *Workforce 2000: Work and workers for the twenty-first century*. Indianapolis, IN: Hudson Institute.

Katchadourian, H. A., & Boli, J. (1985). *Careerism and intellectualism among college students*. San Francisco: Jossey-Bass.

King, M. C. (1988). Advising delivery systems. In W. R. Habley (Ed.), *Status and future of academic advising* (pp. 141–149). Iowa City, IA: American College Testing Program.

Kramer, H. C., & Gardner, R. E. (1983). *Advising by faculty*. Washington, DC: National Education Association.

Lee, C. C., & Richardson, B. L. (Eds.). (1991). *Multicultural issues in counseling*. Alexandria, VA: American Association for Counseling and Development.

Meskill, V. P., & Sheffield, W. (1970). A new specialty: Full-time academic counselors. *Personnel and Guidance Journal*, 49, 55–58.

Miller, T. K., & Prince, J. S. (1976). *The future of student affairs: A guide to student development for tomorrow's higher education*. San Francisco: Jossey-Bass.

Moore, K. M. (1976). Faculty advising: panacea or placebo? *Journal of College Student Personnel*, 12, 371–374.

Noel, L., Levitz, R., & Saluri, D. (1985). *Increasing student retention*. San Francisco: Jossey-Bass.

O'Banion, T. (1972). An academic advising model. *Junior College Journal*, 44, 62–69.

O'Banion, T., Fordyce, J. W., & Goodwin, G. (1972). Academic advising in the two-year college: A national survey. *Journal of College Student Personnel*, 22, 483–488.

Olivas, M. A. (1986). *Latino college students*. New York: Teachers College Press, Columbia University.

Pascarella, E. T., & Terenzini, P. T. (1991). *How college affects students*. San Francisco: Jossey-Bass.

Perry, W. G. (1970). *Intellectual and ethical development in the college years*. New York: Holt, Rinehart, & Winston.

Peterson, E. D., & Kramer, G. L. (1984). Computer-assisted advising: The next agenda item for computer development. *NACADA Journal*, 4, 33–40.

Pyle, K. R. (Ed.). (1986). *Guiding the development of foreign students*. New Directions for Student Services, no. 36. San Francisco: Jossey-Bass.

Rich, J. M. (1984). *Professional ethics in education*. Springfield, IL: Charles C. Thomas.

Rickard, S. T. (1988). Toward a professional paradigm. *Journal of College Student Development*, 29, 388–394.

Rudolph, F. (1962). *The American college and university*. New York: Vintage Books.

Schlossberg, N. (1972). A framework for counseling women. *Personnel and Guidance Journal*, 51, 137–143.

Schubert, A. F., & Schubert, G. W. (1983). Academic advising and potential litigation. *NACADA Journal*, 3, 1–11.

Sheffield, W., & Meskill, V. P. (1972). Faculty adviser and academic counselor: A pragmatic marriage. *Journal of College Student Personnel*, 13, 28–30.

Shriberg, A., & Brodzinski, F. R. (Eds.). (1984). *Rethinking services for college athletes*. New Directions for Student Services, no. 28. San Francisco: Jossey-Bass.

Smart, J. C., & Pascarella, E. T. (1987). Influences on the intention to reenter higher education. *Journal of Higher Education*, 58, 306–321.

Sowa, C. J., & Gressard, C. F. (1983). Athletic participation: Its relationship to student development. *Journal of College Student Personnel*, 24, 236–239.

Spencer, R. W., Peterson, E. D., & Kramer, G. L. (1982). Utilizing college advising centers to facilitate and revitalize academic advisement. *NACADA Journal*, 2, 13–23.

Spencer, R. W., Peterson, E. D., & Kramer, G. L. (1983). Designing and implementing a computer-assisted academic advisement program. *Journal of College Student Personnel*, 24, 513–518.

Srebnik, D. S. (1988). Academic advising evaluation: A review of assessment instruments. *NACADA Journal*, 8, 52–62.

Stewart, S. S. (Ed.). (1983). *Commuter students: Enhancing their educational experiences*. New Directions for Student Services, no. 24. San Francisco: Jossey-Bass.

Sue, D. W., & Morishima, J. K. (1982). *The mental health of Asian Americans*. San Francisco: Jossey-Bass.

Teague, G. V., & Grites, T. J. (1980). Faculty contracts and academic advising. *Journal of College Student Personnel*, 21, 40–44.

Theophilides, C., Terenzini, P. T., & Lorang, W. (1984). Freshman and sophomore experiences and changes in major field. *Review of Higher Education*, 7, 261–278.

Tinto, V. (1987). *Leaving college*. Chicago, IL: University of Chicago Press.

Trombley, T. B. (1984). An analysis of the complexity of academic advising tasks. *Journal of College Student Personnel*, 25, 234–239.

Upcraft, M. L. (Ed.). (1984). *Orienting students to college*. New Directions for Student Services, no. 25. San Francisco: Jossey-Bass.

Upcraft, M. L., & Gardner, J. N. (1989). *The freshman year experience*. San Francisco: Jossey-Bass.

Walsh, E. M. (1979). Revitalizing academic advisement. *Personnel and Guidance Journal*, 57, 446–449.

Willie, C. V., & McCord, A. (Eds.). (1972). *Black students in white colleges*. New York: Praeger.

Winston, R. B., Ender, S. C., & Miller, T. K. (1982). *Developmental approaches to academic advising*. New Directions for Student Services, no. 17. San Francisco: Jossey-Bass.

Winston, R. B., Miller, T. K., Ender, S. C., & Grites, T. J. (1984). *Developmental academic advising*. San Francisco: Jossey-Bass.

Wright, D. J. (Ed.). (1987). *Responding to the needs of today's minority students*. New Directions for Student Services, no. 38. San Francisco: Jossey-Bass.

Young, D. P. (1984). Legal issues regarding academic advising: An update. *NACADA Journal*, 4, 89–95.

Index

About the Author

VIRGINIA N. GORDON is Assistant Dean of the University College at The Ohio State University and Director of the National Clearinghouse for Academic Advising. She has published two books related to academic advising, and her many articles have appeared in journals such as the *Journal of College Student Personnel* and the *NACADA Journal*.